CASENOTE® Legal Briefs®

ADMINISTRATIVE LAW

Keyed to Courses Using

Funk, Shapiro, and Weaver's
Administrative Procedure and Practice:
A Contemporary Approach
Seventh Edition

Authored by: Publisher's Editorial Staff

ASPEN PUBLISHING

This publication is designed to provide accurate and authoritative information in regard to the subject matter covered. It is sold with the understanding that the publisher is not engaged in rendering legal, accounting, or other professional services. If legal advice or other expert assistance is required, the services of a competent professional person should be sought.

— From a Declaration of Principles adopted jointly by a Committee of the American Bar Association and a Committee of Publishers and Associates

To contact Customer Service, e-mail customer.service@aspenpublishing.com, call 1-800-950-5259, or mail correspondence to:

Aspen Publishing
Attn: Order Department
1 Wall Street
Burlington, MA 01803

1 2 3 4 5 6 7 8 9 0

ISBN 979-8-8890-6800-6

ABOUT ASPEN PUBLISHING

Aspen Publishing is a leading provider of legal education content and digital learning solutions in the United States and globally. Our innovative products and platforms—designed based on best practices in learning science—engage students and enhance outcomes. From textbooks and audiobooks authored by renowned experts to digital platforms and products like LEAF, Connected eBooks, Connected Quizzing, PracticePerfect, and JD-Next, we empower the next generation of legal professionals with innovative, trusted, and accessible resources.

The Aspen Casebook Series, affectionately known as the "red and black" casebooks among law faculty and students, includes hundreds of highly regarded textbooks across more than 80 disciplines. These range from foundational courses like Torts and Contracts to emerging electives such as Sustainability and the Law of Policing. Our study aids, including the popular *Examples & Explanations* series, help law students master complex topics with clarity and confidence.

Aspen's expertise extends to undergraduate education with our Paralegal, Criminal Justice, and Business Law series, offering the same hallmark quality to a broader audience. JD-Next, our groundbreaking online law school prep course and admissions test, provides a realistic preview of law school, equips students with essential skills for academic success, and evaluates their readiness for legal studies.

Aspen Publishing Is Proud to Be a UWorld Company

Since 2003, UWorld has been a global leader in developing high-quality learning tools for students preparing for high-stakes exams. With a commitment to excellence, UWorld has helped millions of students in undergraduate, graduate, and professional programs in fields such as medicine, nursing, finance, and law achieve their academic and career goals.

Founded by Chandra S. Pemmasani, M.D., during his medical residency, UWorld began focusing on medical education and has since expanded into various academic fields, including law. In 2020, UWorld launched its Legal vertical, starting with its comprehensive Multistate Bar Exam (MBE®) Question Bank, followed by the acquisition of Themis Bar Review, which integrated resources to provide a complete bar exam preparation experience. In 2024, UWorld expanded its offerings by acquiring Aspen Publishing, enhancing its suite of legal education products.

Today, UWorld offers an unparalleled range of study materials that blend active learning methods with expert content, ensuring students and educators can access the most effective resources. From bar preparation to law school success, UWorld is committed to supporting the next generation of legal professionals. Learn more at uworld.com.

Format for the Casenote® Legal Brief

Nature of Case: This section identifies the form of action (e.g., breach of contract, negligence, battery), the type of proceeding (e.g., demurrer, appeal from trial court's jury instructions) or the relief sought (e.g., damages, injunction, criminal sanctions).

Party ID: Quick identification of the relationship between the parties.

Fact Summary: This is included to refresh your memory and can be used as a quick reminder of the facts.

Rule of Law: Summarizes the general principle of law that the case illustrates. It may be used for instant recall of the court's holding and for classroom discussion or home review.

Facts: This section contains all relevant facts of the case, including the contentions of the parties and the lower court holdings. It is written in a logical order to give you a clear understanding of the case. The plaintiff and defendant are identified by their proper names throughout and are always labeled with a (P) or (D).

Issue: The issue is a concise question that brings out the essence of the opinion as it relates to the section of the casebook in which the case appears. Both substantive and procedural issues are included if relevant to the decision.

Concurrence/Dissent: All concurrences and dissents are briefed whenever they are included by the casebook author.

Analysis: This last paragraph gives you a broad understanding of where the case "fits in" with other cases in the section of the book and with the entire course. It is a hornbook-style discussion indicating whether the case is a majority or minority opinion and comparing the principal case with other cases in the casebook. It may also provide analysis from restatements, uniform codes, and law review articles.

Holding and Decision: This section offers a clear and in-depth discussion of the rule of the case and the court's rationale. It is written in easy-to-understand language and answers the issue presented by applying the law to the facts of the case. When relevant, it includes a thorough discussion of the exceptions to the case as listed by the court, any major cites to the other cases on point, and the names of the judges who wrote the decisions.

Quicknotes: Conveniently defines legal terms found in the case.

Palsgraf v. Long Island R.R. Co.

Injured bystander (P) v. Railroad company (D)

N.Y. Ct. App., 248 N.Y. 339, 162 N.E. 99 (1928).

NATURE OF CASE: **Appeal from judgment affirming verdict for plaintiff seeking damages for personal injury.**

FACT SUMMARY: **Helen Palsgraf (P) was injured on R.R.'s (D) train platform when R.R.'s (D) guard helped a passenger aboard a moving train, causing his package to fall on the tracks. The package contained fireworks which exploded, creating a shock that tipped a scale onto Palsgraf (P).**

RULE OF LAW

The risk reasonably to be perceived defines the duty to be obeyed.

FACTS: Helen Palsgraf (P) purchased a ticket to Rockaway Beach from R.R. (D) and was waiting on the train platform. As she waited, two men ran to catch a train that was pulling out from the platform. The first man jumped aboard, but the second man, who appeared as if he might fall, was helped aboard by the guard on the train who had kept the door open so they could jump aboard. A guard on the platform also helped by pushing him onto the train. The man was carrying a package wrapped in newspaper. In the process, the man dropped his package, which fell on the tracks. The package contained fireworks and exploded. The shock of the explosion was apparently of great enough strength to tip over some scales at the other end of the platform, which fell on Palsgraf (P) and injured her. A jury awarded her damages, and R.R. (D) appealed.

ISSUE: Does the risk reasonably to be perceived define the duty to be obeyed?

HOLDING AND DECISION: (Cardozo, C.J.) Yes. The risk reasonably to be perceived defines the duty to be obeyed. If there is no foreseeable hazard to the injured party as the result of a seemingly innocent act, the act does not become a tort because it happened to be a wrong as to another. If the wrong was not willful, the plaintiff must show that the act as to her had such great and apparent possibilities of danger as to entitle her to protection. Negligence in the abstract is not enough upon which to base liability. Negligence is a relative concept, evolving out of the common law doctrine of trespass on the case. To establish liability, the defendant must owe a legal duty of reasonable care to the injured party. A cause of action in tort will lie where harm, though unintended, could have been averted or avoided by observance of such a duty. The scope of the duty is limited by the range of danger that a reasonable person could foresee. In this case, there was nothing to suggest from the appearance of the parcel or otherwise that the parcel contained fireworks. The guard could not reasonably have had any warning of a threat to Palsgraf (P), and R.R. (D) therefore cannot be held liable. Judgment is reversed in favor of R.R. (D)

DISSENT: (Andrews, J.) The concept that there is no negligence unless R.R. (D) owes a legal duty to take care as to Palsgraf (P) herself is too narrow. Everyone owes to the world at large the duty of refraining from those acts that may unreasonably threaten the safety of others. If the guard's action was negligent as to those nearby, it was also negligent as to those outside what might be termed the "danger zone." For Palsgraf (P) to recover, R.R.'s (D) negligence must have been the proximate cause of her injury, a question of fact for the jury.

ANALYSIS

The majority defined the limit of the defendant's liability in terms of the danger that a reasonable person in defendant's situation would have perceived. The dissent argued that the limitation should not be placed on liability, but rather on damages. Judge Andrews suggested that only injuries that would not have happened but for R.R.'s (D) negligence should be compensable. Both the majority and dissent recognized the policy-driven need to limit liability for negligent acts, seeking, in the words of Judge Andrews, to define a framework "that will be practical and in keeping with the general understanding of mankind." The Restatement (Second) of Torts has accepted Judge Cardozo's view.

Quicknotes

FORESEEABILITY A reasonable expectation that change is the probable result of certain acts or omissions.

NEGLIGENCE Conduct falling below the standard of care that a reasonable person would demonstrate under similar conditions.

PROXIMATE CAUSE The natural sequence of events without which an injury would not have been sustained.

Note to Students

Aspen Publishing is proud to offer *Casenote® Legal Briefs*—continuing thirty years of publishing America's best-selling legal briefs.

Casenote® Legal Briefs are designed to help you save time when briefing assigned cases. Organized under convenient headings, they show you how to abstract the basic facts and holdings from the text of the actual opinions handed down by the courts. Used as part of a rigorous study regimen, they can help you spend more time analyzing and critiquing points of law than on copying bits and pieces of judicial opinions into your notebook or outline.

Casenote® Legal Briefs should never be used as a substitute for assigned casebook readings. They work best when read as a follow-up to reviewing the underlying opinions themselves. Students who try to avoid reading and digesting the judicial opinions in their casebooks or online sources will end up shortchanging themselves in the long run. The ability to absorb, critique, and restate the dynamic and complex elements of case law decisions is crucial to your success in law school and beyond. It cannot be developed vicariously.

In addition to *Casenote® Legal Briefs*, Aspen Publishing offers the following study aids:

- *Casenote® Legal Briefs*
- *Emanuel® Law Outlines*
- Emanuel® *Law in a Flash* Flash Cards
- Emanuel® *CrunchTime® Series*

Each of these series is designed to provide you with easy-to-understand explanations of complex points of law. Each volume offers guidance on the principles of legal analysis and, consulted regularly, will hone your ability to spot relevant issues. We have titles that will help you prepare for class, prepare for your exams, and enhance your general comprehension of the law along the way.

To find out more about our law school tools for success, visit us at *www.AspenPublishing.com* or e-mail us at *customer.service@aspenpublishing.com*. We'll be happy to assist you.

How to Brief a Case

A. Decide on a Format and Stick to It

Structure is essential to a good brief. It enables you to arrange systematically the related parts that are scattered throughout most cases, thus making manageable and understandable what might otherwise seem to be an endless and unfathomable sea of information. There are, of course, an unlimited number of formats that can be utilized. However, it is best to find one that suits your needs and stick to it. Consistency breeds both efficiency and the security that when called upon you will know where to look in your brief for the information you are asked to give.

Any format, as long as it presents the essential elements of a case in an organized fashion, can be used. Experience, however, has led *Casenote® Legal Briefs* to develop and utilize the following format because of its logical flow and universal applicability.

NATURE OF CASE: This is a brief statement of the legal character and procedural status of the case (e.g., "Appeal of a burglary conviction").

There are many different alternatives open to a litigant dissatisfied with a court ruling. The key to determining which one has been used is to discover *who is asking this court for what.*

This first entry in the brief should be kept as *short as possible.* Use the court's terminology if you understand it. But since jurisdictions vary as to the titles of pleadings, the best entry is the one that addresses who wants what in this proceeding, not the one that sounds most like the court's language.

RULE OF LAW: A statement of the general principle of law that the case illustrates (e.g., "An acceptance that varies any term of the offer is considered a rejection and counteroffer").

Determining the rule of law of a case is a procedure similar to determining the issue of the case. Avoid being fooled by red herrings; there may be a few rules of law mentioned in the case excerpt, but usually only one is *the* rule with which the casebook editor is concerned. The techniques used to locate the issue, described below, may also be utilized to find the rule of law. Generally, your best guide is simply the chapter heading. It is a clue to the point the casebook editor seeks to make and should be kept in mind when reading every case in the respective section.

FACTS: A synopsis of only the essential facts of the case, i.e., those bearing upon or leading up to the issue.

The facts entry should be a short statement of the events and transactions that led one party to initiate legal proceedings against another in the first place. While some cases conveniently state the salient facts at the beginning of the decision, in other instances they will have to be culled from hiding places throughout the text, even from concurring and dissenting opinions. Some of the "facts" will often be in dispute and should be so noted. Conflicting evidence may be briefly pointed up. "Hard" facts must be included. Both must be *relevant* in order to be listed in the facts entry. It is impossible to tell what is relevant until the entire case is read, as the ultimate determination of the rights and liabilities of the parties may turn on something buried deep in the opinion.

Generally, the facts entry should not be longer than three to five *short* sentences.

It is often helpful to identify the role played by a party in a given context. For example, in a construction contract case the identification of a party as the "contractor" or "builder" alleviates the need to tell that that party was the one who was supposed to have built the house.

It is always helpful, and a good general practice, to identify the "plaintiff" and the "defendant." This may seem elementary and uncomplicated, but, especially in view of the creative editing practiced by some casebook editors, it is sometimes a difficult or even impossible task. Bear in mind that the *party presently* seeking something from this court may not be the plaintiff, and that sometimes only the cross-claim of a defendant is treated in the excerpt. Confusing or misaligning the parties can ruin your analysis and understanding of the case.

ISSUE: A statement of the general legal question answered by or illustrated in the case. For clarity, the issue is best put in the form of a question capable of a "yes" or "no" answer. In reality, the issue is simply the Rule of Law put in the form of a question (e.g., "May an offer be accepted by performance?").

The major problem presented in discerning what is *the* issue in the case is that an opinion usually purports to raise and answer several questions. However, except for rare cases, only one such question is really the issue in the case. Collateral issues not necessary to the resolution of the matter in controversy are handled by the court by language known as *"obiter dictum"* or merely *"dictum."* While dicta may be included later in the brief, they have no place under the issue heading.

To find the issue, ask *who wants what* and then go on to ask *why did that party succeed or fail in getting it.* Once this is determined, the "why" should be turned into a question.

The complexity of the issues in the cases will vary, but in all cases a single-sentence question should sum up the issue. *In a few cases,* there will be two, or even more rarely, three issues of equal importance to the resolution of the case. Each should be expressed in a single-sentence question.

Since many issues are resolved by a court in coming to a final disposition of a case, the casebook editor will reproduce the portion of the opinion containing the issue or issues most relevant to the area of law under scrutiny. A noted law professor gave this advice: "Close the book; look at the title on the cover." Chances are, if it is Property, you need not concern yourself with whether, for example, the federal government's treatment of the plaintiff's land really raises a federal question sufficient to support jurisdiction on this ground in federal court.

The same rule applies to chapter headings designating sub-areas within the subjects. They tip you off as to what the text is designed to teach. The cases are arranged in a casebook to show a progression or development of the law, so that the preceding cases may also help.

It is also most important to remember to *read the notes and questions* at the end of a case to determine what the editors wanted you to have gleaned from it.

HOLDING AND DECISION: This section should succinctly explain the rationale of the court in arriving at its decision. In capsulizing the "reasoning" of the court, it should always include an application of the general rule or rules of law to the specific facts of the case. Hidden justifications come to light in this entry: the reasons for the state of the law, the public policies, the biases and prejudices, those considerations that influence the justices' thinking and, ultimately, the outcome of the case. At the end, there should be a short indication of thedisposition or procedural resolution of the case (e.g., "Decision of the trial court for Mr. Smith (P) reversed").

The foregoing format is designed to help you "digest" the reams of case material with which you will be faced in your law school career. Once mastered by practice, it will place at your fingertips the information the authors of your casebooks have sought to impart to you in case-by-case illustration and analysis.

B. Be as Economical as Possible in Briefing Cases

Once armed with a format that encourages succinctness, it is as important to be economical with regard to the time spent on the actual reading of the case as it is to be economical in the writing of the brief itself. This does not mean "skimming" a case. Rather, it means reading the case with an "eye" trained to recognize into which "section" of your brief a particular passage or line fits and having a system for quickly and precisely marking the case so that the passages fitting any one particular part of the brief can be easily identified and brought together in a concise and accurate manner when the brief is actually written.

It is of no use to simply repeat everything in the opinion of the court; record only enough information to trigger your recollection of what the court said. Nevertheless, an accurate statement of the "law of the case," i.e., the legal principle applied to the facts, is absolutely essential to class preparation and to learning the law under the case method.

To that end, it is important to develop a "shorthand" that you can use to make marginal notations. These notations will tell you at a glance in which section of the brief you will be placing that particular passage or portion of the opinion.

Some students prefer to underline all the salient portions of the opinion (with a pencil or colored underliner marker), making marginal notations as they go along. Others prefer the color-coded method of underlining, utilizing different colors of markers to underline the salient portions of the case, each separate color being used to represent a different section of the brief. For example, blue underlining could be used for passages relating to the rule of law, yellow for those relating to the issue, and green for those relating to the holding and decision, etc. While it has its advocates, thecolor-coded method can be confusing and time-consuming (all that time spent on changing colored markers). Furthermore, it can interfere with the continuity and concentration many students deem essential to the reading of a case for maximum comprehension. In the end, however, it is a matter of personal preference and style. Just remember, whatever method you use, underlining must be used sparingly or its value is lost.

If you take the marginal notation route, an efficient and easy method is to go along underlining the key portions of the case and placing in the margin alongside them the following "markers" to indicate where a particular passage or line "belongs" in the brief you will write:

N	(NATURE OF CASE)
RL	(RULE OF LAW)
I	(ISSUE)
HL	(HOLDING AND DECISION, relates to the RULE OF LAW behind the decision)
HR	(HOLDING AND DECISION, gives the RATIONALE or reasoning behind the decision)
HA	(HOLDING AND DECISION, applies the general principle(s) of law to the facts of the case to arrive at the decision)

Remember that a particular passage may well contain information necessary to more than one part of your brief, in which case you simply note that in the margin. If you are using the color-coded underlining method instead of marginal notation, simply make asterisks or checks in the margin next to the passage in question in the colors that indicate the additional sections of the brief where it might be utilized.

The economy of utilizing "shorthand" in marking cases for briefing can be maintained in the actual brief writing process itself by utilizing "law student shorthand" within the brief. There are many commonly used words and phrases for which abbreviations can be substituted in your briefs (and in your class notes also). You can develop abbreviations that are personal to you and which will save you a lot of time. A reference list of briefing abbreviations can be found on page x of this book.

C. Use Both the Briefing Process and the Brief as a Learning Tool

Now that you have a format and the tools for briefing cases efficiently, the most important thing is to make the time spent in briefing profitable to you and to make the most advantageous use of the briefs you create. Of course, the briefs are invaluable for classroom reference when you are called upon to explain or analyze a particular case. However, they are also useful in reviewing for exams. A quick glance at the fact summary should bring the case to mind, and a rereading of the rule of law should enable you to go over the underlying legal concept in your mind, how it was applied in that particular case, and how it might apply in other factual settings.

As to the value to be derived from engaging in the briefing process itself, there is an immediate benefit that arises from being forced to sift through the essential facts and reasoning from the court's opinion and to succinctly express them in your own words in your brief. The process ensures that you understand the case and the point that it illustrates, and that means you will be ready to absorb further analysis and information brought forth in class. It also ensures you will have something to say when called upon in class. The briefing process helps develop a mental agility for getting to the *gist* of a case and for identifying, expounding on, and applying the legal concepts and issues found there. The briefing process is the mental process on which you must rely in taking law school examinations; it is also the mental process upon which lawyers rely in serving their clients and in making a living.

Abbreviations for Briefs

acceptance	acp
affirmed	aff
answer	ans
assumption of risk	a/r
attorney	atty
beyond a reasonable doubt	b/r/d
bona fide purchaser	BFP
breach of contract	br/k
cause of action	c/a
common law	c/l
Constitution	Con
constitutional	con
contract	K
contributory negligence	c/n
cross	x
cross-complaint	x/c
cross-examination	x/ex
cruel and unusual punishment	c/u/p
defendant	D
dismissed	dis
double jeopardy	d/j
due process	d/p
equal protection	e/p
equity	eq
evidence	ev
exclude	exc
exclusionary rule	exc/r
felony	f/n
freedom of speech	f/s
good faith	g/f
habeas corpus	h/c
hearsay	hr
husband	H
injunction	inj
in loco parentis	ILP
inter vivos	I/v
joint tenancy	j/t
judgment	judgt
jurisdiction	jur
last clear chance	LCC
long-arm statute	LAS
majority view	maj
meeting of minds	MOM
minority view	min
Miranda rule	Mir/r
Miranda warnings	Mir/w
negligence	neg
notice	ntc
nuisance	nus
obligation	ob
obscene	obs
offer	O
offeree	OE
offeror	OR
ordinance	ord
pain and suffering	p/s
parol evidence	p/e
plaintiff	P
prima facie	p/f
probable cause	p/c
proximate cause	px/c
real property	r/p
reasonable doubt	r/d
reasonable man	r/m
rebuttable presumption	rb/p
remanded	rem
res ipsa loquitur	RIL
respondeat superior	r/s
Restatement	RS
reversed	rev
Rule Against Perpetuities	RAP
search and seizure	s/s
search warrant	s/w
self-defense	s/d
specific performance	s/p
statute	S
statute of frauds	S/F
statute of limitations	S/L
summary judgment	s/j
tenancy at will	t/w
tenancy in common	t/c
tenant	t
third party	TP
third party beneficiary	TPB
transferred intent	TI
unconscionable	uncon
unconstitutional	unconst
undue influence	u/e
Uniform Commercial Code	UCC
unilateral	uni
vendee	VE
vendor	VR
versus	v
void for vagueness	VFV
weight of authority	w/a
weight of the evidence	w/e
wife	W
with	w/
within	w/i
without	w/o
without prejudice	w/o/p
wrongful death	wr/d

Table of Cases

CHAPTER 1

Administrative Law Practice

Quick Reference Rules of Law

Fund for Animals, Inc. v. Rice

Public interest group (P) v. Government agency (D)

85 F.3d 535 (11th Cir. 1996)

NATURE OF CASE: Action seeking injunction against agency decision.

FACT SUMMARY: Fund for Animals (P) challenged the Fish and Wildlife Service's (D) decision to issue a permit for a landfill on a site Fund for Animals (P) claimed would threaten endangered species.

RULE OF LAW

[No rule is provided; the case excerpt in the casebook gives only the facts and issues to show an example of an administrative law case.]

FACTS: Sarasota County applied for a permit with the United States Army Corps of Engineers (the Corps) (D) to build a landfill. The Corps (D) could grant a permit only if the proposed project was consistent with the rules of the Environmental Protection Agency (D) and did not adversely affect a species covered under the Endangered Species Act. Accordingly, the Fish and Wildlife Service (the FWS) (D) was required to conduct an environmental assessment of Sarasota County's proposed landfill. The FWS (D) gave its approval to the project but Fund for Animals (Fund) (P) complained that it hadn't considered the effect on the endangered Florida panther and Eastern Indigo snake. The FWS (D) then issued a Biological Opinion that addressed concerns regarding those species and concluded that the project was unlikely to jeopardize the panther and snake. The opinion did include recommendations for certain preservation measures. Fund (P) then filed suit against all the agencies involved with approving the permit. After some modifications, the permit was approved on April 13, 1995, and Fund (P) amended their complaint and sought injunctive relief. The district court ruled against Fund (P) and it appealed.

HOLDING AND DECISION: (Dubina, J.) The district court did not act arbitrarily or capriciously in approving the permit for the Sarasota project or in relying on the Biological Opinion of the the Fish and Wildlife Service (D). Affirmed.

ANALYSIS

This is a standard case in terms of the parties involved. Government agencies usually make decisions that affect private parties differently. When it reaches the stage of litigation, one party seeks to overturn the decision while another desires to uphold it.

Quicknotes

INJUNCTIVE RELIEF A court order issued as a remedy, requiring a person to do, or prohibiting that person from doing, a specific act.

CHAPTER 2

Rulemaking

Quick Reference Rules of Law

CHAPTER 2

13. *Motor Vehicle Manufacturers Assoc. v. State Farm Mutual Automobile Ins. Co.* When an agency modifies or rescinds a previously promulgated rule, it is required to supply a satisfactory, rational analysis supporting its decision. *19*

Natural Resources Defense Council, Inc. v. EPA

Advocacy organization (P) v. Agency (D)

956 F.3d 1134 (2020)

NATURE OF CASE: Petition for writ of mandamus to compel agency to respond to administrative petition.

FACT SUMMARY: The Natural Resources Defense Council (the NRDC) (P), an environmental advocacy organization, sought to compel the Environmental Protection Agency (the EPA) (D) to respond to NRDC's (P) administrative petition requesting that the EPA (D) end the use in pet products of a pesticide known as tetrachlorvinphos (TCVP), which is known to cause neurodevelopment problems in children, arguing that the EPA's (D) delay in responding for over a decade was egregious.

RULE OF LAW

A writ of mandamus compelling an agency to respond to an administrative petition will be granted where the agency's delay in responding to the administrative petition is "egregious."

FACTS: Under the Federal Insecticide, Fungicide, and Rodenticide Act (FIFRA), 7 U.S.C. §§ 136 et seq., the Environmental Protection Agency (the EPA) (D) is tasked with determining which pesticides may be registered for sale and distribution in the American market, and the EPA (D) may not approve registration of a pesticide that would cause "unreasonable adverse effects" to the environment or human health. In 2009, the Natural Resources Defense Council (the NRDC) (P), an environmental advocacy organization, submitted an administrative petition (Administrative Petition) to cancel the registration of a pesticide called tetrachlorvinphos (TCVP) for use in household pet products, because it came to be known that TCVP causes neurodevelopment health problems in children. It was believed that millions of children could come in direct contact with TCVP through their pets that were being treated with TCVP products such as flea and tick shampoos, powders, and collars. For over seven years, the parties litigated over the Administrative Petition, and the EPA (D) changed its position as to the risks posed by TCVP. In 2016, the EPA (D) stated its intention to issue a final (revised) response to the petition "within 90 days," but it did not. Instead, the EPA (D) sent the NRDC (P) a cursory letter in March 2017, stating that it intended to review pet-care uses of TCVP and issue a proposed decision in several months, between July and September 2017, alongside its scheduled review of all other TCVP uses. However, again, the EPA's (D) stated deadline came and passed without action. The EPA (D) asserted that during this time it was attempting to secure data about pet collars from Hartz Mountain Corp. (Hartz) the only remaining pet collar registrant, but, again, the EPA (D) failed to act for another two years. Then, in 2019, the NRCD (P) filed with the federal Ninth Circuit Court of Appeal a petition for a writ of mandamus to compel the EPA (D) to issue a final response to the Administrative Petition. Five days later, the EPA (D), for the first time, took action to compel Hartz to perform the study that the EPA (D) had requested in 2017.

ISSUE: Will a writ of mandamus compelling an agency to respond to an administrative petition be granted where the agency's delay in responding to the administrative petition is "egregious"?

HOLDING AND DECISION: (Gould, J.) Yes. A writ of mandamus compelling an agency to respond to an administrative petition will be granted where the agency's delay in responding to the administrative petition is "egregious." In determining that an agency's delay has been sufficiently egregious to warrant the remedy of mandamus, the courts consider a six-factor standard—the so-called "TRAC factors"—established in *Telecomms. Research and Action Ctr. (TRAC) v. FCC*, 750 F.2d 70, 79–80 (D.C. Cir. 1984). Those factors are: (1) the time agencies take to make decisions must be governed by a rule of reason; (2) where Congress has provided a timetable or other indication of the speed with which it expects the agency to proceed in the enabling statute, that statutory scheme may supply content for this rule of reason; (3) delays that might be reasonable in the sphere of economic regulation are less tolerable when human health and welfare are at stake; (4) the court should consider the effect of expediting delayed action on agency activities of a higher or competing priority; (5) the court should also take into account the nature and extent of the interests prejudiced by delay; and (6) the court need not find any impropriety lurking behind agency lassitude in order to hold that agency action is unreasonably delayed. The most important of these factors is the first factor, the "rule of reason." Circuit courts have concluded that a reasonable time for agency action is typically counted in weeks or months, not years. Here, more than ten years have passed since the Natural Resources Defense Council (the NRDC) (P) first filed its Administrative Petition. Notably, it has repeatedly taken the action of the NRDC (P) or a court to prompt any movement by the Environmental Protection Agency (the EPA) (D). Despite the EPA's (D) representations to this court, to the NRDC (P), and to the public that it planned to issue a

Continued on next page.

final decision within 90 days of completing a revised risk assessment, which the EPA (D) completed in December 2016, the EPA (D) never made such a response, and it has repeatedly delayed its review ever since. Whether the time is measured from 2009 (the year the NRDC (P) first filed its Administrative Petition) or March 2017 (the date that a final response should have been made according to the EPA's (D) own representations), the EPA (D) has stretched the rule of reason beyond its limits. Thus, this factor supports mandamus relief. The other *TRAC* factors also support mandamus relief. The second and sixth factors merit little discussion because Congress has supplied no specific timetable for this type of EPA (D) action except that it occurs "within a reasonable time," and because there is no dispute that the court need not find any impropriety lurking behind agency lassitude in order to hold that agency action is unreasonably delayed. This leaves the third, fourth, and fifth factors: whether "human health and welfare are at stake," "the effect of expediting delayed action on agency activities of a higher or competing priority," and "the nature and extent of the interests prejudiced by delay." These factors strongly support the NRDC's (P) petition for mandamus relief. For these reasons, the EPA's (D) delay has been egregious, and the NRDC's (P) petition for a writ of mandamus is granted.

ANALYSIS

The issuance by a court of a writ of mandamus directing a federal agency to act is considered an extraordinary remedy that is justified only in exceptional circumstances, but as this case illustrates, mandamus is warranted in those rare instances when an agency's delay has been "egregious." Notwithstanding that the grant of a writ of mandamus is an exceptional remedy, the Ninth Circuit Court of Appeals indicated that it granted three such writs over a five-year period, in circumstances materially similar to those presented by this case, to compel Environmental Protection Agency (the EPA) (D) action in response to serious dangers to human health. One argument that the EPA (D) made in its defense was that because the EPA (D) by its nature regulates almost entirely in the realm of human health and welfare, any acceleration of action on the Natural Resources Defense Council's (P) petition would delay other agency actions that also impact human health. The court rejected this argument, finding, in part, that the EPA's (D) contention that it could not prioritize the known dangers of tetrachlorvinphos (TCVP) to children's health ahead of 300 other regularly-scheduled pesticide registration reviews—for which it had identified no specific danger—was not an acceptable justification for the considerable human health interests prejudiced by the delay.

Quicknotes

WRIT OF MANDAMUS A court order issued commanding a public or private entity, or an official thereof, to perform a duty required by law.

Arkansas Power & Light Co. v. Interstate Commerce Commission

Utility company (P) v. Government agency (D)

725 F.2d 716 (D.C. Cir. 1984)

NATURE OF CASE: Appeal from agency rejection of petition for rulemaking.

FACT SUMMARY: Arkansas Power & Light Co. (P) petitioned the Interstate Commerce Commission (D) to collect certain data so that it could review rates that railroads charged for certain shippers.

RULE OF LAW

Courts will compel agencies to institute rulemaking proceedings only in extremely rare circumstances.

FACTS: Arkansas Power & Light Co. (P) and other utility companies wanted review of rates that "captive" shippers were charged by railroads. They petitioned the Interstate Commerce Commission (the ICC) (D) to institute rulemaking to collect data so that the rates could be approved. The ICC (D) concluded that development of a nationwide database was unnecessary, not required by statute and too burdensome. The ICC (D) decided to retain a system whereby companies could obtain the needed data on an individual basis for rate approvals. Arkansas Power & Light Co. (P) filed suit to compel the rulemaking and collection of a database.

ISSUE: Will courts commonly compel agencies to institute rulemaking proceedings?

HOLDING AND DECISION: (Edwards, J.) No. Courts will compel agencies to institute rulemaking proceedings only in extremely rare circumstances. Review of agency decisions is limited to ensuring that the agency has adequately explained the facts and policy concerns it relied on and that the facts have some factual basis. In the present case, the Interstate Commerce Commission (the ICC) (D) clearly decided that there were important reasons for not instituting rulemaking to collect data from all carriers. The reasons had a factual basis and were not arbitrary. Accordingly, there is absolutely no basis for the court to step in and compel agency action in this matter. The ICC's (D) decision not to engage in rulemaking is affirmed.

ANALYSIS

The Interstate Commerce Commission (D) apparently believed that making decisions on rates was best handled on an individual case basis. The agency (D) thought that the plaintiff utility companies would have adequate information available without an established database for the entire nation. Given the narrow standard of review, this explanation was more than adequate for the court.

Quicknotes

RULEMAKING The promulgation of a rule governing a particular activity by an administrative agency, acting within the scope of its power pursuant to statute.

Massachusetts v. Environmental Protection Agency

Coalition (P) v. Government agency (D)

549 U.S. 497 (2007)

NATURE OF CASE: Review of denial of rulemaking petition by agency.

FACT SUMMARY: A coalition of state and local governments and private organizations (collectively, "coalition") (P) petitioned the Environmental Protection Agency (D) to regulate greenhouse gas emissions pursuant to the Clean Air Act.

RULE OF LAW

Agency action is arbitrary and capricious when the agency fails to base its denial of the rulemaking petition in the statute at issue, offering no reasoned explanation for its refusal to reach a determination on the substantive matter of the petition.

FACTS: A coalition of state and local governments and private organizations (collectively, "coalition") (P) petitioned the Environmental Protection Agency (the EPA) (D) to regulate greenhouse gas emissions from new motor vehicles pursuant to the Clean Air Act (the CAA). Upon requesting and receiving more than 50,000 public comments on the issues raised in the rulemaking petition, the EPA (D) denied the petition. Specifically, the EPA (D) concluded that the CAA did not authorize it to issue regulations to address global climate change, and, even if the EPA (D) did have the authority to set greenhouse gas emissions standards, it would decline to do so because such regulation would conflict with other administration priorities.

ISSUE: Is agency action arbitrary and capricious when the agency fails to base its denial of the rulemaking petition in the statute at issue, offering no reasoned explanation for its refusal to reach a determination on the substantive matter of the petition?

HOLDING AND DECISION: (Stevens, J.) Yes. Agency action is arbitrary and capricious when the agency fails to base its denial of the rulemaking petition in the statute at issue, offering no reasoned explanation for its refusal to reach a determination on the substantive matter of the petition. Here, the Environmental Protection Agency (the EPA) (D) erred in concluding that the Clean Air Act (the CAA) did not authorize it to issue mandatory regulations to address global climate change. Indeed, the CAA requires the EPA (D) either to determine that greenhouse gases do not contribute to climate change or to provide a reasonable explanation as to why it cannot or will not exercise its discretion to determine whether said gases contribute to climate change. And notwithstanding the EPA's (D) broad discretion in choosing how to efficiently allocate limited resources to carry out its delegated responsibilities, it is the intent of Congress to constrain agency discretion in pursuing priorities of the President. As such, and without reaching the question of whether policy concerns can inform the EPA's (D) actions upon making an endangerment finding, if the EPA (D) ultimately makes such a finding, it is clear that the denial of the rulemaking petition was arbitrary and capricious. Remanded for further proceedings.

ANALYSIS

The initial petitioners in *Massachusetts v. Environmental Protection Agency*, a group of private organizations, were joined, prior to review in the D.C. Circuit, by the intervenor Massachusetts and other state and local governments. In dissent here, Chief Justice Roberts writes of his concern that a state has little or no authority to bring suit against the federal government, and that the majority has devised a new doctrine of state standing to support its result. Furthermore, Article III standing requirements, argues the Chief Justice, should not be relaxed because asserted injuries are pressed by a state. In other words, the complaint of Massachusetts that it faces impending loss of coastal land does not meet the particularized injury requirement set forth in *Lujan v. Defenders of Wildlife*, 504 U.S. 555 (1992). In short, the dissent concludes, the relaxation of Article III standing requirements improperly expands the role of courts.

Quicknotes

RULEMAKING The promulgation of a rule governing a particular activity by an administrative agency, acting within the scope of its power pursuant to statute.

JEM Broadcasting Company, Inc. v. Federal Communications Commission

Radio station (P) v. Government agency (D)

22 F.3d 320 (D.C. Cir. 1994)

NATURE OF CASE: Appeal from denial of license application.

FACT SUMMARY: JEM Broadcasting Company, Inc. (P) submitted a radio license application containing inconsistent information to the Federal Communications Commission (D), which refused to allow correction of the error.

RULE OF LAW

Rules of agency organization, procedure, and practice are exempt from the general notice and comment rulemaking requirements.

FACTS: In July 1988, JEM Broadcasting Company, Inc. (JEM) (P) submitted a license application for a radio station in Arkansas. When the Federal Communications Commission (the FCC) (D) reviewed the application, it determined that JEM (P) had provided inconsistent information that could not be resolved from the application documents. Therefore, the FCC (D) used its 1985 "hard look" regulations, which established a fixed filing window for substantially complete applications. Those applications that did not include the requisite information were returned without any opportunity to fix the errors under the "hard look" rules. JEM (P) contended that the "hard look" rules should not be applied because they were not promulgated with notice and comment in violation of the Administrative Procedure Act (APA).

ISSUE: Are rules of agency organization, procedure, and practice exempt from the general notice and comment rulemaking requirements?

HOLDING AND DECISION: (Edwards, J.) Yes. Rules of agency organization, procedure, and practice are exempt from the general notice and comment rulemaking requirements. The Administrative Procedure Act (the APA) generally requires notice and comment before new regulations are promulgated. However, there is an exception to this general rule for procedural regulations, as opposed to substantive rules that alter the rights and interests of parties affected by the regulations. *Air Transport Association of America v. Department of Transportation*, 900 F.2d 369 (D.C. 1990), suggested notice and comment was required when the promulgated rules encoded a substantive value judgment although nominally procedural. That decision might appear to inform this case, but the "value judgment" rationale was extended too far, the court vacated that judgment, and it has no precedent here. In the present case, it is unquestioned that the Federal Communications Commission (the FCC) (D) can set a deadline for applications. Although the "hard look" rules are significant, they do not change the substantive standards by which the FCC (D) evaluates applications. Thus, they are mostly procedural and are not required to go through notice and comment before being adopted.

ANALYSIS

The court considered JEM's (P) argument that the "hard look" regulations were substantive because they sacrificed applications with minor errors for the sake of efficiency. However, they held that this view would swallow up the procedural exception. *Air Transport Association of America v. Department of Transportation*, 900 F.2d 369 (D.C. 1990) that seemed to support this argument is no longer good law.

Quicknotes

ADMINISTRATIVE PROCEDURE ACT (APA) Enacted in 1946 to govern practices and proceedings before federal administrative agencies.

RULEMAKING The promulgation of a rule governing a particular activity by an administrative agency, acting within the scope of its power pursuant to statute.

United States v. Allegheny-Ludlum Steel Corp.

Federal government (D) v. Shipper (P)

406 U.S. 742 (1972)

NATURE OF CASE: Challenge to agency regulation.

FACT SUMMARY: Allegheny-Ludlum Steel Corp. (P) complained that the Interstate Commerce Commission (D) should have held hearings before promulgating rules regarding railroad rates.

RULE OF LAW

Informal rulemaking is permitted where the governing statute does not require that rules be made on the record.

FACTS: The Interstate Commerce Commission (the ICC) (D) regulated railroad rates. Congress passed the Esch Car Service Act of 1917 (the Esch Act), which allowed the ICC (D) to establish reasonable rules and regulations on its own initiative without requiring that they be inside "on the record." The ICC (D) used informal rulemaking to set some rates and Allegheny-Ludlum Steel Corp. (Allegheny-Ludlum) (P), a shipper, sought judicial review, complaining that a hearing should have been held.

ISSUE: Is informal rulemaking permitted where the governing statute does not require that rules be made on the record?

HOLDING AND DECISION: (Rehnquist, J.) Yes. Informal rulemaking is permitted where the governing statute does not require that rules be made on the record. According to 5 U.S.C. §§ 556 and 557, rulemaking procedure includes a hearing before the promulgation of the new regulation. However, these sections apply only when the statute requires rules be made "on the record." In the present case, the Esch Car Service Act of 1917 (the Esch Act) does not absolutely require that the rules be made on the record. While the precise words "on the record" are not the only factor to be considered, the language of the Esch Act does not indicate that formal rulemaking was to be involved.

ANALYSIS

The formal rulemaking procedures of 5 U.S.C. §§ 556 and 557 include a trial-type proceeding. A hybrid type of rulemaking has also arisen where Congress has expressly required it. Hybrid rulemaking is more burdensome than informal rulemaking, but less burdensome than the formal type.

Quicknotes

RULEMAKING The promulgation of a rule governing a particular activity by an administrative agency, acting within the scope of its power pursuant to statute.

United States v. Florida East Coast Railway Co.

Federal government (D) v. Railroad company (P)

410 U.S. 224 (1973)

NATURE OF CASE: Appeal of nullification of certain boxcar compensation rules.

FACT SUMMARY: The Interstate Commerce Commission (D) adopted rules regarding per diem charges on boxcars following an informal conference.

RULE OF LAW

The Interstate Commerce Commission need not hold a formal hearing prior to establishing rules with respect to car service by common carriers.

FACTS: Amendments to the Interstate Commerce Act empowered the Interstate Commerce Commission (the ICC) (D) to adopt rules with respect to car service by common carriers and particularly to the compensation to be paid car owners for borrowed boxcars. The ICC (D) obtained data on freight-car demand from various carriers. In response to concerns expressed by various carriers, the ICC (D) held an informal conference. The ICC (D) subsequently published rule proposals inviting criticism. The proposals were then adopted. The ICC's (D) actions were challenged for failure to hold a formal hearing. The lower court invalidated the ICC's (D) actions.

ISSUE: Must the Interstate Commerce Commission hold a formal hearing prior to establishing rules with respect to car service by common carriers?

HOLDING AND DECISION: (Rehnquist, J.) No. The Interstate Commerce Commission (the ICC) (D) need not hold a formal hearing prior to establishing rules with respect to car service by common carriers. The Administrative Procedure Act states the evidentiary requirements for formal hearings but does not mandate that formal hearings always be held. When a statute does not expressly require a formal hearing, the agency in question may, when conducting rulemaking, take evidence by written submission if the agency believes a formal hearing unnecessary. Here, the ICC (D) took extensive steps to obtain evidence through written submission. Since this Court has already held that the Interstate Commerce Act does not require hearings, the ICC's (D) actions were proper. Reversed.

ANALYSIS

The Court's opinion here took a very narrow view of the necessity for formal hearings. The Interstate Commerce Act amendment in question did contain language suggesting a hearing would be necessary, but the Court found the language insufficient to trigger the requirement of a hearing. It would seem only statutes clearly spelling out the requirement of a hearing will bring the Administrative Procedure Act's rules for formal hearings into play.

Quicknotes

APA § 553 Establishes the minimum requirements of public rulemaking procedure.

INTERSTATE COMMERCE ACT § 1(14) Allows the Commission to prescribe per diem charges for the use of railroad cars owned by another.

PRETERMINATION HEARING A hearing held prior to the termination of a property interest.

RULEMAKING The promulgation of a rule governing a particular activity by an administrative agency, acting within the scope of its power pursuant to statute.

Vermont Yankee Nuclear Power Corp. v. Natural Resources Defense Council, Inc.

Nuclear power plant (D) v. Environmental group (P)

435 U.S. 519 (1978)

NATURE OF CASE: Appeal in connection with review of agency rulemaking procedure.

FACT SUMMARY: The Natural Resources Defense Council, Inc. (P) challenged a rule promulgated by the Atomic Energy Commission (D) because of alleged procedural defects in the rulemaking process.

RULE OF LAW

The adequacy of the record in a rulemaking proceeding does not depend on the type of procedural devices employed but turns on whether the agency has followed the statutory mandate of the Administrative Procedure Act.

FACTS: The Natural Resources Defense Council, Inc. (the NRDC) (P) challenged a rule promulgated by the Atomic Energy Commission (the AEC) (D) on the basis it was denied the opportunity for discovery and cross-examination and thus a meaningful opportunity to participate in the rulemaking proceedings. The reviewing court agreed that the procedures followed by the AEC (D) during promulgation of the rule were inadequate and remanded the rule to the AEC (D). The United States Supreme Court, however, found the reviewing court to be in error in requiring the AEC (D) to grant additional procedural rights in the exercise of its rulemaking functions.

ISSUE: Does the adequacy of the record in an agency rulemaking proceeding depend on the type of procedural devices, "or does it turn" on whether the agency has followed the statutory mandate of the Administrative Procedure Act?

HOLDING AND DECISION: (Rehnquist, J.) Yes. The adequacy of the record in an agency rulemaking proceeding is not correlated directly to the type of procedural devices employed but turns on whether the agency has followed the statutory mandate of the Administrative Procedure Act. Vermont Yankee's (D) contention fails because the Atomic Energy Commission (the AEC) (D) was well within its authority on the waste disposal and fuel reprocessing issues as they applied in individual license proceedings. However, the court of appeals was incorrect in its invalidation of the AEC's (D) rulemaking proceeding. Absent constitutional restraints or extremely compelling circumstances, the administrative agencies should be free to fashion their own rules of procedure and to pursue methods of inquiry capable of permitting them to discharge their duties. There are three compelling reasons why the agencies' discretion should be determinative. First, if courts continually review agency proceedings to determine whether the agency employed procedures that were what the court perceived to be the best or correct results, judicial review would be totally unpredictable. Second, the fact that the court looked only at the record and not at information available to the AEC (D) when it decided to structure the proceedings in a certain way is an example of Monday morning quarterbacking that would compel the agency to conduct all rulemaking proceedings with the full panoply of procedural devices normally associated only with adjudicatory hearings. Finally, and perhaps most importantly, this type of review misconceives the standard for judicial review of an agency rule; rulemaking need not be based solely on the transcript of a hearing. In fact, in a case like this there need not be a formal hearing. Reversed.

ANALYSIS

Executive Order 12044 concerned President Carter's directive to the agencies to "adopt procedures to improve existing and future regulations." 43 Fed. Reg. 12661. The order called for greater involvement by the public. This consisted, in part, of suggestions concerning published notice, conferences, hearings, and direct mailing. Gellhorn, W., *Admin. Law*, 203-204.

Quicknotes

5 U.S.C. § 553 Establishes minimum requirements of public rulemaking procedure.

ADJUDICATORY PROCEEDING A hearing conducted by an administrative agency resulting in a final judgment regarding the rights of the parties involved.

JUDICIAL REVIEW The authority of the courts to review decisions, actions, or omissions committed by another agency or branch of government.

Chocolate Manufacturers Association v. Block

Trade group (P) v. Government agency (D)

755 F.2d 1098 (4th Cir. 1985)

NATURE OF CASE: Appeal from decision denying relief from an administrative rule.

FACT SUMMARY: The Chocolate Manufacturers Association (P) challenged, on inadequate-notice grounds, a United States Department of Agriculture (D) rule that prohibited the use of chocolate-flavored milk in the federally funded Special Supplemental Food Program for Women, Infants, and Children.

RULE OF LAW

The notice in the Federal Register that an agency must give of a proposed rulemaking must contain either the terms or substance of the proposed rule or a description of the subjects and issues involved.

FACTS: The Special Supplemental Food Program for Women, Infants, and Children (the WIC Program) was established by Congress in 1972 to assist pregnant, postpartum, and breastfeeding women, infants, and children from families with inadequate income whose physical and mental health were in danger because of inadequate nutrition or health care. In 1979, Congress extended the WIC Program and redefined the term "supplemental foods" that the program was established to provide. This redefinition stated that the United States Department of Agriculture (the USDA) (D) must assure that the fat, sugar, and salt content of foods prescribed by the WIC Program were appropriate. The USDA (D) then published for comment the proposed rule at issue here, which proposed a maximum sugar content for authorized cereals but did not discuss sugar in relation to flavoring in milk. The USDA (D) notice allowed 60 days for comment and specifically invited comment on the entire scope of the proposed rule. Of the over 1,000 comments received, 78 recommended that flavored milk be deleted from the WIC Program's list of approved foods. The USDA (D) did delete flavored milk from the list, and the Chocolate Manufacturers Association (the CMA) (P) challenged the rule on the grounds that it did not provide the disallowance of flavored milk would be considered. The lower court denied the CMA (P) any relief and it appealed.

ISSUE: Must the notice in the Federal Register that an agency must give of a proposed rulemaking contain either the terms or substance of the proposed rule or a description of the subjects and issues involved?

HOLDING AND DECISION: (Sprouse, J.) Yes. Section 4 of the Administrative Procedure Act requires that the notice in the Federal Register that an agency must give of a proposed rulemaking contain either the terms or substance of the proposed rule or a description of the subjects and issues involved. The purpose of the notice-and-comment procedure is both to allow the agency to benefit from the experience and input of the parties who file comments and to see to it that the agency maintains a flexible and open-minded attitude toward its own rules. There is no question that an agency may promulgate a final rule that differs in some particulars from its proposal, but it does not have carte blanche to establish a rule contrary to its original proposal simply because it receives suggestions to alter it during the comment period. If the final rule materially alters the issues involved in the rulemaking or if it substantially departs from the terms or substance of the proposed rule, the notice is inadequate. Here, the final rule was an outgrowth of the original rule proposed, but perhaps not a logical outgrowth. In all the activities setting out and discussing food packaging, including the proposed rule and its preamble, the United States Department of Agriculture (D) never suggested that flavored milk be removed from the Women, Infants, and Children (the WIC Program). At the time of the proposed rulemaking, neither Chocolate Manufacturers Association (P) nor the general public could have any indication that flavored milk was not part of the WIC Program acceptable diet. Reversed and remanded.

ANALYSIS

Section 553 of the Administrative Procedure Act has been and remains the foremost example of federal rulemaking. Section 553's provisions detail the procedure an agency must follow in promulgating a rule. These provisions state the general public must be given a chance to comment in writing or orally about the rule to be promulgated, and the agency promulgating the rule must incorporate in the final rule a statement of its basis and purpose.

Home Box Office v. Federal Communications Commission

Television network (P) v. Government agency (D)

567 F.2d 9 (D.C. Cir. 1977)

NATURE OF CASE: Review of an informal rulemaking procedure.

FACT SUMMARY: Ex parte comments were received in connection with an informal rulemaking procedure.

RULE OF LAW

The public record must reflect the representations made to an agency so that relevant information supporting or refuting those representations may be brought to the attention of the reviewing courts by persons participating in agency proceedings.

FACTS: Ex parte comments were received in connection with an informal rulemaking proceeding dealing with subscription television. A participant in the proceeding, and an amicus before the court, Geller (P), filed a petition with the Federal Communications Commission (the FCC) (D) to disclose ex parte communications during the proceedings. The FCC (D) took no action and Geller (P) sought judicial review of the FCC's (D) order promulgating four amendments regulating subscription television. The court of appeals sua sponte ordered the FCC (D) to disclose the ex parte contacts. The FCC (D) did so and showed that the competing industry representatives had a great voice in the outcome of the proceedings.

ISSUE: Must the public record reflect what representations were made to an agency so that relevant information supporting or refuting those representations may be brought to the attention of the reviewing courts by persons participating in agency proceedings?

HOLDING AND DECISION: (Per curiam) Yes. The public record must reflect the representations made to an agency so that relevant information supporting or refuting those representations may be brought to the attention of the reviewing courts by persons participating in agency proceedings. Here, the evidence is consistent with the claim of undue industry influence over the Federal Communications Commission (the FCC) (D) proceedings. The presence of secrecy makes it difficult to judge the truth even when later disclosed by the FCC (D). Secrecy is inconsistent with fundamental notions of fairness implicit in due process. Therefore, once a notice of proposed rulemaking has been issued, discussion with interested parties should be prohibited, and if made, a written document or a summary of any oral communications must be placed in the public file immediately after the communication so that interested parties may comment.

ANALYSIS

The courts encouraged agencies to use an informal rulemaking procedure. However, they became afraid that this informal procedure would fall victim to too much political pressure. Therefore, the courts are demanding that these procedures become more judicial in nature. Gellhorn, quoting Robinson, 64 *Va. L. Rev.* 227-230.

Quicknotes

AMICUS BRIEF A brief submitted by a third party, not a party to the action, that contains information for the court's consideration in conformity with its position.

DUE PROCESS The constitutional mandate requiring the courts to protect and enforce individuals' rights and liberties consistent with prevailing principles of fairness and justice and prohibiting the federal and state governments from such activities that deprive its citizens of a life, liberty, or property interest.

EX PARTE A proceeding commenced by one party without providing any opposing parties with notice or that is uncontested by an adverse party.

SUA SPONTE An action taken by the court by its own motion and without the suggestion of one of the parties.

Sierra Club v. Costle

Environmental protection group (P) v. Government agency (D)

657 F.2d 298 (D.C. Cir. 1981)

NATURE OF CASE: Appeal from decision denying relief in a challenge to an agency rule.

FACT SUMMARY: The Sierra Club (P) and the Environmental Defense Fund (P) challenged the Environmental Protection Agency's (D) adoption of the 1.2 lbs./MBtu standard for power plants using coal fuel to generate power.

RULE OF LAW

The 1977 Amendments to the Clean Air Act provide that all relevant documents that become available after a proposed rule has been published shall be placed in the docket as soon as possible after their availability.

FACTS: The Environmental Defense Fund (the EDF) (P) and the Sierra Club (P) challenged a rule promulgated by Costle (D) and the Environmental Protection Agency (EPA) (D) that adopted a 1.2 lbs./MBtu standard for power plants using coal fuel to generate power. The EDF (P) objected that comments regarding the adopted standard were filed after the close of the official comment period and that meetings between EPA (D) officials and various government and private parties interested in the outcome of the final rule took place after the close of the comment period. The EDF (P) alleged that such "late" comments, mostly from representatives of the coal or utility industries, and the meetings persuaded the EPA (D) to back away from adopting a .55 lb./MBtu limit and instead to adopt the more lenient 1.2 lbs./MBtu standard. The EDF (P) also alleged that some post-comment communications were not docketed by the EPA (D) in violation of the 1977 Amendments to the Clean Air Act (the Act) and that, therefore, the EDF (P) was not able to adequately respond to those documents before the 1.2 lbs./MBtu standard was adopted. The lower court ruled in favor of the EPA (D), and the EDF (P) appealed.

ISSUE: Do the 1977 Amendments to the Clean Air Act provide that all documents that become available after a proposed rule has been published and which the Administrator determines are of central relevance to the rulemaking shall be placed in the docket as soon as possible after their availability?

HOLDING AND DECISION: (Wald, J.) Yes. The 1977 Amendments to the Clean Air Act (the Act) provide that all relevant documents that become available after a proposed rule has been published shall be placed in the docket as soon as possible after their availability. This provision is not limited to the comment period, and it apparently allows the Environmental Protection Agency (the EPA) (D) not only to put documents in the record after the comment period is over, but also to define which documents are "of central relevance" so as to require that they be placed in the docket. The EPA (D) thus has the authority to place post-comment documents into the docket, but it need not do so in all instances. The Act does not expressly treat the issue of post-comment period meetings with individuals outside the EPA (D). Oral face-to-face discussions are not prohibited anywhere, anytime, in the Act. But at least some adequate summary of them must be made in order to preserve the integrity of the rulemaking docket. Docketing of such summaries may be needed to give practical effect to the provisions of the Act that demand that all documents of central relevance to the rulemaking shall be placed in the docket post haste. It was not unlawful in this case for EPA (D) not to docket a meeting since EPA (D) makes no effort to base the rule on any information arising from that meeting. In sum, EPA's (D) adoption of the 1.2 lbs./MBtu emissions ceiling was free from procedural error. Affirmed.

ANALYSIS

In the above case, the comment period regarding the proposed emissions ceiling ran from September 19, 1978, to January 15, 1979. After January 15, the Environmental Protection Agency (the EPA) (D) received almost 300 written submissions on the proposed rule that were accepted by the EPA (D) and entered on its administration docket. The EPA (D) did not officially reopen the comment period, and it did not notify the public through the Federal Register that it had received and was entering "late" comments. Of the late comments, the Environmental Defense Fund (the EDF) (P) claimed that at least 30 were from representatives of the coal or utility industries and 22 were submitted by members of Congress as advocates of those interests. The EDF (P) characterized such comments and meetings that took place after the comment period closed as an "ex parte blitz" by the coal industry to force the EPA (D) to adapt a higher emissions ceiling.

Quicknotes

CLEAN AIR ACT § 307 Requires that documents relevant to rulemaking under the Act be docketed.

Chevron v. Natural Resources Defense Council, Inc.

Civil company (D) v. Environmental group (P)

467 U.S. 837 (1984)

NATURE OF CASE: Appeal from review of an Environmental Protection Agency (D) regulation.

FACT SUMMARY: The Environmental Protection Agency (D) passed a regulation incorporating a broader definition of an air pollution "source" than it had used previously.

RULE OF LAW

Where Congress has left an open question in its legislation, judicial review of an agency's interpretation of that question must be limited to whether the agency's construction is legitimate.

FACTS: In the 1977 Amendments to the Clean Air Act, Congress limited the issuance of permits to stationary sources of air pollution to those meeting strict requirements. The legislation was unclear as to what the term "stationary source" meant. The Environmental Protection Agency (the EPA) (D) passed a regulation applying the strict standard to each individual emitting source. The EPA (D) later revised the regulation to allow all emitting sources in a single plant to be treated as a single source for the purposes of the legislation. The Natural Resources Defense Council, Inc. (P) filed a petition for review of this regulation. The court of appeals found the EPA's (D) interpretation inconsistent with the policy of the legislation. The EPA (D) appealed, and the United States Supreme Court granted certiorari.

ISSUE: Must judicial review of an agency's interpretation of a question left open in legislation by Congress be limited to whether the agency's construction is legitimate?

HOLDING AND DECISION: (Stevens, J.) Yes. Where Congress has left an open question in legislation, judicial review of the agency's interpretation of that question must be limited to whether the agency's construction is legitimate. In this case Congress did not clearly define "stationary source." The legislative history is not clear as to whether "stationary source" should have a plant-wide definition. The Environmental Protection Agency's (D) construction is reasonable in light of the plain English of the statute as well as the competing interests involved. The judiciary may not review an agency's authority in light of the policy of the statute but only based on the reasonableness of the language. Reversed.

ANALYSIS

In a 1989 law review article, Justice Scalia delineated two categories of congressional ambiguity, each requiring a different standard of review by the judiciary. Where Congress clearly intended a certain result, but was unclear about it, the court must resolve the issue as a question of law. On the other hand, where congressional vagueness was intentionally meant to delegate authority to an agency, the standard of *Chevron* must apply. *Chevron, U.S.A., Inc. v. Natural Resources Defense Council, Inc.*, 467 U.S. 837 (1984). See Scalia, "Judicial Deference to Administrative Interpretations of Law," 1989 *Duke L.J.* 511, 516.

Quicknotes

INTERPRETATION The determination of the meaning of a statute.

JUDICIAL REVIEW The authority of the courts to review decisions, actions, or omissions committed by another agency or branch of government.

STATUTORY CONSTRUCTION The examination and interpretation of statutes.

West Virginia v. EPA

State (P) v. Federal agency (D)

142 S. Ct. 2587 (2022)

NATURE OF CASE: Challenge to a federal agency's authority to adopt a regulatory scheme absent express congressional authority.

FACT SUMMARY: A novel generation-shifting approach to reducing carbon emissions from power plants, adopted by the Environmental Protection Agency (the EPA) (D) under the authority of Section 111 of the Clean Air Act, was challenged as beyond the EPA's (D) authority absent express congressional authority.

RULE OF LAW

The generation-shifting "best system of emission reduction" (BESR) identified by the Environmental Protection Agency (the EPA) in the Clean Power Plan is not within the authority granted to the EPA in Section 111(d) of the Clean Air Act, given that such a BESR scheme would substantially restructure the nation's energy market and was not expressly authorized by Congress.

FACTS: The Clean Air Act authorizes the Environmental Protection Agency (the EPA) (D) to regulate power plants by setting a "standard of performance" for their emission of certain pollutants into the air. Under one presidential administration (President Obama), the EPA (D) promulgated the Clean Power Plan, addressing carbon dioxide emissions from existing coal- and natural-gas-fired power plants. For authority, the EPA (D) cited Section 111 of the Clean Air Act (CAA). The EPA (D) determines the emissions limit for emissions governed by the CAA, which specifies that an emission limit should reflect the "best system of emission reduction (BSER). . . that has been adequately demonstrated" for a given source of air pollution. Prior to the Clean Power Plan, the EPA (D) had set performance standards based on "engineering control" measures that would reduce pollution by causing plants to operate more cleanly. Under the Clean Power Plan, the BSER included "generation shifting," at the grid level, which involved a shift in electricity production from higher-emitting to lower-emitting producers. For example, one of these generation shifts was from existing coal-fired power plants, which would make less power, to natural-gas-fired plants, which would make more. This would reduce carbon dioxide emissions because natural gas plants produce less carbon dioxide per unit of electricity generated than coal plants. Another shift was to cleaner sources, such as renewables, primarily wind and solar, of electricity production. In litigation that followed, some states and private parties challenged the EPA's (D) authority to use a generation-shifting approach absent express congressional authority to do so and contended that the EPA (D) was restricted to limiting emissions through the use of engineering controls. The EPA (D) argued that "best system" encompassed other ways of limiting emissions and that generation shifting was a "best system," because it resulted in greater emissions reductions than could be achieved only through engineering controls. If the EPA's (D) generation-shifting BSER were used, it was projected to restructure the nation's overall mix of electricity generation to transition from 38 percent to 27 percent coal by 2030. The issue reached the United States Supreme Court.

ISSUE: Is the generation-shifting "best system of emission reduction" (BSER) identified by the Environmental Protection Agency (the EPA) in the Clean Power Plan within the authority granted to the EPA in Section 111(d) of the Clean Air Act, given that such a BESR scheme would substantially restructure the nation's energy market and was not expressly authorized by Congress?

HOLDING AND DECISION: (Roberts, C.J.) No. The generation-shifting "best system of emission reduction" (BSER) identified by the Environmental Protection Agency (the EPA) in the Clean Power Plan is not within the authority granted to the EPA in Section 111(d) of the Clean Air Act, given that such a BSER scheme would substantially restructure the nation's energy market and was not expressly authorized by Congress. The issue here is whether restructuring the nation's overall mix of electricity generation to transition from 38 percent to 27 percent coal by 2030 can be the BSER within the meaning of Section 111. Precedent teaches that there are extraordinary cases "in which the history and the breadth of the authority that [an agency] has asserted," and the "economic and political significance" of that assertion, provide a reason to hesitate before concluding that Congress meant to confer such authority. Under this body of law, known as the major questions doctrine, given both separation of powers principles and a practical understanding of legislative intent, the agency must point to "clear congressional authorization" for the authority it claims. This is a major questions case. The EPA (D) claimed to discover an unheralded power representing a transformative expansion of its regulatory authority in the vague language of a long-extant, but rarely used, statute designed as a gap filler. That discovery allowed it to adopt a regulatory program that Congress had conspicuously declined to enact itself. Given these circumstances, there is every

Continued on next page.

reason to hesitate before concluding that Congress meant to confer on the EPA (D) the authority it claims under Section 111(d). Prior to 2015, the EPA (D) had always set emissions limits under Section 111 based on the application of measures that would reduce pollution by causing the regulated source to operate more cleanly. It had never devised a cap by looking to a "system" that would reduce pollution simply by "shifting" polluting activity "from dirtier to cleaner sources." Given these circumstances, the Court's precedents counsel skepticism toward the EPA's (D) claim that Section 111 empowers it to devise carbon emissions caps based on a generation-shifting approach. To overcome that skepticism, the EPA (D) must—under the major questions doctrine—point to "clear congressional authorization" to regulate in that manner. Capping carbon dioxide emissions at a level that will force a nationwide transition away from the use of coal to generate electricity may be a sensible "solution to the crisis of the day," [alluding to global warming and climate change], but it is not plausible that Congress gave the EPA (D) the authority to adopt on its own such a regulatory scheme in Section 111(d). A decision of such magnitude and consequence rests with Congress itself, or an agency acting pursuant to a clear delegation from that representative body.

DISSENT: (Kagan, J.) The majority's decision rests on one claim alone: that generation shifting is just too new and too big a deal for Congress to have authorized it in Section 111's general terms. But that is wrong. A key reason Congress makes broad delegations like Section 111 is so an agency can respond, appropriately and commensurately, to new and big problems. The majority today overrides that legislative choice. In so doing, it deprives EPA (D) of the power needed—and the power granted—to curb the emission of greenhouse gases. The majority conveniently ignores the text of the Clean Air Act and conjures the "major questions doctrine" so it can prevent agencies from doing important work, notwithstanding that is what Congress directed. Agency delegations of the magnitude at issue here go back to the nation's founding. Congress has always delegated and continues to do so — including on important policy issues. As the Court itself has recognized, it is often "unreasonable and impracticable" for Congress to do anything else. In all times, but ever more in our increasingly complex society, Congress simply cannot do its job absent an ability to delegate power under broad general directives. Why wouldn't Congress instruct the EPA (D) to select "the best system of emission reduction," rather than try to choose that system itself? Congress knows that systems of emission reduction lie not in its own but in the EPA's (D) unique expertise. Additionally, Congress knows that without delegation and expertise of agencies, Congress itself cannot keep regulatory schemes working across time. The "best system of emission reduction" is not today what it was yesterday and will surely be something different tomorrow. So, for this reason too, a rational Congress delegates. It enables an agency to adapt old regulatory approaches to new times, to ensure that a statutory program remains effective. In sum, Congress knows how government works in ways courts do not and what mix of legislative and administrative action conduces to good policy. For these reasons, the majority should not replace its ideas of delegation for those of Congress, as already stated in the Clean Air Act.

ANALYSIS

This decision has been criticized as adopting a rule that will block agencies from adopting new measures that significantly depart from prior measures in addressing new and pressing national problems. The decision states that there are "extraordinary" cases "in which the history and the breadth of the authority that [an agency] has asserted," and the "economic and political significance" of that assertion, provide a reason to hesitate before concluding that Congress meant to confer such authority. However, the Court does not announce any standards for when such an "extraordinary" case is presented, thus leaving it entirely to courts to decide, based solely on the courts' own views of the proper role of regulatory agencies, whether to require express authority from Congress in addition to the authority Congress has already delegated statutorily, for any given agency action. Ostensibly, this could result in agencies avoiding addressing large, immediate issues for fear of having their efforts blocked by the courts based only on the courts' standardless views. On the other hand, the decision could also have the effect of forcing Congress to pass new and specific legislation to address large, new problems like climate change. In any event, after *West Virginia,* once a court has decided it is faced with a "major question," agency action will be presumed invalid absent a clear congressional statement that such action is authorized.

Quicknotes

MAJOR QUESTIONS DOCTRINE Statutory interpretation doctrine pursuant to which a court will presume that Congress has not delegated to an agency the authority to act on an issue the court deems to be of major political or economic significance, despite there being statutory authority for such action, thus requiring clear congressional authorization for the agency to act.

Motor Vehicle Manufacturers Assoc. v. State Farm Mutual Automobile Ins. Co.

[Parties not identified.]

463 U.S. 29 (1983)

NATURE OF CASE: Appeal from decision finding agency action arbitrary and capricious.

FACT SUMMARY: The National Highway Traffic Safety Administration (the NHTSA) (D) appealed from a decision of the court of appeals, finding that the revocation of the requirement that new motor vehicles produced after September 1982 be equipped with passive restraints to protect occupants in the event of a collision was arbitrary and capricious.

RULE OF LAW

When an agency modifies or rescinds a previously promulgated rule, it is required to supply a satisfactory, rational analysis supporting its decision.

FACTS: Standard 208 is a rule promulgated by the Department of Transportation dealing with motor vehicle occupant safety. From the time that it was originally issued in 1967, the standard has been subject to constant rescission, modification, and amendment. In 1969, the standard first included a requirement that cars come equipped with a passive restraint system. Between 1976 and 1980, a mandatory passive restraint requirement was issued. The two systems that would satisfy the standard would be an air bag system or a passive seat belt system, with the choice of system being left up to the manufacturer. It was assumed that manufacturers would install approximately 60 percent air bags and 40 percent passive belts. By 1981, the manufacturers planned to produce 99 percent of their cars equipped with passive belts. In 1981, even though studies, surveys, and other empirical evidence indicated that the use rate associated with the passive belts was more than double that associated with manual belts, the National Highway Traffic Safety Administration (the NHTSA) (D) concluded that the safety benefits associated with the standard's implementation did not justify the costs of implementing the standard. In that same year, the NHTSA (D), without considering the possible use of air bags, rescinded the passive restraint requirement. The court of appeals found that the NHTSA's (D) revocation of the passive restraint requirement was arbitrary and capricious, and the NHTSA (D) appealed.

ISSUE: When an agency rescinds or modifies a previously promulgated rule, is it required to supply a satisfactory, rational analysis supporting its decision?

HOLDING AND DECISION: (White, J.) Yes. When an agency rescinds or modifies a previously promulgated rule, it is required to supply a satisfactory, rational analysis supporting its decision. A change or rescission is akin to the promulgation of the rule itself and is subject to the same arbitrary and capricious standard. The agency may be required to more fully justify its decision than if the agency had not acted in the first instance. The agency must show a rational connection between the facts found and the decision rendered. If an agency relies on improper facts or fails to consider important aspects of the problem or renders a decision that runs contrary to the evidence, its decision may be considered arbitrary and capricious. The National Traffic and Motor Vehicle Safety Act of 1966 mandates the achievement of traffic safety. Given the conceded effectiveness of air bags, the logical response to the manufacturers' actions would have been to require air bags. Not only was this not done, it appears that the NHTSA (D) did not even consider it. A rational rescission decision cannot be made without the consideration of technologically feasible alternatives of proven value. Further, the empirical evidence runs counter to the agency's determination that the safety aspects associated with the use of passive belts could not be determined. The empirical evidence indicates that there is a doubling of use of passive belts over the use of manual belts, and the safety benefits associated with the increased use of safety belts is unquestioned. Finally, the NHTSA (D) has failed to articulate a basis for not requiring nondetachable passive belts. By failing to consider feasible, logical alternatives and dismissing the safety benefits associated with passive restraints in light of the evidence, the NHTSA (D) has failed to present an adequate basis or explanation for rescinding the mandatory passive restraint requirement. Vacated and remanded.

CONCURRENCE AND DISSENT: (Rehnquist, J.) The majority correctly concludes that the National Highway Traffic Safety Administration (the NHTSA) (D) must provide a rational explanation for changing course and rescinding Standard 208, and that the NHTSA (D) arbitrarily failed to consider the benefits of air bags. Contrary to the majority's holding, however, the NHTSA (D) met that requirement here with respect to automatic seatbelts. The Agency's changed view seems to result from the election of a president from a different political party, but that fact alone is a reasonable basis for an agency to reevaluate its priorities and change course to match the

Continued on next page.

views of a new administration, so long as the agency's change stays within congressionally defined boundaries.

ANALYSIS

Standard setting by the National Highway Traffic Safety Administration (D) has proved most troublesome. Initial promulgation of standards was in large part mere adoptions of already existing standards. The promulgation of new standards is associated with a whole host of problems, including the problem of obtaining accurate information and the problem of enforcement and the problems that may be encountered in negotiating such standards with industry and other interest groups.

Quicknotes

ARBITRARY AND CAPRICIOUS STANDARD Standard imposed in reviewing the decision of an agency or court that the decision may have been made in disregard of the facts or law.

CHAPTER 3

Adjudication

Quick Reference Rules of Law

CHAPTER 3

National Labor Relations Board v. Local Union No. 25, International Brotherhood of Electrical Workers

Government agency (P) v. Labor union (D)

586 F.2d 959 (2d Cir. 1978)

NATURE OF CASE: Petition for enforcement of order invalidating a collective bargaining agreement.

FACT SUMMARY: An administrative law judge ruled that the Union (D) had engaged in unfair labor practices and that a provision of the collective bargaining agreement was illegal.

RULE OF LAW

The Administrative Procedure Act requires that there be adequate notice, argument, and evidence before an administrative law judge makes a decision.

FACTS: Flores filed a complaint with the National Labor Relations Board (NLRB) (P) that the Union (D) failed to provide him with job referrals because he was not a Union (D) member. The administrative law judge (ALJ), hearing the case agreed and found that the Union (D) had engaged in unfair labor practices. The ALJ then went beyond the NLRB (P) complaint and found that a provision of the collective bargaining agreement at issue was illegal and invalidated it. The Union (D) claimed that they were denied a fair hearing on this issue because there was no notice, argument, or evidence presented on the legality of the agreement's clause.

ISSUE: Does the Administrative Procedure Act require that there be adequate notice, argument, and evidence before an administrative law judge makes a decision?

HOLDING AND DECISION: (Lumbard, J.) Yes. The Administrative Procedure Act (the APA) requires that there be adequate notice, argument, and evidence before an administrative law judge (ALJ) makes a decision. APA § 554 requires that there be notice to the parties before an ALJ rules on an issue. In the present case, the judge hearing the National Labor Relations Board's (P) complaint on behalf of Flores went ahead and ruled on the validity of the collective bargaining agreement even though the issue was not raised in the complaint or in oral argument, nor was there any evidence presented. Accordingly, the Union (D) did not receive the requisite notice and the decision cannot be enforced.

ANALYSIS

Different states handle administrative law judges in various manners. In some, the judges are hired by the agencies themselves. In others, there are central panels of judges not controlled by the agency.

Quicknotes

APA § 554 Provides for procedures in agency adjudications.

COLLECTIVE BARGAINING Negotiations between an employer and employee that are mediated by a specified third party.

Southwest Sunsites, Inc. v. Federal Trade Commission

Land developer (P) v. Government agency (D)

785 F.2d 1431 (9th Cir. 1986)

NATURE OF CASE: Appeal from agency cease-and-desist order.

FACT SUMMARY: Southwest Sunsites, Inc. (P) complained that the Federal Trade Commission (D) had applied a new standard with regard to deceptive practices without advance notice.

RULE OF LAW

The notice requirement of the Administrative Procedure Act is satisfied where the parties understood the relevant issues and were afforded a full opportunity to justify their conduct.

FACTS: Southwest Sunsites, Inc. (Southwest) (P) sold undeveloped land in rural west Texas to out-of-state purchasers. The Federal Trade Commission (the FTC) (D) filed a complaint against Southwest (P) contending that it was engaged in unfair and deceptive practices with regard to the sales. The complaint argued that Southwest (P) misrepresented the investment potential of the land and its suitability for use and value. An administrative law judge dismissed the complaint, finding that the representations did not have the tendency and capacity to mislead. The FTC (D), applying a different standard, found that the representations were likely to mislead reasonable consumers, and reversed and issued a cease-and-desist order. Southwest (P) appealed.

ISSUE: Is the notice requirement of the Administrative Procedure Act satisfied where the parties understood the relevant issues and were afforded a full opportunity to justify their conduct?

HOLDING AND DECISION: (Beezer, J.) Yes. The notice requirement of the Administrative Procedure Act (the APA) is satisfied where the parties understood the relevant issues and were afforded a full opportunity to justify their conduct. The APA requires that parties involved in agency complaints be "timely informed of the matters of fact and law asserted." In the present case, the standard used by the Federal Trade Commission (the FTC) (D) was different from that used by the judge, but it imposed a greater burden on the agency since probable deception and detriment to the consumer had to be expressly proved. Thus, the administrative law judge's finding was based on a standard that was narrower and completely subsumed by the FTC's (D) new standard. Accordingly, Southwest Sunsites, Inc. (P) had a more than adequate opportunity to respond to the complaint. The FTC's (D) cease-and-desist order is affirmed.

ANALYSIS

This case involves an unusual situation. The court correctly ruled that the "likely" standard applied by the Federal Trade Commission (D) was harder to reach than the "tendency" standard used by the administrative law judge (ALJ). Thus, the ALJ and the agency must have had wildly different views of the facts involved to come to opposite conclusions.

Quicknotes

ADMINISTRATIVE LAW JUDGE (ALJ) A judge who presides over administrative hearings.

ADMINISTRATIVE PROCEDURE ACT (APA) Enacted in 1946 to govern practices and proceedings before federal administrative agencies.

CEASE-AND-DESIST ORDER An order from a court or administrative agency prohibiting a person or business from continuing a particular course of conduct.

NOTICE AND COMMENT RULEMAKING Informal rulemaking.

John D. Copanos and Sons, Inc. v. Food and Drug Administration

Drug manufacturer (P) v. Government agency (D)

854 F.2d 510 (D.C. Cir. 1988)

NATURE OF CASE: Petition for review of agency's rejection of application.

FACT SUMMARY: The Food and Drug Administration (D) withdrew its approval of Kanasco's (P) drug applications due to a record of manufacturing violations.

RULE OF LAW

Agencies may summarily withdraw approval for applications after providing the party with due notice.

FACTS: John D. Copanos & Sons, Inc. and Kanasco (P) manufactured and distributed human and veterinary drugs. In March 1987, the Food and Drug Administration (the FDA) (D) published a Notice of Opportunity for a Hearing proposing to withdraw Kanasco's (P) applications for new drugs on the grounds Kanasco's (P) manufacturing was substandard. Over a three-year period, periodic inspections of Kanasco's (P) facilities had resulted in numerous violations and evidence that false records were submitted to cover up other violations. Kanasco (P) requested a hearing, but in August 1987, the FDA (D) summarily withdrew the applications. Kanasco (P) petitioned for review on the ground it had not received adequate notice of the basis for the action.

ISSUE: May agencies summarily withdraw approval for applications after providing the party with due notice?

HOLDING AND DECISION: (Ginsburg, J.) Yes. Agencies may summarily withdraw approval for applications after providing the party with due notice. The Federal Food, Drug, and Cosmetic Act (the Act) prohibits the introduction of new drugs without prior Food and Drug Administration (FDA) (D) approval. The Act also established procedures whereby the FDA (D) can withdraw approval after due notice to the applicant. One of the grounds for withdrawal is substandard manufacturing by the applicant. This provision does not guarantee an applicant a hearing in all circumstances since the agency may summarily withdraw approval where there is no "genuine and substantial issue of fact that requires a hearing." Thus, notice being critical, it must contain enough information to provide the applicant with a genuine opportunity to identify the material issues of fact in the context of the action. In the present case, Kanasco (P) was not confronted with any significant ambiguity regarding the type of information that would warrant an agency hearing. Considering the context of the prior proceedings and violations, the hearing notice certainly advised Kanasco (P) of the type of information it would need to submit to command a hearing. Even without specific instructions telling Kanasco (P) what to produce, they have failed to identify any evidence that might have been presented but for lack of notice. Accordingly, the petition for review is denied.

ANALYSIS

The narrow grounds for Kanasco's (P) petition for review should be noted. In this case, they were not challenging the Food and Drug Administration's (the FDA's) (D) finding directly but arguing only that the lack of proper notice had invalidated the subsequent summary decision. The court did take the FDA (D) to task for not making it easier to more clearly identify the exact violations that formed the basis for the approval withdrawal.

Quicknotes

FEDERAL FOOD, DRUG, AND COSMETIC ACT Consumer-protection statute authorizing promulgation of rules governing food, drugs, and cosmetics. It gives the U.S. Food and Drug Administration (FDA) authority to oversee the safety of food, drugs, medical devices and cosmetics.

Wallace v. Bowen

Social Security applicant (P) v. Government agency (D)

869 F.2d 187 (3d Cir. 1989)

NATURE OF CASE: Petition for review of agency denial of benefits.

FACT SUMMARY: Wallace (P) appealed his denial of social security disability benefits, which was based on reports that were not available for cross-examination at the hearing, claiming violations of his statutory and constitutional due process rights and that one administrative law judge's decision was not supported by substantial evidence.

RULE OF LAW

Agencies may not make adjudications based on post-hearing reports that are not subject to cross-examination.

FACTS: In February 1985, Wallace (P) suffered a heart attack while working and a stroke a month later. The stroke may have resulted in the loss of vision in one eye. Wallace (P) applied for disability benefits and supplemental security income based on his condition. After his claims were denied, Wallace (P) was granted a hearing before an administrative law judge (ALJ) in which he introduced doctors' reports about his ailments. After the hearing, the ALJ sent Wallace (P) to two doctors, both of whom reported back that his impairments did not meet the required criteria. Thus, the ALJ ruled that Wallace (P) was not disabled under the terms of the Social Security Act. Wallace (P) sought review, arguing that he did not have an opportunity to cross-examine the two post-hearing reports.

ISSUE: May agencies make adjudications based on post-hearing reports that are not subject to cross-examination?

HOLDING AND DECISION: (Sloviter, J.) No. Agencies may not make adjudications based on post-hearing reports that are not subject to cross-examination. Section 205 of the Social Security Act provides that upon denial of a claim, applicants are entitled to a hearing where a decision will be based on evidence adduced at the hearing. A full disclosure of the facts at a hearing requires the opportunity for cross-examination, which is an element of fundamental fairness to the applicant. Even where an opinion is wholly medical, cross-examination could reveal what evidence a doctor considered or failed to consider in formulating a conclusion. Accordingly, an applicant must have the opportunity to cross-examine any post-hearing reports that are relied upon by the administrative law judge when such cross-examination may be required for a full and accurate disclosure of the facts. Therefore, Wallace's petition for review is upheld; the judgment is vacated, and the case is remanded.

ANALYSIS

The court found that the two post-hearing reports by the doctors in this case were substantially relied upon by the administrative law judge (ALJ). The ALJ even had remarked in the opinion that he had relied "in particular" on the report of the doctor who ruled that Wallace's (P) visual impairment was not sufficient to qualify. Thus, there was little question that cross-examination could have affected the result here.

Quicknotes

ADMINISTRATIVE LAW JUDGE (ALJ) A judge who presides over administrative hearings.

SOCIAL SECURITY ACT § 205 Reasonable notice and an opportunity for a hearing must be given to an applicant who requests it after an unfavorable determination of claim.

Professional Air Traffic Controllers Organization v. Federal Labor Relations Authority

Union (D) v. Government agency (P)

685 F.2d 547 (D.C. Cir. 1982)

NATURE OF CASE: Evidentiary hearing to determine nature, extent, and effect of ex parte communications in unfair labor practice case.

FACT SUMMARY: While the Federal Labor Relations Authority (P) was deciding a case involving Professional Air Traffic Controllers Organization (D), board members had ex parte contacts with some interested parties.

RULE OF LAW

Undisclosed improper ex parte communications during agency proceedings do not necessarily void an agency decision.

FACTS: The Professional Air Traffic Controllers Organization (PATCO) (D) was the exclusive bargaining representative for air traffic controllers when negotiations over a new contract stalled in 1981. PATCO (D) struck the Federal Aviation Administration (FAA) on August 3, 1981. The government obtained a restraining order against the strike and then fired 11,000 controllers who failed to return to work two days later. The FAA also filed an unfair labor practice charge against PATCO (D) with the Federal Labor Relations Authority (FLRA) (P) alleging that the strike was unfair and seeking revocation of PATCO's (D) certification as the bargaining representative for the controllers. While the FLRA (P) was hearing the case, Board members who were deciding the case had brief encounters with interested parties to the case and did not disclose them. After PATCO's (D) certification was revoked, it sought to invalidate the decision based on the ex parte communications. The court ordered an evidentiary hearing.

ISSUE: Do undisclosed improper ex parte communications during agency proceedings necessarily void an agency decision?

HOLDING AND DECISION: (Edwards, J.) No. Undisclosed improper ex parte communications during agency proceedings do not necessarily void an agency decision. The Civil Service Reform Act requires that Federal Labor Relations Authority (FLRA) (D) hearings be conducted in accordance with the Administrative Procedure Act. As such, ex parte communications with interested parties during agency adjudications are prohibited if they are not made public and are relevant to the merits of the proceeding. Disclosure of ex parte communications can usually solve any problems that may arise since it prevents the appearance of any impropriety. Thus, it is often the first remedy. If it isn't sufficient, the violating party may have to show cause why the proceeding should not be dismissed or denied on account of the violation. Thus, agency proceedings that have been blemished by ex parte communications are voidable based on whether the process was irrevocably tainted so as to make the ultimate judgment unfair. There are no mechanical rules to apply; rather, each case must be looked at given the surrounding circumstances. In the present case, there is insufficient reason to vacate the FLRA decision. While the ex parte communications at issue should have been disclosed, there does not appear to be any evidence that the proceedings were prejudiced against the Professional Air Traffic Controllers Organization (D). Authority's decision affirmed.

ANALYSIS

The court looked closely at three contacts with the Federal Labor Relations Authority (FLRA) (P) board members. As it turned out, the court had the most problem with a dinner between a different union's leader and a board member, where the union leader tried to convince the board member not to severely punish the union. The court found this totally unacceptable behavior but obviously found that no party had benefitted from this contact.

Quicknotes

ADMINISTRATIVE PROCEDURE ACT § 557(D) Governs ex parte communications in agency proceedings.

CIVIL SERVICE REFORM ACT OF 1978 Requires that the Federal Labor Relations Authority (FRLA) conduct hearings in accordance with the Administrative Procedure Act.

EX PARTE A proceeding commenced by one party without providing any opposing parties with notice or that is uncontested by an adverse party.

Stone v. Federal Deposit Insurance Corporation

Federal employee (P) v. Employer (D)

179 F.3d 1368 (Fed. Cir. 1999)

NATURE OF CASE: Appeal from final decision of the Merit Systems Protection Board.

FACT SUMMARY: The Merit Systems Protection Board sustained a decision by an administrative law judge that Stone's (P) removal from his position as a federal bank examiner had not violated due process.

RULE OF LAW

The introduction of new and material information by means of ex parte communications to the deciding official undermines a public employee's due process right to notice and the opportunity to respond.

FACTS: Stone (P) allegedly falsified forms for approved leave from his position as a GS-12 bank examiner in the Federal Deposit Insurance Corporation's (FDIC's) (D) Division of Supervision. The FDIC (D) began removal proceedings, and a deciding official recommended that Stone (P) be terminated. When Stone (P) appealed his dismissal to the Merit Systems Protection Board (the Board), Stone's (P) attorney requested relevant documents from the FDIC (D). Stone (P) then discovered that the deciding official had received an ex parte memorandum urging his removal. Stone (P) alleged that the ex parte communication was a violation of his right to due process and should automatically void his dismissal. The administrative law judge found there was nothing wrong with the ex parte communications and the Board sustained Stone's (P) dismissal. On appeal, Stone (P) alleged that a violation of his due process rights had occurred.

ISSUE: Does the introduction of new and material information by means of ex parte communications to the deciding official undermine a public employee's due process right to notice and the opportunity to respond?

HOLDING AND DECISION: (Gajarsa, J.) Yes. The introduction of new and material information by means of ex parte communications to the deciding official undermines a public employee's due process right to notice and the opportunity to respond. A public employee is entitled to notice and an opportunity to respond prior to removal from office. In determining whether new and material information was introduced, the Merit Systems Protection Board (the Board) must determine whether the ex parte communication was so substantial and likely to cause prejudice that no employee can fairly be required to be subjected to a deprivation of property under such circumstances. Where a procedural due process violation has occurred because of ex parte communications, such a violation is not subject to the harmless error test. Here Stone (P) had a property interest in continued employment with the Federal Deposit Insurance Corporation (D); thus, he was entitled to meaningful notice of the reasons for his removal and a meaningful opportunity to respond. Vacated and remanded.

ANALYSIS

The facts and circumstances of each individual case must be considered. The court listed several factors for the Board to consider. Whether the information was cumulative; whether the ex parte communications were of the type likely to result in undue pressure on the deciding official to rule in a particular manner; and whether the employee knew of the error and had a chance to respond are among the factors to consider.

Quicknotes

ADMINISTRATIVE LAW JUDGE (ALJ) A judge who presides over administrative hearings.

DUE PROCESS CLAUSE Language in the Fifth and Fourteenth Amendments to the U.S. Constitution providing that no person shall be deprived of "life, liberty, or property, without due process of law."

EX PARTE A proceeding commenced by one party without providing any opposing parties with notice or that is uncontested by an adverse party.

MATERIALITY Importance; the degree of relevance or necessity to the particular matter.

NOTICE Communication of information to a person by an authorized person or an otherwise proper source.

Londoner v. Denver

Property owner (P) v. City council (D)

210 U.S. 373 (1908)

NATURE OF CASE: Appeal of a tax assessment.

FACT SUMMARY: Londoner (P) contended the Denver City Council (D) denied him due process by imposing an assessment of paving costs without notice and an evidentiary hearing.

RULE OF LAW

Due process requires that the taxpayers be afforded notice and an evidentiary hearing before a tax is set by an agency.

FACTS: The Denver City Council (Council) (D), under statutory authority, approved an assessment on Londoner's (P) property for the costs of paving a public street. Before approving the assessment, the Council (D) gave notice to Londoner (P) and afforded an opportunity to file written objections to the assessment. Londoner's (P) objections consisted of allegations that the hearing procedures, precluding the presentation of evidence, denied due process. The Colorado courts rejected Londoner's (P) contentions, and the United States Supreme Court took jurisdiction.

ISSUE: Does due process require that the taxpayers be afforded notice and an evidentiary hearing before a tax is set by an agency?

HOLDING AND DECISION: (Moody, J.) Yes. Due process requires that the taxpayers be afforded notice and an evidentiary hearing before a tax is set by an agency. While there are few constitutional restrictions on a state legislature's power to tax, there are limitations imposed where this power is delegated to an administrative agency. In such a case, as here, more than an opportunity to tender written objections to the tax is required by due process. The taxpayer must be allowed to present evidence in support of his allegations, and an opportunity to participate in oral argument. The failure to afford such opportunities in this case renders the assessments invalid as adopted through a denial of due process. Reversed.

ANALYSIS

This case illustrates the general requirement that agencies exercising taxation or economic regulation follow formal procedures. This requirement can have several sources including the agency's enabling statute, its own procedural requirements, the Administrative Procedure Act, federal common law, and judicial decisions.

Quicknotes

EVIDENTIARY HEARING Hearing pertaining to the evidence of the case.

NOTICE Communication of information to a person by an authorized person or an otherwise proper source.

PROCEDURAL DUE PROCESS The constitutional mandate that if the state or federal government acts so as to deny a citizen of a life, liberty or property interest the individual is first entitled to notice and the right to be heard.

Bi-Metallic Investment Company v. State Board of Equalization

Property owner (P) v. State board (D)

239 U.S. 441 (1915)

NATURE OF CASE: Certiorari review of lawsuit seeking to enjoin board's order and alleging violation of the Fourteenth Amendment.

FACT SUMMARY: Bi-Metallic Investment Company (Bi-Metallic) (P) sued Colorado (D) to enjoin enforcement of an order increasing property taxes in Denver. Bi-Metallic (P) argued that it was entitled to an opportunity to be heard in opposition to the order and that having its property taken without due process is a violation of the Fourteenth Amendment.

RULE OF LAW

Where an agency rule will apply to a vast number of people, the Constitution does not require that each be given an opportunity to be heard directly for the purpose of arguing in favor for or against its adoption.

FACTS: The Colorado Tax Commission (D) and the State Board of Equalization (D) ordered a 40 percent increase in the valuation of all taxable property in the city of Denver. Bi-Metallic Investment Company (Bi-Metallic) (P), the owner of certain real estate in Denver, sought to enjoin enforcement of the order. It argued that it had been afforded no opportunity to be heard in opposition to the order and was thus threatened with deprivation of property without due process of law. The Supreme Court of Colorado ordered dismissal of Bi-Metallic's (P) claim, and Bi-Metallic (P) appealed to the United States Supreme Court, alleging a violation of its Fourteenth Amendment rights. The United States Supreme Court granted review.

ISSUE: Where an agency rule will apply to a vast number of people, does the Constitution require that each be given an opportunity to be heard directly for the purpose of arguing in favor for or against its adoption?

HOLDING AND DECISION: (Holmes, J.) No. Agency orders and rules that will affect vast numbers of people may be adopted without affording every interested party a direct opportunity to be heard. In cases such as the present one, it would be impractical to allow all individuals affected to offer a direct voice in support of or in opposition to an order. Thus, the Constitution is satisfied by the fact that, as voters, the taxpayers involved exercised power, remote or direct, over those responsible for the order. This case differs from *Londoner v. Denver*, 210 U.S. 373 (1908), because that determination involved a specific tax levy on a small number of exceptionally affected individuals, while the order at issue here affects an entire county of citizens. [Affirmed.]

ANALYSIS

The result of this case is opposite to that reached in *Londoner v. Denver*, 210 U.S. 373 (1908). However, the apparent conflict between the two cases is explained by the observation that *Bi-Metallic* involved so-called "legislative" facts whereas *Londoner* was a case that presented an issue requiring evaluation of "adjudicative" facts. "Legislative" facts are those that primarily involve determinations of broad policies or principles of general application, e.g., whether every tract of land in a large city has been under-assessed for property tax purposes. In resolving issues pertaining to "legislative" as opposed to "adjudicative" facts, administrative agencies may dispense with the practice of according every interested party an opportunity to be heard.

Quicknotes

ADMINISTRATIVE ORDER The final disposition of an administrative hearing or the interpretation or application of a statute.

FOURTEENTH AMENDMENT Declares that no state shall make or enforce any law that shall abridge the privileges or immunities of citizens of the United States; no state shall deny to any person within its jurisdiction the equal protection of the laws.

FOURTEENTH AMENDMENT DUE PROCESS CLAUSE Provides that protections mandated by the U.S. Constitution and observed by the federal government are equally applicable, and therefore must be observed by the states.

RULEMAKING The promulgation of a rule governing a particular activity by an administrative agency, acting within the scope of its power pursuant to statute.

Paul v. Davis

Police chief (D) v. Alleged shoplifter (P)

424 U.S. 693 (1976)

NATURE OF CASE: Suit against two police chiefs claiming defamation that allegedly violated the Due Process Clause of the Fourteenth Amendment.

FACT SUMMARY: Davis (P) sued Paul (D), the police chief of Louisville, Kentucky, and McDaniel (D), the police chief in Jefferson County, Kentucky, seeking redress for an alleged violation of his constitutional rights.

RULE OF LAW

A government official's defamation of a person does not constitute a deprivation of the liberty interest guaranteed by the Due Process Clause of the Fourteenth Amendment.

FACTS: Police chiefs Paul (D) and McDaniel (D) alerted local merchants to possible shoplifters who might be operating in the Louisville, Kentucky, area during the 1972 Christmas season. The chiefs (D) distributed a flyer to approximately 800 area merchants; the five-page flyer presented names and photographs of persons alleged to be shoplifters. Davis's (P) picture appeared in the flyer [because he had been arrested in Louisville, though not convicted, on a shoplifting charge]. Davis (P) sued Paul (D) and McDaniel (D) in U.S. District Court, alleging that the chiefs (D) had defamed him in violation of the liberty interest secured by the Fourteenth Amendment's Due Process Clause. [The trial judge granted the police chiefs' (D) motion to dismiss. The court of appeals reversed, holding that Davis's (P) complaint stated a claim upon which relief could be granted because, the appellate court reasoned, the complaint alleged facts that constituted a denial of due process under the Fourteenth Amendment.] Paul (D) and McDaniel (D) petitioned the United States Supreme Court for further review.

ISSUE: Does a government official's defamation of a person constitute a deprivation of the liberty interest guaranteed by the Due Process Clause of the Fourteenth Amendment?

HOLDING AND DECISION: (Rehnquist, J.) No. A government official's defamation of a person does not constitute a deprivation of the liberty interest guaranteed by the Due Process Clause of the Fourteenth Amendment. Davis (P) asserts that the flyer impermissibly deprived him of some "liberty" protected by the Fourteenth Amendment; the designation of him as an "active shoplifter," he contends, would effectively prohibit him from entering business establishments for fear of being suspected of shoplifting, and, if he were apprehended, would seriously impair his future employment opportunities. Such allegations seem to state a claim for defamation—specifically, a claim for defamation per se, given the accusation of criminal misconduct against Davis (P)—that would be actionable in almost every state. A study of our decisions, however, convinces us that they do not support Davis's (P) attempt to use defamation as a violation of due process under the Fourteenth Amendment. The words "liberty" and "property," as used in the Fourteenth Amendment, do not single out reputation for special protection, and we therefore hold that the interest in reputation asserted here is neither "liberty" nor "property" that is protected from government deprivation without due process of law. Reversed.

DISSENT: (Brennan, J.) Police officials now may brand innocent persons as criminals without constitutional limitation under the Due Process Clause. All the protections of a criminal trial are meaningless because people can now be arbitrarily punished as criminals by the very officials whose duty it is to enforce the laws fairly against all persons.

ANALYSIS

The ready existence of state-law remedies strongly influenced the majority's holding in *Paul v. Davis.* As excerpted in the casebook, Justice Brennan's dissent overlooks that larger context, assuming instead that reputation equates with the liberty interests indisputably implicated by criminal proceedings.

Quicknotes

FOURTEENTH AMENDMENT Declares that no state shall make or enforce any law that shall abridge the privileges or immunities of citizens of the United States; no state shall deny to any person within its jurisdiction the equal protection of the laws.

FOURTEENTH AMENDMENT DUE PROCESS CLAUSE Provides that protections mandated by the U.S. Constitution and observed by the federal government are equally applicable, and therefore must be observed by the states.

Bishop v. Wood

Discharged police officer (P) v. Municipal official (D)

426 U.S. 341 (1976)

NATURE OF CASE: Appeal from affirmance of summary judgment for defendant municipality in action challenging constitutionality of municipal employee's discharge.

FACT SUMMARY: Bishop (P), a police officer, asserted, inter alia, that because the reasons given for his discharge by the municipality (D) for which he worked were false and incorrect, he was deprived of a constitutionally protected liberty interest, notwithstanding that the reasons were communicated to him in private and later during pretrial discovery.

RULE OF LAW

Where the reasons for a municipal employee's discharge are false and communicated to employee in private, such false reasons do not deprive the employee of an interest in liberty protected by Due Process Clause of the Fourteenth Amendment.

FACTS: Acting on the recommendation of the chief of police (D), the city manager (D) of a municipality terminated Bishop's (P) employment as a police officer, on grounds of insubordination, causing low morale, and conduct unsuited to an officer, without affording Bishop (P) a hearing to determine the sufficiency of the cause for his discharge. The reasons for Bishop's (P) discharge were communicated orally to him in private and were not made public. Bishop (P) sued the municipal officials (D) in federal district court, asserting that (1) his employment status was a property interest protected by the Due Process Clause of the Fourteenth Amendment, and (2) assuming that the explanation for his discharge was false, that the false explanation deprived him of an interest in liberty protected by that Clause. The asserted reasons for Bishop's (P) discharge were set forth in answers to Bishop's (P) interrogatories. Bishop (P) responded by presenting evidence that he was a competent police officer, that he was respected by his peers, and that the municipality's (D) reasons for discharging him were false and incorrect. The district court granted summary judgment against Bishop (P), the Fourth Circuit Court of Appeals affirmed, and the United States Supreme Court granted certiorari. As to Bishop's (P) first claim, the Court held that because Bishop (P) could be discharged at will, he had no property interest that was protected by the Due Process Clause.

ISSUE: Where the reasons for a municipal employee's discharge are false and communicated to employee in private, do such false reasons deprive the employee of an interest in liberty protected by Due Process Clause of the Fourteenth Amendment?

HOLDING AND DECISION: (Stevens, J.) No. Where the reasons for a municipal employee's discharge are false and communicated to employee in private, such false reasons do not deprive the employee of an interest in liberty protected by Due Process Clause of the Fourteenth Amendment. First, even assuming that the reasons for Bishop's (P) discharge were false and incorrect, because the reasons for Bishop's (P) discharge were not made public, Bishop's (P) interest in his "good name, reputation, honor, or integrity" was not impaired. Nor can the communication of such reasons as answers to interrogatories during pretrial discovery provide retroactive support for Bishop's (P) claim since the statement of those reasons was made in the course of a judicial proceeding that did not commence until after Bishop (P) had suffered his alleged injury. Second, although the truth or falsity of the city manager's (D) explanation determines whether or not the decision to discharge Bishop (P) was correct or prudent, the truth or falsity of such explanation neither enhances nor diminishes Bishop's (P) claim that his constitutionally protected interest in liberty was impaired. Affirmed.

ANALYSIS

The Court explained that a contrary holding in this case would enable every discharged employee to assert a constitutional claim merely by alleging that their former supervisor made a mistake. The Court also emphasized that the federal courts are not the appropriate forum in which to review the multitude of personnel decisions that are made daily by public agencies, notwithstanding the harsh reality that numerous individual mistakes are inevitable in the day-to-day administration of people's affairs, and that the Constitution cannot be construed to require federal judicial review for every such error. The Court further explained that in the absence of any claim that a public employer was motivated by a desire to curtail or to penalize the exercise of an employee's constitutionally protected rights, it must be presumed that official action was regular and, if erroneous, can best be corrected in other ways. In other words, the Due Process Clause of the Fourteenth Amendment is not a

Continued on next page.

guarantee against incorrect or ill-advised personnel decisions.

Quicknotes

FOURTEENTH AMENDMENT DUE PROCESS CLAUSE Provides that protections mandated by the U.S. Constitution and observed by the federal government are equally applicable, and therefore must be observed by the states.

INTERROGATORIES A method of pretrial discovery in which written questions are provided by one party to another who must respond in writing under oath.

PRETRIAL DISCOVERY Pretrial procedure during which each party makes certain information available to the other.

Codd v. Velger

Employer (D) v. Employee (P)

429 U.S. 624 (1977)

NATURE OF CASE: Appeal from denial of agency employment hearing.

FACT SUMMARY: Velger (P) was dismissed as a police officer and claimed he was due a hearing because of stigmatizing information placed in his file.

RULE OF LAW

Hearings mandated by the Due Process Clause are required only when there is a clear factual dispute.

FACTS: Velger (P) was a police officer in New York City in a probationary position. He was dismissed, apparently because he had put a gun to his head in a suicide attempt. Velger (P) then obtained a job with the Penn-Central Railroad Police Department but was dismissed when a Penn-Central officer was shown his New York City file. Velger (P), who ordinarily wasn't entitled to a hearing as probationary employee, claimed that a hearing was required because of the stigmatizing information in his file that prevented him from finding similar employment. The court decided that Velger (P) did not prove that he had been stigmatized and Velger (P) appealed. The court of appeals held that the finding of no stigma was clearly erroneous. The United States Supreme Court granted certiorari.

ISSUE: Are hearings mandated by the Due Process Clause required only when there is a clear factual dispute?

HOLDING AND DECISION: (Per curiam) Yes. Hearings mandated by the Due Process Clause are required only when there is a clear factual dispute. Whether the report in Velger's (P) file was stigmatizing need not be determined in this case because Velger (P) has failed to prove another essential element. Nowhere in the pleadings is there any assertion that the report of the suicide attempt is substantially false. The absence of this allegation is fatal to any claim or request for a hearing. If there is no factual dispute at issue, the hearing usually required by the Due Process Clause would be rendered meaningless. Thus, Velger (P) is not entitled to a hearing.

DISSENT: (Stevens, J.) The purpose of a hearing is twofold. First, it is to establish the truth or falsity of the charges, and second, to also provide a basis for deciding what action is warranted. Even if the charge is clearly true, procedural safeguards still must be observed.

ANALYSIS

The dissent made a valid point when it said that the government should carry the burden in these instances. Justice Stewart argued that the agency employer should at least have to show that the denial of due process was harmless error. It is unclear from the majority opinion just how much Velger (P) would have to allege regarding the facts in order to sufficiently justify the hearing.

Quicknotes

DUE PROCESS CLAUSE Clauses found in the Fifth and Fourteenth Amendments to the United States Constitution providing that no person shall be deprived of "life, liberty, or property, without due process of law."

Cleveland Bd. of Education v. Loudermill

Public employer (D) v. Employee (P)

470 U.S. 532 (1985)

NATURE OF CASE: Constitutional challenge to Ohio employment pretermination procedures.

FACT SUMMARY: Cleveland Board of Education (D) terminated James Loudermill's (P) employment without providing him an opportunity to respond to the allegation he had lied on his employment application.

RULE OF LAW

The Due Process Clause requires an employee receive a pretermination opportunity to respond coupled with statutory post-termination administrative procedures.

FACTS: James Loudermill (P) applied for and received a position as a security guard with the Cleveland Board of Education (the Board) (D). Loudermill (P) stated on his employment application that he had never been convicted of a felony. Eleven months later, as a routine audit, the Board (D) learned Loudermill (P) had been convicted several years earlier of grand larceny. The Board (D) terminated Loudermill's (P) employment based on his dishonesty in completing the employment application. Loudermill (P) was not given a pretermination opportunity to respond to the charge of dishonesty or challenge his dismissal. He appealed his dismissal to the Cleveland Civil Service Commission (the Commission) and argued he thought the conviction was for a misdemeanor. The appointed referee recommended reinstatement and the case was referred to the full Commission. The Commission orally announced it would uphold the dismissal. Loudermill (P) filed a complaint in the federal District Court for the Northern District of Ohio alleging the Ohio statute was unconstitutional for failure to provide an employee the pretermination opportunity to respond to charges, thus depriving discharged employees of liberty and property without due process. The district court dismissed for failure to state a claim, and the case was appealed to the United States Supreme Court.

ISSUE: Does the Due Process Clause require an employee receive a pretermination opportunity to respond coupled with statutory post-termination procedures?

HOLDING AND DECISION: (White, J.) Yes. The Due Process Clause requires an employee receive a pretermination opportunity to respond coupled with statutory post-termination administrative procedures. The Due Process clause requires an individual receive an opportunity to be heard before being deprived of liberty or property. An employee with a constitutionally protected property interest in his employment should receive some sort of hearing prior to discharge. A pretermination hearing is of obvious value to reach an accurate discharge decision and at least provides the employer notice of the existence of disputes about facts. The risk of error is substantially reduced. Loudermill's (P) discharge involves arguable issues and was not based on the objective question of his ex-felon status but on the subjective determination he lied on his application form. His explanation is at least plausible in light of the fact he received a suspended six-month sentence and a fine. The District Court erred in dismissing the claim.

ANALYSIS

The United States Supreme Court affirmed the Sixth Circuit Court of Appeals decision that the federal District Court for the Northern District of Ohio erred and remanded the case. The Court noted the pretermination hearing is not the forum for an employee to argue for the employer to be lenient or depart from legal requirements. The hearing is an opportunity for the employee to state facts and arguments that might enlighten the employer as to the propriety of the discharge versus continued employment. Ohio now requires public sector employers to issue employees Loudermill hearings or letters prior to discharge.

Quicknotes

DUE PROCESS CLAUSE Language in the Fifth and Fourteenth Amendments to the U.S. Constitution providing that no person shall be deprived of "life, liberty, or property, without due process of law."

PRETERMINATION HEARING A hearing held prior to the termination of a property interest.

Shands v. City of Kennett

Volunteer firemen (P) v. City government (D)

993 F.2d 1337 (8th Cir. 1993)

NATURE OF CASE: Appeal from judgment notwithstanding the verdict in action for deprivation of due process.

FACT SUMMARY: Several volunteer firemen (P) were dismissed from their positions and claimed that they were deprived of their constitutional rights without due process.

RULE OF LAW

Government employees are entitled to procedural due process in connection with employment discharges only when they have been deprived of a constitutionally protected liberty or property interest.

FACTS: The Kennett City Council (the Council) (D) dismissed several volunteer firemen (P) when they undermined the authority of the Fire Chief with respect to another employment decision. At a Council (D) meeting, the dismissed firemen told their side of the case and were allowed to question some witnesses. Still, the Council (D) voted not to reinstate them and released a statement that the men (P) had not been dismissed for any illegal or immoral activities but rather, as the result of personnel matters. The dismissed firemen (P) then filed suit alleging that there had been false and stigmatizing statements made against them to the media and that they were entitled to a fair hearing in order to clear their names. The firemen (P) earned a favorable verdict but the court granted Kennett's (D) motion for judgment notwithstanding the verdict and the firemen (P) appealed.

ISSUE: Are government employees entitled to procedural due process in connection with employment discharges only when they have been deprived of a constitutionally protected liberty or property interest?

HOLDING AND DECISION: (Wollman, J.) Yes. Government employees are entitled to procedural due process in connection with employment discharges only when they have been deprived of a constitutionally protected liberty or property interest. To establish a protected liberty interest, a dismissed government employee must show that an official publicly made untrue charges that would stigmatize him so as to seriously damage the employee's standing in the community or prevent further employment. In the present case, the only public statements on the record about the dismissed firemen (P) expressly said that the dismissals were for "personnel" reasons and for being "insubordinate." These statements did not create the level of stigma that implicates a constitutionally protected liberty interest. The requisite stigma has generally been found in cases involving accusations of dishonesty, immorality, criminality, or racism. A mere charge of insubordination is insufficient. Accordingly, the dismissed firemen (P) were not entitled to a hearing regarding their dismissal. Affirmed.

ANALYSIS

There are often two steps to the due process claim. If a court decides that a hearing was required, it must then be decided what that entails. Sometimes, an administrative hearing is necessary. Other times, the courts have found that a fuller trial-type proceeding with notice and evidentiary rulings is required.

Quicknotes

DUE PROCESS The constitutional mandate requiring the courts to protect and enforce individuals' rights and liberties consistent with prevailing principles of fairness and justice and prohibiting the federal and state governments from such activities that deprive its citizens of a life, liberty, or property interest.

JUDGMENT NOTWITHSTANDING THE VERDICT (JNOV) A judgment entered by the trial judge reversing a jury verdict if the jury's determination has no basis in law or fact.

Mathews v. Eldridge

Social Security Administration (D) v. Disability benefits recipient (P)

424 U.S. 319 (1976)

NATURE OF CASE: Appeal concerning constitutional validity of procedures on termination of disability benefits.

FACT SUMMARY: Eldridge (P) had his disability benefits terminated and brought suit.

RULE OF LAW

The Due Process Clause does not require an evidentiary hearing prior to termination of disability benefits.

FACTS: The state agency and the Social Security Administration (D) terminated Eldridge's (P) disability benefits. The relevant administrative procedure was the provision of the opportunity for a claimant to assert his claim prior to any administrative action, a right to an evidentiary hearing, and subsequent judicial review before the claim became final. Instead of requesting reconsideration, Eldridge (P) commenced an action challenging the constitutional validity of the administrative procedures. The district court held that the administrative procedures pursuant to which Eldridge's (P) benefits had been terminated abridged his right to procedural due process. The court of appeals affirmed. The dispute centered on what kind of procedure was required when benefits were initially terminated, pending review. The courts below held that due process required an evidentiary hearing prior to termination.

ISSUE: Does the Due Process Clause require an evidentiary hearing prior to termination of disability benefits?

HOLDING AND DECISION: (Powell, J.) No. The Due Process Clause does not require an evidentiary hearing prior to termination of disability benefits. Only in *Goldberg v. Kelly*, 397 U.S. 254 (1970), has this Court held that due process requires an evidentiary hearing prior to a temporary deprivation because in that case it was emphasized that welfare assistance is given to persons on the very margin of subsistence. Eligibility for disability benefits, on the other hand, is not based on financial need. The probable value of additional procedural safeguards is not great because termination of disability benefits turns on the routine medical reports of physicians. In considering the public interest, experience with the constitutionalizing of government procedures suggests that the ultimate additional cost in terms of money and administrative burden would be substantial. The judgment of the court of appeals is reversed.

ANALYSIS

In the wake of *Eldridge*, the Court has in several cases held that due process requires administrators to conduct informal "consultative" hearings prior to depriving a person of a property or liberty interest. One such instance is where a utility wants to terminate a customer's service for nonpayment of bills, see *Memphis Light, Gas & Water Div. v. Craft*, 436 U.S. 1 (1977). In such a case, under the *Eldridge* test, a consumer's interest in maintaining services and the risk of erroneous termination outweigh the utility's interests in summary termination. Another example is where a school district wants to terminate a tenured employee for cause. In that case, due process requires that the employee be given an opportunity to present his or her side of the facts prior to termination, see *Cleveland Bd. of Educ. v. Loudermill*, 470 U.S. 532 (1985). In rare instances, even a postdeprivation hearing will satisfy due process requirements, as where there is a potentially imminent threat to public safety, see *North American Cold Storage Co. v. Chicago*, 211 U.S. 306 (1908).

Quicknotes

DUE PROCESS The constitutional mandate requiring the courts to protect and enforce individuals' rights and liberties consistent with prevailing principles of fairness and justice and prohibiting the federal and state governments from such activities that deprive its citizens of a life, liberty, or property interest.

Board of Curators of the University of Missouri v. Horowitz

State university (D) v. Medical school student (P)

435 U.S. 78 (1978)

NATURE OF CASE: Appeal from reinstatement of action protesting a student's dismissal from school.

FACT SUMMARY: When Horowitz (P) was dismissed from medical school for unsatisfactory performance, she filed suit, alleging that the Board of Curators (D) had not accorded her procedural due process.

RULE OF LAW
A formal hearing is not required to dismiss a student for unsatisfactory performance based on the academic judgment of school officials.

FACTS: As Horowitz (P) progressed through medical school, several faculty members expressed dissatisfaction with her clinical performance during her first year. Faculty dissatisfaction with her performance continued during the following year. The Council on Evaluation finally recommended that, absent radical improvement, Horowitz (P) be dropped from school. Horowitz (P) was permitted to take a set of oral and practical examinations as an "appeal" of the eventual decision not to permit her to graduate. Only two of seven practicing physicians in the area who evaluated Horowitz (P) recommended that she be graduated on schedule. Following her dismissal, Horowitz (P) filed suit, alleging she had not been accorded procedural due process prior to that dismissal. After a trial, the district court dismissed her complaint. The court of appeals reversed. The University's Board of Curators (D) appealed.

ISSUE: Is a formal hearing required to dismiss a student for unsatisfactory performance based on the academic judgment of school officials?

HOLDING AND DECISION: (Rehnquist, J.) No. A formal hearing is not required to dismiss a student for unsatisfactory performance based on the academic judgment of school officials. The ultimate decision to dismiss Horowitz (P) was careful and deliberate. These procedures were sufficient under the Due Process Clause of the Fourteenth Amendment. The determination whether to dismiss a student for academic reasons requires an expert evaluation of cumulative information and is not readily adapted to the procedural tools of judicial or administrative decision-making. There is no reason to further enlarge the judicial presence in the academic community and thereby risk deterioration of many beneficial aspects of the faculty-student relationship. Reversed.

ANALYSIS

The Court referred to its prior decision in *Goss v. Lopez*, 419 U.S. 565 (1975), in making a distinction between students who are dismissed for disciplinary purposes and those who are dismissed for academic reasons. In *Goss*, the Court felt that suspensions of students for disciplinary reasons have sufficient resemblance to traditional judicial and administrative fact-finding to call for a "hearing" before the relevant school authority. Even in the context of a school disciplinary proceeding, however, the Court stopped short of requiring a formal hearing.

Quicknotes

FOURTEENTH AMENDMENT Declares that no state shall make or enforce any law that shall abridge the privileges or immunities of citizens of the United States; no state shall deny to any person within its jurisdiction the equal protection of the laws.

PROCEDURAL DUE PROCESS The constitutional mandate that if the state or federal government acts so as to deny a citizen of a life, liberty, or property interest the person is first entitled to notice and the right to be heard.

Gabrilowitz v. Newman

College student (P) v. University official (D)

582 F.2d 100 (1st Cir. 1978)

NATURE OF CASE: Appeal from order granting preliminary injunction involving student disciplinary action.

FACT SUMMARY: Steven A. Gabrilowitz (P) faced criminal charges and civil university disciplinary charges for the same conduct involving his alleged assault with intent to rape another student. Gabrilowitz (P) requested counsel of his choice to advise him at the disciplinary hearing so that he might be informed about the consequences of his defense, or lack thereof, on his criminal prosecution.

RULE OF LAW

A student is unconstitutionally deprived of due process when forced to make defense decisions at a disciplinary hearing without the benefit of legal counsel in the face of a pending criminal action arising from the same set of facts.

FACTS: Steven A. Gabrilowitz (P), a senior at the University of Rhode Island (U.R.I.) (D), allegedly assaulted another student with intent to rape. The South Kingstown, Rhode Island, Police Department charged Gabrilowitz (P) for the alleged assault and U.R.I. (D) sent Gabrilowitz (P) a letter informing him the campus police had charged him with violating the U.R.I. Community Standards of Behavior. The letter outlined the disciplinary hearing rules, including the exclusion of legal counsel at the hearing. Gabrilowitz (P) sought a preliminary injunction restraining U.R.I. (D) from conducting the hearing unless he is allowed to be represented by the attorney of his choice. The United States District Court for the District of Rhode Island granted the preliminary injunction and U.R.I. officials (D) appealed.

ISSUE: Is a student unconstitutionally deprived of due process when forced to make defense decisions at a disciplinary hearing without the benefit of legal counsel in the face of a pending criminal action arising from the same set of facts?

HOLDING AND DECISION: (Bownes, J.) Yes. A student is unconstitutionally deprived of due process when forced to make defense decisions at a disciplinary hearing without the benefit of legal counsel in the face of a pending criminal action arising from the same set of facts. Gabrilowitz's (P) counsel stated at oral argument that counsel at the disciplinary hearing would not participate in any capacity except sitting at Gabrilowitz's (P) side for consultation and advice, so the Court proceeds under that scenario. The University of Rhode Island (U.R.I.) (D) first argues the criminal and civil actions are unrelated, but this Court rejects that assertion. Gabrilowitz (P) is impaled on the horns of a legal dilemma in that a full defense and his testimony at the disciplinary hearing might jeopardize his criminal defense while failure to mount a full defense with testimony at his disciplinary hearing could result in the loss of his college degree and a seriously blemished reputation. Most courts have declined to grant students the right to counsel in disciplinary hearings, but those cases did not involve a related criminal action. In the absence of compelling precedent, the Court applies the due process balancing test delineated in *Mathews v. Eldridge*, 424 U.S. 319 (1976). The need for counsel at this hearing seems obvious; while it will not eliminate risk, it enables Gabrilowitz (P) to make an informed, intelligent choice between the risks presented. Counsel's principal function will be to advise Gabrilowitz (P) to safeguard him from self-incrimination. U.R.I. (D) will be aware of the presence of an outsider, but this emphasizes the gravity of the matter and sets no financial or administrative burden on U.R.I (D). This decision sets precedent only for this truly unusual situation. The denial of counsel for advice and consultation deprives Gabrilowitz (P) of due process of law. Affirmed.

DISSENT: (Campbell, J.) The pendency of criminal charges must be irrelevant to potential due process violations for lack of counsel at a separate civil proceeding. These facts are similar to convicts involved in prison disciplinary proceedings while facing pending criminal charges arising out of the same incident. This Court held the potential for self-incrimination there required the presence of counsel. The Supreme Court disagreed in *Baxter v. Palmigiano*, 425 U.S. 308 (1976), and that is the closest precedent here. The majority opinion likely opens the door to students insisting upon counsel in almost all student disciplinary proceedings because most serious actions involve at least colorable misdemeanors. Counsel could provide passive assistance through pre-hearing consultations or periodic consultations during the hearing but outside the room.

ANALYSIS

Gabrilowitz v. Newman is the exception to the majority of cases that have determined students do not have the right to counsel in disciplinary proceedings. The

Continued on next page.

exception, however, only provides assistance of counsel rather than representation by counsel. The courts continue to defer to the administrative procedures of higher education institutions despite the similarity of the proceedings to criminal prosecutions.

Quicknotes

PRELIMINARY INJUNCTION A judicial mandate issued to require or restrain a party from certain conduct; used to preserve a trial's subject matter or to prevent threatened injury.

Osteen v. Henley

Student (P) v. University (D)

13 F.3d 221 (7th Cir. 1993)

NATURE OF CASE: Appeal from school's decision to expel student.

FACT SUMMARY: Osteen (P) was expelled for two years from Northern Illinois University (D) for fighting.

RULE OF LAW

There is no constitutional right to counsel in student disciplinary proceedings.

FACTS: Osteen (P), a football player at Northern Illinois University (University) (D), hit two students and broke their noses after an argument involving his friends. Osteen (P) admitted his guilt to the charges at a meeting with the University's (D) judicial officer but requested a hearing regarding the proposed sanction. At the hearing, Osteen (P) was represented by a student advocate, but the appeals board approved the recommended two-year expulsion, as did the University's (D) vice-president. Osteen (P) sought judicial review of this decision.

ISSUE: Is there a constitutional right to counsel in student disciplinary hearings?

HOLDING AND DECISION: (Posner, C.J.) No. There is no constitutional right to counsel in student disciplinary proceedings. The application of the Due Process Clause to student disciplinary hearings has not been resolved definitively by the courts. However, it is at least arguable that when faced with serious charges, a student is entitled to consult with a lawyer. But there does not seem to be any right to have a lawyer perform the traditional functions of a trial lawyer at the proceeding. To recognize that right would force disciplinary hearings into the mold of adversary litigation and would severely increase their cost and complexity. Since there is no real danger that schools will engage in unwarranted expulsions without this right, there is no reason to think that students' rights will be violated. Furthermore, the consequence to a student such as Osteen (P), who may still enroll in other colleges, is not so severe as to entitle him to litigation-type procedural protections. Therefore, Osteen's (P) claim for review is denied.

ANALYSIS

The court went on to note that it doubted that any student disciplinary hearing could rise to the level requiring the right of counsel. The decision also rejected Osteen's (P) claim that the interruption of himself and his advocate at the hearing by the board was a denial of due process. The court found that the interruptions related only to times where Osteen (P) was attempting to revisit the issue of guilt.

Quicknotes

DUE PROCESS CLAUSE Language in the Fifth and Fourteenth Amendments to the U.S. Constitution providing that no person shall be deprived of "life, liberty, or property, without due process of law."

Withrow v. Larkin

Medical board (D) v. Physician (P)

421 U.S. 35 (1975)

NATURE OF CASE: Appeal of order enjoining an administrative hearing.

FACT SUMMARY: The district court enjoined the Wisconsin Medical Examining Board (D) from holding a contested hearing to determine whether Larkin (P) had engaged in prohibited acts.

RULE OF LAW

The performance of both prosecutorial and adjudicative functions by the same agency officials is not per se a denial of due process.

FACTS: The Wisconsin Medical Examining Board (the Board) (D) held an investigative hearing to determine whether Larkin (P) had committed certain proscribed acts within his medical practice. As a result of the investigation, the Board (D) notified Larkin (P) that it would hold a contested hearing to determine whether his medical license should be suspended. Larkin (P) brought suit to enjoin the contested hearing on the basis that it was improper for the Board (D) to adjudicate the same case it had investigated. The district court granted the injunction holding that the Board (D) could not properly rule on the same charges it investigates. The Board (D) appealed.

ISSUE: Is the performance of both investigatory and adjudicative functions by the same agency officials per se a denial of due process?

HOLDING AND DECISION: (White, J.) No. The performance of both investigatory and adjudicative functions by the same agency officials is not per se a denial of due process. There is a presumption of honesty and integrity in adjudications. As a result, the performance of these two functions is not a denial of due process unless this presumption is overcome by a showing of bias on the part of those performing the dual functions of investigation and adjudication. Such bias will not be implied merely by the performance of these functions by the same entity. In this case, the only evidence offered of the impropriety of the contested hearing was the performance of both functions by the same officials. This was insufficient to constitute a denial of due process. Reversed.

ANALYSIS

Some commentators argue that combining adjudicatory and prosecutorial functions, even if not inherently unconstitutional, is fundamentally unfair. An empirical study conducted by Professor Richard Posner, *The Behavior of Administrative Agencies*, 1 J. Legal Stud. 305 (1972), found that dismissal rates did not reflect a reluctance of agencies to dismiss complaints when performing both prosecutorial and adjudicative functions. Regardless of this empirical evidence, veteran administrators continue to argue that dual functions inhibit an agency from reaching a just conclusion.

Quicknotes

LICENSE A right that is granted to a person allowing him or her to conduct an activity that without such permission he or she could not lawfully do, and which is unassignable and revocable at the will of the licensor.

PER SE By itself; without more; taken alone; not requiring additional evidence for proof; as a matter of law.

PROCEDURAL DUE PROCESS The constitutional mandate that if the state or federal government acts so as to deny a citizen of a life, liberty, or property interest the person is first entitled to notice and the right to be heard.

Torres v. Mukasey

Applicant for asylum (P) v. Government department (D)

551 F.3d 616 (7th Cir. 2008)

NATURE OF CASE: Appeal of denial of application for asylum.

FACT SUMMARY: Torres's (P) petition for asylum and protection under the Convention Against Torture was denied by the Department of Justice (D), U.S. Attorney General Michael Mukasey, because of inconsistencies between Torres's (P) oral testimony and his application for asylum.

RULE OF LAW

When the credibility determination of the immigration judge (IJ) is not supported by substantial evidence that bears a legitimate nexus to the findings, and when the improper behavior of the IJ at the immigration hearing renders the IJ's credibility determination unreliable, the reviewing court will not defer to the conclusions of the IJ.

FACTS: Torres (P) petitioned the Department of Justice (DOJ) (D) for asylum and protection under the Convention Against Torture (CAT) because of persecution he endured as a soldier in the Honduran army. The alleged persecution was a result of his membership in a social group—namely, his family. Upon denial of his petition for asylum by the immigration judge (IJ), Torres (P) sought review before the Board of Immigration Appeals (BIA). The BIA affirmed the decision of the IJ, and Torres (P) appealed to the instant court. Following a review of the record, the appeals court found error in the IJ's substantive analysis and in his conduct at Torres's (P) hearing. Specifically, the appeals court determined that the record supported Torres's (P) assertion that he was tortured and abused because of the military desertions of each of his three older brothers. In rejecting the IJ's conclusions, the appeals court found no inconsistencies in Torres's (P) testimony, which established that Torres's (P) commanding officer repeatedly targeted Torres (P) because of his family history. Additionally, the appeals court determined that, in his oral testimony, Torres (P) sufficiently explained omissions in his written asylum application. As such, the appeals court found that Torres's (P) family history was the nexus for his mistreatment, and that the establishment of this nexus supported Torres's (P) credibility, without which Torres (P) could not sustain his burden of proof.

ISSUE: Must the reviewing court defer to the conclusions of the immigration judge (IJ) when the credibility determination of the IJ is not supported by substantial evidence that bears a legitimate nexus to the findings, and when the improper behavior of the IJ at the immigration hearing renders the IJ's credibility determination unreliable?

HOLDING AND DECISION: (Kanne, J.) No. When the credibility determination of the immigration judge (IJ) is not supported by substantial evidence that bears a legitimate nexus to the findings, and when the improper behavior of the IJ at the immigration hearing renders the IJ's credibility determination unreliable, the reviewing court will not defer to the conclusions of the IJ. In fact, the IJ's improper conduct—specifically, the IJ's overactive role during the immigration hearing, his demonstrated impatience and hostility towards Torres (P), and his reliance on personal knowledge beyond the record facts, provides sufficient basis to remand the case for further proceedings. Evaluating the IJ's findings under the substantial evidence standard, it is clear the IJ failed to base his credibility determination on specific, cogent reasons that bear a legitimate nexus to the findings. Instead, the IJ adopted an inquisitorial role in Torres's (P) hearing, focusing on purported inconsistencies in Torres's (P) testimony regarding the involvement in and motivation for the torture of Torres (P) by his commanding officer. Thus, because the IJ ignored the consistent and credible testimony of Torres (P), and his convincing explanations for discrepancies in the material facts of the asylum application, the denial of same by the IJ and the Board of Immigration Appeals are vacated and remanded for further proceedings.

ANALYSIS

In *Torres*, the Seventh Circuit encouraged the Board of Immigration Appeals to assign a different immigration judge (IJ) to the case on remand. In *Huang v. Gonzales*, 403 F.3d 945 (7th Cir. 2005), the Seventh Circuit took similar action, upon similar circumstances, in encouraging assignment of a different IJ on remand. See also, *Ali v. Mukasey*, 529 F.3d 478 (2d Cir. 2008); *Wang v. Attorney General of the United States*, 423 F.3d 260 (3d Cir. 2005); *Reyes-Melendez v. I.N.S.*, 342 F.3d 1001 (9th Cir. 2003). Insofar as the conduct of the IJ affects a credibility finding, specifically when the IJ relies on his own personal experience, wholly unsupported by specific and cogent reasons that bear no legitimate nexus

Continued on next page.

to the finding, case law suggests a nationwide trend of biased immigration hearings.

Quicknotes

ASYLUM A place of protection or refuge.

EVIDENCE Any type of proof offered at a trial in order to prove or disprove a disputed fact or issue.

Jackson v. Veterans Administration

Employee (P) v. Employer (D)

768 F.2d 1325 (Fed. Cir. 1985)

NATURE OF CASE: Appeal of agency employment discharge.

FACT SUMMARY: Jackson (P) was discharged from the Veterans Administration (D) due to allegations of sexual harassment of a subordinate, which were disputed.

RULE OF LAW

A board must articulate sound reasons, based on the record of evidence, when its evaluation of testimony is contrary to that of the presiding official.

FACTS: Jackson (P) worked as a supervisor in the Veterans Administration (D). He was accused of sexual harassment, involving five separate incidents of misconduct, and was dismissed. A presiding official conducted a hearing and reversed the removal based on a determination that none of the incidents were established by a preponderance of the evidence. The agency requested a review and the board (D) reversed, concluding that two of the incidents were supported by the evidence. In the first incident, a subordinate employee claimed that Jackson (P) had kissed her while she was on the telephone, and the second incident involved his request for a kiss so that the employee could leave early. Jackson (P) appealed the board's (D) ruling.

ISSUE: Must a board articulate sound reasons, based on the record of evidence, when its evaluation of testimony is contrary to that of the presiding official?

HOLDING AND DECISION: (Nies, J.) Yes. A board must articulate sound reasons, based on the record of evidence, when its evaluation of testimony is contrary to that of the presiding official. The issue is whether the board's evaluation of the weight of the evidence is reasonable and supported by substantial evidence, taking into consideration that the presiding official made a different evaluation after actually hearing the witnesses. In the present case, the presiding official decided that the first alleged incident was unproven because it came down to conflicting accounts that could not be corroborated by other witnesses. Given these circumstances, the board (D) should not have reversed the presiding official given that his decision was largely based on credibility determinations. However, with regard to the second alleged incident, the presiding official apparently ignored the account of a witness who corroborated the testimony and did not discredit it. Therefore, the board (D) was certainly entitled to weigh this evidence on its own and find that a preponderance of evidence showed Jackson's (P) guilt. Jackson's (P) claim for review is denied.

ANALYSIS

A board must have "substantial evidence" to support its determination when there is a factual dispute. When there is a dispute as to the legal issues involved, courts may simply look to see whether the agency action at issue conforms to the applicable law. It is a more difficult matter when the dispute revolves around a matter that is not clearly legal or factual.

Quicknotes

PREPONDERANCE OF THE EVIDENCE A standard of proof requiring the trier of fact to determine whether the fact sought to be established is more probable than not.

SEXUAL HARASSMENT An employment discrimination subjecting persons to verbal or physical abuse of a sexual nature.

National Labor Relations Board v. Hearst Publications

Labor board (P) v. News publisher (D)

322 U.S. 111 (1944)

NATURE OF CASE: Appeal of a National Labor Relations Board bargaining order.

FACT SUMMARY: The National Labor Relations Board (the NLRB) (P) found that newsboys selling Hearst (D) newspapers were employees under the National Labor Relations Act (the NLRA) and, therefore, Hearst (D) was ordered to engage in collective bargaining with their representative.

RULE OF LAW

A reviewing court must accept an agency's application of a broad statutory term if such application is supported in the record and has a reasonable basis in law.

FACTS: Several Hearst (D) newspapers were distributed in Los Angeles through vendors, called newsboys. The price at which the newsboys bought the papers from Hearst (D) and the price they could charge the public were set by Hearst (D). The location, conditions, and hours within which the papers could be sold were determined either expressly or implicitly by Hearst (D). The newsboys organized to bargain collectively, claiming they were "employees" under the National Labor Relations Act (the NLRA). Hearst (D) refused to bargain, contending the newsboys were independent contractors and therefore not protected by the NLRA. The National Labor Relations Board (the NLRB) (P) concluded the newsboys were employees and ordered Hearst (D) to bargain. The court of appeals made an independent evaluation of the record and found the newsboys were independent contractors. The NLRB (P) appealed.

ISSUE: Must a reviewing court accept an agency's application of a broad statutory term if such application is supported in the record and has a reasonable basis in law?

HOLDING AND DECISION: (Rutledge, J.) Yes. A reviewing court must accept an agency's application of a broad statutory term if such application is supported in the record and has a reasonable basis in the law. Congress has vested the duty of administering the National Labor Relations Act (the NLRA) in the National Labor Relations Board (the NLRB) (P). The NLRB's (P) experience in dealing with labor matters makes it a logical choice to determine the application of broad statutory terms within the context of national labor policy. Therefore, the NLRB's (P) application of the term "employee" within the present context must be upheld if supported in the record and if reasonably based in law. The measure of control over the newsboy's activities exercised by Hearst (D) is sufficient evidence for the NLRB (P) to conclude the existence of an employer-employee relationship under recognized legal principles. Therefore, the court of appeals improperly substituted its own application of the term. Reversed.

ANALYSIS

In *Gary v. Powell*, 314 U.S. 402 (1941), the Court laid the foundation for *Hearst*. It held that where a term's definition is delegated to an agency, the development of the definition will be upheld in respect of the delegation. After the *Hearst* decision, Congress amended the National Labor Relations Act (the NLRA) to exclude persons having a common-law independent contractor status. In *Hearst*, the court of appeals' holding of independent contractor status was based on common-law interpretations, while National Labor Relations Board's determination of employee status was a modification of the common-law idea of independent contractor status as equivalent to employee status under the NLRA.

Quicknotes

COLLECTIVE BARGAINING Negotiations between an employer and employee that are mediated by a specified third party.

DELEGATION The authorization of one person to act on another's behalf.

INDEPENDENT CONTRACTOR A party undertaking a particular assignment for another who retains control over the manner in which it is executed.

QUESTION OF FACT An issue relating to a factual assertion that is disputed at trial and left to the jury to resolve.

QUESTION OF LAW An issue regarding the legal significance of a particular act or event, which is usually left to the judge to ascertain.

Evening Star Newspaper Company v. Kemp

Employer (D) v. Employee (P)

533 F.2d 1224 (D.C. Cir. 1976)

NATURE OF CASE: Appeal of order awarding benefits to widow of employee.

FACT SUMMARY: Kemp (P) was killed by his own gun while on the job for Evening Star (D) but not engaged with company business.

RULE OF LAW

Decisions by administrative law judges should be upheld on judicial review unless they are irrational or unsupported by substantial evidence on the record.

FACTS: Kemp (P) was employed by Evening Star (D) as a truck driver to deliver newspapers. Between delivery runs there was an hour of time where Kemp (P) was "on the clock" but allowed to do whatever he wanted. On August 10, 1971, Kemp (P) was working on his own car in a garage where the Evening Star (D) mechanics worked during this hour period. A friend began playing with a gun that Kemp (P) kept in his own car and accidentally killed Kemp (P). At a hearing before an administrative law judge (ALJ) to determine whether Kemp's widow (P) was entitled to compensation under a worker's compensation law, the ALJ found for the widow (P) because Kemp's death occurred in the course of his employment. The Department of Labor's Benefits Review Board affirmed and Evening Star (D) appealed.

ISSUE: Should decisions by administrative law judges be upheld on judicial review unless they are irrational or unsupported by substantial evidence on the record?

HOLDING AND DECISION: (Van Pelt, Sr. J.) Yes. Decisions by administrative law judges should be upheld on judicial review unless they are irrational or unsupported by substantial evidence on the record. The role of judicial review of agency adjudications is not to make independent decisions based on its own evaluation, but rather only to make sure that the decision was not arbitrary and capricious. In the present case, the administrative law judge (the ALJ) expressly found that Kemp (P) was killed during an enforced lull, a condition required by the employment. His presence at the garage was clearly acquiesced in by Evening Star (D) and the ALJ found that the handgun that killed Kemp (P) was sometimes carried by him for protection while delivering newspapers. Given these findings, it cannot be said the activity that Kemp (P) was engaged in was so totally unreasonable to sever the connection between the employee and the employment. Thus, the ALJ's ruling was neither unreasonable nor unsupported by the evidence. Accordingly, it must be affirmed.

DISSENT: (Danaher, Sr. J.) Kemp (P) was not engaged at the time of the injury in an activity of benefit to Evening Star (D). Thus, his death did not arise out of the employment.

ANALYSIS

The dissent pointed out the administrative law judge seemed to go out of his way to develop a record that would support compensation for the widow (P). The dissent noted that it felt that many of the facts puts on the record were hardly relevant. The majority, on the other hand, seemed more concerned with deferring to the factual record and findings.

Quicknotes

JUDICIAL REVIEW The authority of the courts to review decisions, actions, or omissions committed by another agency or branch of government.

Durrah v. Washington Metropolitan Area Transit Authority

Employee (P) v. Employer (D)

760 F.2d 322 (D.C. Cir. 1985)

NATURE OF CASE: Petition for review of denial of benefits claim.

FACT SUMMARY: Durrah (P) was a special police officer for the Washington Metropolitan Area Transit Authority (D) and was injured when he left his guard post to buy a soda.

RULE OF LAW

Employees need not be engaged directly in an activity to the benefit of the employer at the time of an injury to be entitled to workers' compensation.

FACTS: Durrah (P) worked as a special police officer for the Washington Metropolitan Area Transit Authority (WMATA) (D) and was posted at a guard post during the overnight shift at a large bus depot. At 4:00 a.m., Durrah (P) left his spot to buy a soda from a vending machine in the employees' lounge on the premises. Durrah (P) was supposed to obtain a substitute to cover his post when he took such a break but failed to do so on this occasion. On returning to his post, Durrah (P) slipped on a staircase and injured his knee. An administrative law judge (ALJ) denied Durrah's (P) claim for benefits because Durrah (P) had left his post without permission. The Benefits Review Board affirmed the ALJ. Durrah (P) petitioned for review.

ISSUE: Do employees need to be engaged directly in an activity to the benefit of the employer at the time of an injury to be entitled to workers' compensation?

HOLDING AND DECISION: (Ginsburg, J.) No. Employees need not be engaged directly in an activity to the benefit of the employer at the time of an injury to be entitled to workers' compensation. If the "obligations or conditions" of employment create a "zone of danger" out of which an injury arises, then it is covered by workers' compensation. In the present case, it is clear even if Durrah (P) had found a replacement for his post before leaving to buy the soda, his injury still would have occurred in the same place and in the same manner. The activity of going to the employees' lounge for a break was anticipated and expected by the Washington Metropolitan Area Transit Authority (WMATA) (D) and Durrah's (P) violation of a policy did not place him in the path of any additional risks. The injury clearly resulted from an activity that was incidental to the employment. Accordingly, the administrative law judge's ruling was unsupported by the law and reason behind workers' compensation. Reversed and remanded.

ANALYSIS

The court noted that the violation of policy fell far short of disconnecting Durrah (P) from the service of his employer. The court noted that Durrah (P) could have been disciplined in a separate proceeding. But eliminating his right to compensation was not properly at issue.

Quicknotes

JUDICIAL REVIEW The authority of the courts to review decisions, actions, or omissions committed by another agency or branch of government.

WORKERS' COMPENSATION Fixed awards provided to employees for job-related injuries.

ZONE OF DANGER For purposes of tort liability, the requirement that the plaintiff be within the area of risk of injury from the defendant's conduct in order to recover for negligence.

Citizens to Preserve Overton Park v. Volpe

Memphis citizens group (P) v. Secretary of Transportation (D)

401 U.S. 402 (1971)

NATURE OF CASE: Suit to set aside administrative action.

FACT SUMMARY: A group of concerned citizens (P) sued the Secretary of Transportation (D), challenging his decision to construct a highway through a public park.

RULE OF LAW

When reviewing administrative decisions that are not supported by formal factual findings, courts should determine the scope of the appropriate official's authority, whether that authority was abused, and whether all applicable procedural requisites have been observed.

FACTS: The Citizens to Preserve Overton Park (Citizens) (P) sued Secretary Volpe (D) of the Department of Transportation. He was accused of violating the Department of Transportation Act and the Federal Aid Highway Act by approving plans to construct a six-lane highway through Overton Park, a popular recreation site. The Citizens (P) assailed the Secretary (D) for his failure to state the factual findings upon which he based his decision. The Citizens (P) also alleged the Secretary (D) failed to explain why he believed, as required by statute, that no feasible alternative location was available and that all possible steps had been taken to minimize harm to the park. The Citizens (P) sought to have the Secretary's (D) decision nullified, but the district court granted the Secretary's (D) motion for summary judgment, basing its ruling on the contents of affidavits that had been prepared specifically in response to the litigation. The court of appeals affirmed, but the United States Supreme Court granted a stay and agreed to review the decisions below. On appeal, the Citizens (P) sought either a de novo review of the Secretary's (D) decision or application of the substantial evidence test.

ISSUE: When reviewing administrative decisions that are not supported by formal factual findings, should courts determine the scope of the appropriate official's authority, whether that authority was abused, and whether all applicable procedural requisites have been observed?

HOLDING AND DECISION: (Marshall, J.) Yes. When reviewing administrative decisions that are not supported by formal factual findings, courts should determine the scope of the appropriate official's authority, whether that authority was abused, and whether all applicable procedural requisites have been observed. This case is not one in which the Court may appropriately undertake a de novo review of the Secretary of the Department of Transportation's (D) decision since it presents neither a circumstance in which an adjudicatory proceeding was supported by inadequate fact-finding procedures, nor one in which new issues are raised in a proceeding to enforce nonadjudicatory agency action. Likewise, the substantial evidence test should not be applied to the Secretary's (D) action since his decision was neither the product of a public adjudicatory hearing nor an exercise of the rulemaking function. However, the applicable statutes clearly mandate that the Secretary (D) shall act only when all effective alternative sites for highway construction have been ruled out and, even then, only after taking all available steps to minimize harm to the chosen location. The court need not confine its review to agency affidavits. The Citizens (P) were entitled to a review of the Secretary's (D) deliberative processes, which took account of more evidence than that upon which the lower courts based their decisions. Therefore, it is necessary that this case be remanded for reconsideration, based on broader evidence of whether the Secretary (D) observed the required procedure of investigating alternative routes and insuring only minimal harm to Overton Park. In reviewing the Secretary's (D) decision, the district court may undertake the unusual procedure of requiring the administrative officials to reveal the thought processes used to arrive at their conclusions. Although the district court need not adopt this drastic course, it may resort to this procedure as a means of compensating for the lack of any factual findings upon which to predicate its decision. Reversed and remanded.

ANALYSIS

The principal significance of *Citizens to Preserve Overton Park v. Volpe* rests in its concern with insuring that judicial review of administrative decisions will be meaningful. To that end, the *Overton Park* Court countenanced the extraordinary procedure of probing the deliberative processes of administrative officials. It seems clear that the provisions of the Administrative Procedure Act calling for judicial review of administrative determinations cannot be implemented in the absence of a record sufficient to accommodate review, and that

Continued on next page.

when such a record is absent, the courts must choose between ordering its compilation or undertaking their own review de novo.

Quicknotes

DE NOVO The review of a lower court decision by an appellate court, which is hearing the case as if it had not been previously heard and as if no judgment had been rendered.

JUDICIAL REVIEW The authority of the courts to review decisions, actions, or omissions committed by another agency or branch of government.

CHAPTER 4

Choice of Procedures and Nonlegislative Rules

Quick Reference Rules of Law

National Labor Relations Board v. Bell Aerospace Company Division of Textron Inc.

Government agency (D) v. Aerospace products manufacturer (P)

416 U.S. 267 (1974)

NATURE OF CASE: Appeal from denial of enforcement of an agency order.

FACT SUMMARY: Bell (P) opposed a representation election on the grounds its buyers were "managerial employees" and were thus not covered by the National Labor Relations Act or entitled to elect union representation.

RULE OF LAW

The National Labor Relations Board is not precluded from announcing new principles in an adjudicative proceeding.

FACTS: Bell Aerospace (Bell) (P), which operated a plant engaging in research and development in the design and fabrication of aerospace products, opposed the petition of its employee buyers in the purchasing and procurement department for an election to decide whether a union would be certified as the buyers' bargaining representative. Bell (P) contended that the buyers were "managerial employees" and were not covered by the National Labor Relations Act (the NLRA), and therefore, were not entitled to the NLRA's protections. The National Labor Relations Board (the NLRB) (D), after a representation hearing, issued an order holding that the buyers did constitute an appropriate unit for the purpose of collective bargaining and directed an election. An election was held and the union was certified by the NLRB (D) as the exclusive bargaining representative for Bell's (P) buyers. Bell (P), encouraged by an Eighth Circuit Court of Appeals decision holding that "managerial employees" were not covered by the NLRA, moved the NLRB (D) for reconsideration of its order. The NLRB (D) denied the motion. Bell (P) then petitioned for review of the NLRB's (D) order, and the NLRB (D) cross-petitioned for enforcement. The Second Circuit Court of Appeals denied enforcement and the NLRB (D) appealed.

ISSUE: Is the NLRB precluded from announcing new principles in an adjudicative proceeding?

HOLDING AND DECISION: (Powell, J.) No. The National Labor Relations Board (the NLRB) (D) is not precluded from announcing new principles in an adjudicative proceeding; the choice between rulemaking and adjudication lies within the NLRB's (D) discretion in the first instance. In this case, there is ample indication that adjudication is especially appropriate. The duties of buyers vary widely depending on the company or industry. It is doubtful whether any generalized standard could be framed that would have more than marginal utility. The NLRB (D) thus has reason to proceed with caution, developing its standards in a case-by-case manner with attention to the specific character of the buyer's authority and duties in each company. The NLRB's (D) decision that adjudication best serves this purpose is entitled to great weight, and the agency has discretion to decide that the adjudicative procedures in this case may also produce the relevant information necessary for a mature and fair consideration of the issues. [Affirmed in part, reversed in part, and remanded.]

ANALYSIS

When the Taft-Hartley Act of 1947 was passed, both the U.S. Senate and the House of Representatives (the House) voiced concern over the National Labor Relations Board (D) broad reading of the term "employee," which then included those clearly within the managerial hierarchy. The Senate noted that unionization of supervisors had hurt productivity, increased the accident rate, upset the balance of power in collective bargaining, and tended to blur the lines between management and labor. The House echoed the concern for reduction of industrial output and noted that unionization of supervisors had deprived employers of the loyal representatives to which they were entitled.

Quicknotes

MANAGERIAL EMPLOYEE An employee whose duties involve the administration of the business's affairs or the supervising of the work of other employees.

SUPERVISORY EMPLOYEE An employee authorized to implement independent judgment in the management, direction, and discipline of other employees.

TAFT-HARTLEY ACT An amendment to the National Labor Relations Act, imposing limitations on unions and safeguarding the rights of employers.

Retail, Wholesale and Department Store Union v. National Labor Relations Board

Union (D) v. Government agency (P)

466 F.2d 380 (D.C. Cir. 1972)

NATURE OF CASE: Appeal from unfair labor practice decision.

FACT SUMMARY: Coca-Cola (D) complained that a new rule from the National Labor Relations Board (P) about replacing striking workers should not be applied retroactively.

RULE OF LAW

The retroactive application of a new agency rule depends upon a balancing of the danger of reaching a result contrary to law against the negative effect of the retroactive application.

FACTS: Coca-Cola (D) failed to hire workers who were permanently replaced during a strike. At the time, it was a well-settled rule with the National Labor Relations Board (the NLRB) (P) that when an employer replaced a striker, there was no obligation to hire back that employee. However, the NLRB (P) overturned this rule and held that former strikers were entitled to offers of reinstatement when the replacements vacated their positions. The NLRB (P) found that Coca-Cola (D) violated this new rule and imposed backpay liability on the company, although the underlying events occurred before the new rule was adopted. Coca-Cola (D) appealed on the basis of this retroactive application of the new rule.

ISSUE: Does the retroactive application of a new agency rule depend upon a balancing of the danger of reaching a result contrary to law against the negative effect of the retroactive application?

HOLDING AND DECISION: (McGowan, J.) Yes. The retroactive application of a new agency rule depends upon a balancing of the danger of reaching a result contrary to law against the negative effect of the retroactive application. The retroactive application of a new agency rule depends on factors such as whether the case is one of first impression. The Administrative Procedure Act authorizes agencies to conduct formal rulemaking so as to have rules that have prospective application. But many agencies fashion new rules and standards on a case-by-case basis through adjudications. Whether a new rule should be applied retroactively depends on the equities of the particular case, and courts may review this decision without deference to the agency. Among the key considerations are whether the case is one of first impression, whether the new rule is an abrupt departure from the old practice, the extent of reliance on the old rule, and the degree of burden the new rule imposes. The present case involving Coca-Cola (D) is not one of first impression, because the rule was changed in a prior case. Therefore, the reasons for applying it retroactively in the first impression case may not be present in the instant case. Looking at the equities in this case, it appears that Coca-Cola (D) tried to conform its conduct to the well-established and accepted old rule and the burden of imposing the new standard is considerable. Accordingly, it is highly unfair to punish Coca-Cola (D) for failing to conform to a standard subsequently adopted. Therefore, enforcement of the National Labor Relations Board (P) order is denied.

ANALYSIS

The court noted that United States Supreme Court precedent in this area did not establish any bright line guidelines. Agencies can choose not to apply a rule retroactively after it has been adopted in one case. On the other hand, reviewing courts may refuse to enforce retroactive agency orders.

Quicknotes

BALANCING TEST Court's balancing of an individual's constitutional rights against the state's right to protect its citizens.

RETROACTIVE APPLICATION Having an effect on something that occurred in the past.

General Electric Company v. U.S. Environmental Protection Agency

Alleged polluter (D) v. Government agency (P)

53 F.3d 1324 (D.C. Cir. 1995)

NATURE OF CASE: Appeal from fine for illegal polluting.

FACT SUMMARY: General Electric (D) was fined for disposing of toxic materials in a manner that the Environmental Protection Agency (P) believed was impermissible under its interpretation of the regulations.

RULE OF LAW

Agencies may not impose liability where a regulation is not sufficiently clear to provide fair notice to the affected party.

FACTS: General Electric Company (D) had a service shop in Georgia that decommissioned large electric transformers. Inside the transformers were polychlorinated biphenyls (PCB), a dangerous pollutant that had to be disposed of in compliance with Environmental Protection Agency (the EPA) (P) regulations. Essentially, the regulations stated that the PCBs had to be incinerated. General Electric (D) began a process that involved an intermediary step of recycling and distillation before incineration. The EPA (P) charged the company with violating the regulations and assessed a $25,000 fine. An administrative law judge (ALJ) and the Environmental Appeals Board upheld the fine and General Electric (D) petitioned for review.

ISSUE: May agencies impose liability where a regulation is not sufficiently clear to provide fair notice to the affected party?

HOLDING AND DECISION: (Tatel, J.) No. Agencies may not impose liability where a regulation is not sufficiently clear to provide fair notice to the affected party. Ordinarily, an agency's interpretation of its regulations is entitled to a high level of deference. However, it may be overturned if it is plainly wrong. Additionally, an order to comply with an interpretation carries more weight than a decision that a violation has occurred where an interpretation has not been expressly made before. Due process requires that parties receive fair notice before being deprived of property. This fair notice rule applies to both criminal and civil liability. An agency's pre-enforcement efforts to bring about compliance often provide adequate notice. If a regulated party could have identified the standards it was expected to have conformed to through regulations and other agency statements, then that is fair notice. In the instant case, the regulations at issue provide no notice whatsoever with regard to pre-disposal processes such as distillation. It certainly cannot be said that a reasonable person would know that distillation was to be considered a means of disposal. While the Environmental Protection Agency (the EPA) (P) is entitled to conclude that it is, given the area of expertise, it does stray from a common understanding of the terms and would be unexpected without an express statement. Accordingly, General Electric (D) had no fair warning that the EPA (P) would make such an interpretation. Petition for review granted, agency finding vacated, and case remanded.

ANALYSIS

The court left the Environmental Protection Agency (P) with room to apply its interpretation in future cases. But the court clearly found that the interpretation barring General Electric's (D) method to be unnatural given the language of the prior regulations. Thus, it had no difficulty in finding that there was no fair prior warning and notice.

Quicknotes

DUE PROCESS The constitutional mandate requiring the courts to protect and enforce individuals' rights and liberties consistent with prevailing principles of fairness and justice and prohibiting the federal and state governments from such activities that deprive its citizens of a life, liberty, or property interest.

NOTICE Communication of information to a person by an authorized person or an otherwise proper source.

NOTICE AND COMMENT RULEMAKING Informal rulemaking.

American Hospital Association v. Bowen

Trade organization (P) v. Government agency (D)

834 F.2d 1037 (D.C. Cir. 1987)

NATURE OF CASE: Appeal from declaration that documents issued by the Department of Health and Human Services (D) were invalid.

FACT SUMMARY: The American Hospital Association (P) claimed that the Department of Health and Human Services (D) had improperly issued rules and regulations by not first undertaking the notice and comment rulemaking prescribed by the Administrative Procedure Act, 5 U.S.C. § 553.

RULE OF LAW

The requirement of notice and an opportunity for comment does not apply to general statements of policy.

FACTS: When the Department of Health and Human Services (HHS) (D) implemented the system of peer review of Medicare, it issued many documents without first undertaking the notice and comment rulemaking prescribed by the Administrative Procedure Act (the APA), 5 U.S.C. § 553. When the American Hospital Association (AHA) (P) claimed a document soliciting proposed contracts from entities seeking to become peer review organizations (PROs) contained legislative rules, the district court held those parts of the Request for Proposals (the RFP) to be invalid. HHS (D) appealed, claiming the RFP was a nonbinding statement of policy and was therefore exempt from provisions of the APA.

ISSUE: Does the requirement of notice and an opportunity for comment apply to general statements of policy?

HOLDING AND DECISION: (Wald, C.J.) No. The requirement of notice and an opportunity for comment does not apply to general statements of policy. A general statement of policy does not establish a "binding norm" and leaves the agency free to exercise its discretion. Here the Request for Proposals (the RFP) merely established talking points and did not bind either the agency or the peer review organization to which it was sent. The RFP had no present effect and it did not prevent future exercises of agency discretion. The district court wrongly invalidated those parts of the RFP it deemed legislative in character. Reversed.

ANALYSIS

The court contrasted "substantive rules" with "general statements of policy." It found that substantive rules establish standards of conduct that have the force of law. General statements of policy, on the other hand, announce only what the agency seeks to establish as policy.

Quicknotes

ADMINISTRATIVE PROCEDURE ACT (APA) Enacted in 1946 to govern practices and proceedings before federal administrative agencies.

APA § 553 Establishes the minimum requirements of public rulemaking procedure.

NOTICE AND COMMENT RULEMAKING Informal rulemaking.

American Mining Congress v. Mine Safety & Health Administration

Industry organization (P) v. Federal agency (D)

995 F.2d 1106 (D.C. Cir. 1993)

NATURE OF CASE: Petitions for review of rules promulgated by federal agency.

FACT SUMMARY: The American Mining Congress (P) alleged that the Mine Safety and Health Administration (D) should have followed requirements for notice and comment prior to issuing Program Policy Letters regarding the use of x-ray results to diagnose lung disease.

RULE OF LAW

Substantive rules have the force of law if Congress delegated legislative power to the agency and the agency intended to exercise that power in promulgating the rules.

FACTS: Under relevant rules adopted via notice and comment by the Mine Safety and Health Administration (the MSHA) (D), mine operators are required to report within ten days all accidents, occupational injuries, and occupational illnesses that occur at a mine. The MSHA (D), in response to inquiries from mine operators about whether certain x-ray results had to be reported as diagnoses, issued three Program Policy Letters (PPLs) regarding when x-ray results constituted a "diagnosis" without following the notice and comment procedures of the Administrative Procedure Act (the APA), 5 U.S.C. § 553. The American Mining Congress (P) petitioned for judicial review of the MSHA's (D) decision to act without notice and comment in issuing the PPLs. The MSHA (D) claimed that the PPLs were interpretive, not substantive, rules and therefore were exempt from the notice and comment requirements under § 553(b)(3)(A) of the APA.

ISSUE: Do substantive rules have the force of law if Congress delegated legislative power to the agency and the agency intended to exercise that power in promulgating the rules?

HOLDING AND DECISION: (Williams, J.) Yes. Substantive rules have the force of law if Congress delegated legislative power to the agency and the agency intended to exercise that power in promulgating the rules. Only substantive rules are subject to the notice and comment requirements. In determining whether a purported interpretive rule has legal effect, the relevant inquiry is: (1) whether in the absence of the rule there would not be an adequate legislative basis for enforcement action or other agency action; (2) whether the rule has been published in the Code of Federal Regulations; (3) whether the agency expressly invoked its general legislative authority; or (4) whether the rule amends a prior legislative rule. If the answer to any of these inquiries is yes, the rule is legislative and not interpretive. Here the Program Policy Letters were interpretive rules since the agency did not purport to act legislatively. Petitions dismissed.

ANALYSIS

The distinction between those agency pronouncements that are subject to notice and comment requirements and those that are exempt is described by the court as "enshrouded in considerable smog." The court reviewed three types of agency rules. Substantive rules are pronouncements of law. Interpretative rules and general statements of policy are interpretive only and do not amend legislative rules.

Quicknotes

ADMINISTRATIVE PROCEDURE ACT (APA) Enacted in 1946 to govern practices and proceedings before federal administrative agencies.

INTERPRETIVE RULE A rule issued by an administrative agency for the purpose of explaining or interpreting a statute.

NOTICE AND COMMENT RULEMAKING Informal rulemaking.

RULEMAKING The promulgation of a rule governing a particular activity by an administrative agency, acting within the scope of its power pursuant to statute.

Metropolitan School District v. Davila

Local school district (P) v. Department of Education (D)

969 F.2d 485 (7th Cir. 1992)

NATURE OF CASE: Appeal from summary judgment in action challenging agency regulation.

FACT SUMMARY: A Michigan school district (P) claimed that a U.S. Department of Education (D) regulation should have been subject to notice and comment requirements.

RULE OF LAW

Interpretive rules are statements as to what an administrative officer thinks a statute or regulation means and are not subject to notice and comment requirements.

FACTS: Part B of the Individuals with Disabilities Act (the Act) provides federal funding to states to support the education of disabled children. To qualify for the funds, a state must establish a policy of assuring a free education to all disabled children. The Office of Special Education and Rehabilitative Services (OSERS) administers the Act. Davila (D), an administrator for OSERS, sent a letter regarding the policy for states providing educational services to disabled children who are expelled. This position was not made subject to notice and comment requirements. The Metropolitan School District (Metropolitan) (P) sued the U.S. Department of Education (the Department) (D) on behalf of all districts, asserting that the position in Davila's (D) letter imposed a large financial burden and should have been subject to notice and public comment. Both parties moved for summary judgment. The district court granted Metropolitan's (P) motion and the Department (D) appealed.

ISSUE: Are interpretive rules statements as to what an administrative officer thinks a statute or regulation means and not subject to notice and comment requirements?

HOLDING AND DECISION: (Bauer, C.J.) Yes. Interpretive rules are statements as to what an administrative officer thinks a statute or regulation means and are not subject to notice and comment requirements. The Administrative Procedure Act does not require that administrative agencies follow notice and comment procedures in all situations. Interpretive rules and general statements of policy are exempt from this process. The starting point in determining whether a rule is interpretive is the agency's characterization of the rule. An interpretive rule simply states what the agency thinks the underlying statute means and reminds affected parties of existing duties. On the other hand, substantive or legislative rules create new duties, have the force and effect of law, and have effects independent of the statute. Interpretative rules, although entitled to deference, do not bind reviewing courts. In the present case, the letter from Davila (D) purports to be interpretative and satisfies the general test. It relies upon the language of the statute and legislative history. Accordingly, it was not subject to notice and comment. Reversed and remanded for entry of summary judgment in favor of Davila (D) and the Department of Education (D).

ANALYSIS

The distinction between interpretative and legislative rules is a very blurry one, as even many courts have remarked. For a time, some courts used a "substantial impact" test to make the distinction. But this test has fallen out of favor.

Quicknotes

INTERPRETIVE RULE A rule issued by an administrative agency for the purpose of explaining or interpreting a statute.

LEGISLATIVE RULE The promulgation of a rule by an administrative agency, acting within the scope of its power pursuant to statute, enacting a law governing a particular activity.

SUMMARY JUDGMENT Judgment rendered by a court in response to a motion by one of the parties, claiming that the lack of a question of material fact in respect to an issue warrants disposition of the issue without consideration by the jury.

Heckler v. Community Health Services

Secretary, U.S. Dept. of Health and Human Services (D) v. Medicare provider (P)

467 U.S. 51 (1984)

NATURE OF CASE: Review of reversal of administrative determination.

FACT SUMMARY: Community Health Services (CHS) (P) claimed that the U.S. Department of Health and Human Services (D) was estopped from demanding repayment of federal funds CHS (P) had improperly received.

RULE OF LAW

A party claiming an estoppel must have relied on the adversary's conduct in such a manner as to change his or her position for the worse, and the reliance must have been reasonable under the circumstances.

FACTS: Community Health Services (CHS) (P) had received government reimbursement for home health care services it had provided to patients under the Medicare program. In seeking reimbursement, CHS (P) had relied on oral statements made by an insurance company that had acted as a fiscal intermediary in the proceedings. The U.S. Department of Health and Human Services (HHS) (D) later determined that the expenses were not reimbursable under Medicare and notified the insurance company who made a formal demand on CHS (P) for repayment. CHS (P) obtained a temporary injunction pending the outcome of an administrative review. The district court affirmed the administrative determination that HHS (D) should not have paid CHS (P). The court of appeals reversed, holding that the government may be estopped due to the affirmative misconduct of the government employees and the insurance company's erroneous advice. HHS (D) appealed, asserting that an estoppel may not run against the government.

ISSUE: Must a party claiming an estoppel have relied on the adversary's conduct in such a manner as to change his or her position for the worse, and must the reliance have been reasonable under the circumstances?

HOLDING AND DECISION: (Stevens, J.) Yes. A party claiming an estoppel must have relied on the adversary's conduct in such a manner as to change his or her position for the worse, and the reliance must have been reasonable under the circumstances. Here Community Health Services (CHS) (P) did not lose any rights in reliance on the Department of Health and Human Services' (D) misconduct. CHS (P) was merely induced to do something that could be corrected later. It was not reasonable for CHS (P) to rely on oral advice from the insurance company when it knew that fiscal intermediaries did not resolve policy questions. Reversed and remanded.

ANALYSIS

The court found that the elements of estoppel had not been established. Although stopping short of holding that the government may never be estopped, the court here found that the burden was heavier when applied to the government. The interest of the citizenry as a whole in obedience to the rule of law is undermined when the government is unable to enforce the law because the conduct of its agents gave rise to an estoppel.

Quicknotes

AGENT An individual who has the authority to act on behalf of another.

DETRIMENTAL RELIANCE Reliance by one party that is based on the conduct or promises of another, resulting in loss to the party.

EQUITABLE ESTOPPEL A doctrine that precludes a person from asserting a right to which he or she was entitled due to his or her action, conduct, or failure to act, causing another party to justifiably rely on such conduct to his or her detriment.

Office of Personnel Management v. Richmond

Human resources office (D) v. Navy welder (P)

496 U.S. 414 (1990)

NATURE OF CASE: Appeal from an award of damages for loss of disability annuity.

FACT SUMMARY: Richmond (P) retired from his job as a welder after the Office of Personnel Management (D) approved his application for a disability annuity due to his impaired eyesight.

RULE OF LAW

No money shall be drawn from the Treasury but in consequence of appropriations made by law.

FACTS: As a welder for the Navy, Richmond's (P) impaired eyesight qualified him for a disability annuity under 5 U.S.C. § 8337(d). The statute, however, provided that disability payments would end if the retiree earned an amount fairly comparable to the current rate of pay of the position occupied at the time of retirement. The original measuring period for restoration of earning capacity was two years, but after 1982, the measuring period was changed to one year. Upon retirement, Richmond (P) took a part-time job. Concerned about losing his eligibility if he made too much money, Richmond (P) twice consulted the Navy's Civilian Personnel Department and was given advice based on the former two-year eligibility rule. Richmond (P) then worked overtime in the erroneous belief his eligibility would not be affected, and the Office of Personnel Management (OPM) (D) suspended his disability annuity for six months. The court of appeals ruled that estoppel was properly applied against the federal government and ordered the suspended payments restored to Richmond (P). This appeal by OPM (D) followed.

ISSUE: Shall money be drawn from the Treasury but in consequence of appropriations made by law.?

HOLDING AND DECISION: (Kennedy, J.) No. No money shall be drawn from the Treasury, but in consequence of appropriations made by law (Appropriation Clause of the Constitution, Art. I, § 9, cl. 7). Judicial use of the equitable doctrine of estoppel cannot grant a money remedy that Congress has not authorized. The general purpose of the clause is to prevent fraud and corruption. But the direct purpose relevant to this case is to assure that public funds will be spent according to the letter of the difficult judgments reached by Congress as to the common good, and not according to the individual favor of government agents or the individual pleas of litigants. Estoppel claims based on real or imagined claims of misinformation by disgruntled citizens would impose an unpredictable drain on the public. An assertion of estoppel against the government by a claimant seeking public funds has never been upheld, for courts cannot estop the Constitution. Reversed.

ANALYSIS

Because of dicta in the Court's more recent cases, the courts of appeals had begun to apply equitable estoppel against the government. In *Office of Personnel Management v. Richmond*, the Court declared it was not deciding whether an estoppel claim could ever succeed against the government. However, it also declared that it has reversed every finding of estoppel that it has reviewed.

Quicknotes

ANNUITY The payment or right to receive payment of a fixed sum periodically, for a specified time period.

APPROPRIATION In governmental accounting, an expenditure authorized for a specific amount, purpose, and time.

ESTOPPEL An equitable doctrine precluding a party from asserting a right to the detriment of another who justifiably relied on the conduct.

Appeal of Eno (New Hampshire Department of Employment Security)

Applicant for benefits (P) v. State agency (D)

N.H. Sup. Ct., 126 N.H. 650, 495 A.2d 1277 (1985)

NATURE OF CASE: Appeal from denial of unemployment benefits.

FACT SUMMARY: Eno (P) was denied unemployment benefits because the New Hampshire Department of Employment Security (D) claimed that she had made insufficient efforts to find a job.

RULE OF LAW

Agencies deny due process when they apply different standards after causing persons to rely on lesser standards.

FACTS: Eno (P) was laid off from her job in February. In March, she applied for unemployment benefits from the New Hampshire Department of Employment Security (the Department) (D). She was given a pamphlet that stated the conditions of eligibility including a provision for seeking employment. When she appeared to make weekly applications, Eno (P) was asked if she was seeking employment and answered affirmatively. There was no further explanation or inquiry. Eno (P) had been answering want ads by telephone and sending out resumes, but she did not make personal visits to possible employers. The Department (D) later determined that she was ineligible for benefits since she had made insufficient efforts to obtain other employment. Eno (P) appealed.

ISSUE: Do agencies deny due process when they apply different standards after causing persons to rely on lesser standards?

HOLDING AND DECISION: (Souter, J.) Yes. Agencies deny due process when they apply different standards after causing persons to rely on lesser standards. A claim of entitlement to unemployment compensation is a claim to a property interest that is subject to due process guarantees. Thus, the New Hampshire Department of Employment Security (the Department) (D) may not deny a claim by a procedure that is fundamentally unfair. In the present case, it appears that Eno (P) did not comply with the statutory standard for eligibility because she did not make personal visits to potential employers. However, the Department's (D) contacts with Eno (P) indicated that different standards were applicable. When asked whether she was seeking employment, she answered truthfully that she had. Since these answers were accepted without further inquiry, it left Eno (P) with the natural impression that she had satisfied the eligibility conditions. It also signaled to Eno (P) that she should continue on that course. If she had been told that it was insufficient, she could have made a greater effort the following week. Since Eno (P) acted in reliance on the Department's (D) apparent standards, it was unfair to deny her benefits based on more exacting conditions. Reversed and remanded.

ANALYSIS

The court also noted that the New Hampshire Department of Employment Security (the Department) (D) revised its pamphlets after this case. The pamphlet now states that personal visits to employers are expected. The court sympathized with the Department's (D) indication it was understaffed at the time Eno (P) was seeking benefits but found that didn't justify the denial of benefits.

Quicknotes

DUE PROCESS The constitutional mandate requiring the courts to protect and enforce individuals' rights and liberties consistent with prevailing principles of fairness and justice and prohibiting the federal and state governments from such activities that deprive its citizens of a life, liberty, or property interest.

Christensen v. Harris County

[Party not identified] (P) v. County (D)

529 U.S. 576 (2000)

NATURE OF CASE: Certiorari review on agency regulation interpretation with split in Courts of Appeals decisions.

FACT SUMMARY: Harris County (D) wanted to require its employees to take earned compensatory time rather than receive monetary compensation for the overtime hours. The sheriff and 127 deputy sheriffs of Harris County did not want to be forced to take compensatory time. The Department of Labor issued its opinion that Harris County (D) could not force its employees (P) to take compensatory time in the absence of a prior agreement.

RULE OF LAW

Agency interpretations of unambiguous regulations issued in formats lacking the force of law are not entitled to *Chevron*-style or *Auer* deference but may be entitled to respect under *Skidmore* if the interpretations have the power to persuade.

FACTS: The Fair Labor Standards Act (the FLSA) permits states and their political subdivisions to compensate employees for overtime through granting compensatory time ("comp time"). In some circumstances, the employer is liable to pay cash compensation for accrued but unused comp time. Harris County (D) feared the fiscal effect of paying for comp time, so it wanted to institute a policy requiring its employees to take accrued comp time after reaching a predetermined maximum number of hours. Harris County (D) sought an opinion from the Department of Labor, which determined the FLSA does not permit an employer to require its employees take comp time in the absence of a prior agreement. Harris County (D) subsequently instituted a policy in which supervisors set the maximum number of hours to be accumulated, informed employees when the maximum was about to be reached, and requested employees take comp time. If the employees did not do so voluntarily, the supervisor may order comp time taken at set times. The sheriff and 127 deputy sheriffs (Petitioners) (P) filed suit, alleging the policy violated FLSA § 207(o)(5). The district court granted Petitioners (P) summary judgment and the Fifth Circuit Court of Appeals reversed. The courts of appeals are divided on the issue. The United States Supreme Court granted certiorari.

ISSUE: Are agency interpretations of unambiguous regulations issued in formats lacking the force of law entitled to *Chevron*-style or *Auer* deference?

HOLDING AND DECISION: (Thomas, J.) No. Agency interpretations of unambiguous regulations issued in formats lacking the force of law are not entitled to *Chevron*-style or *Auer* deference but may be entitled to respect under *Skidmore* if the interpretations have the power to persuade. Here, Fair Labor Standards Act (the FLSA) § 207(o)(5) requires employers to accommodate employees' reasonable requests to use comp time. The statute has no language prohibiting employers from requiring the use of comp time, so Petitioners (P) cannot prove Harris County (D) violated the FLSA. Petitioners (P) try to get around the obvious language of the statute and argue the Department of Labor (the DOL) opinion is entitled to *Chevron*-style deference as set out in *Chevron U.S.A. Inc. v. Natural Resources Defense Council, Inc.*, 467 U.S. 837 (1984), but this case involves an interpretation contained in an opinion letter, not one arrived at after notice and comment rulemaking. The DOL opinion letter is "entitled to respect" under *Skidmore v. Swift & Co.*, 323 U.S. 134 (1944), to the extent the agency interpretation has the "power to persuade." The agency's interpretation here is unpersuasive as the express language of the statute on compelled use is permissive and certainly does not prohibit the action at issue. Petitioners (P) also argue the opinion letter is entitled to *Auer* deference as delineated in *Auer v. Robbins*, 519 U.S. 452 (1997), but that is warranted only when the statutory language is ambiguous. This language is unambiguous on the issue of compelled comp time. Affirmed.

ANALYSIS

The Department of Labor (the DOL) wanted the Court to defer to its interpretation of its own regulation, but the Court looked at the express language of the statute to find the DOL's interpretation was in direct conflict with the language. The agency could hold a period of notice and comment rulemaking to formally interpret its regulation and thus prohibit compelled compensatory time.

Quicknotes

NOTICE AND COMMENT RULEMAKING Informal rulemaking.

United States v. Mead Corporation

Federal government (P) v. Corporation (D)

533 U.S. 218 (2001)

NATURE OF CASE: Certiorari review granted in tariff assessment action.

FACT SUMMARY: Mead Corporation (Mead) (D) was assessed a tariff on its day planners, and it protested to the United States Customs Service (the Customs Service). The Customs Service issued a ruling letter explaining why Mead (D) was assessed a tariff.

RULE OF LAW

There is a presumption that deference to agency discretion does not exist unless the relevant statute, expressly or impliedly, provides such deference.

FACTS: Mead Corporation (Mead) (D) imports "day planners." [The tariff schedule in regard to day planners is regulated by the Harmonized Tariff Schedule of the United States (the Schedule), which subjects day planners to a tariff of 4.0 percent.] Until 1993, when the United States Customs Service Headquarters issued a "ruling letter" classifying Mead's (D) day planners as "Diaries. . . bound," day planners had been duty-free. In response to Mead's (D) protest of the reclassification, Customs Service Headquarters issued a new letter, never published, and discussed the two definitions of "diary" from the dictionary; it concluded that the definition reflects commercial usage. As for the definition of "bound," Customs Service Headquarters concluded that "bound" meant "reinforcements or fittings of metal, plastics, etc." In the Schedule, Congress had conferred upon the Customs Service the power to issue regulations to establish procedures for the issuance of a binding ruling prior to the entry of the merchandise concerned and to disseminate information necessary to secure uniformity. A ruling letter represents the official position of the Customs Service with respect to a particular transaction or issue described therein. Ruling letters respond to transactions of the moment, so they are not subject to notice and comment before being issued, and although they may be published, they need only be made available for public inspection. In addition, the ruling letter has no bearing on nonparties to the transaction at issue. Forty-six different Customs Service offices issue 10,000-15,000 ruling letters per year. The court of appeals ruled that the Customs Service ruling letters do not fall within deference due pursuant to *Chevron U.S.A. Inc. v. Natural Resources Defense Council, Inc.*, 467 U.S. 837 (1984).

ISSUE: Does a tariff classification ruling by the United States Customs Service deserve judicial deference?

HOLDING AND DECISION: (Souter, J.) No. There is a presumption that deference to agency discretion does not exist unless the relevant statute, expressly or impliedly, provides such deference. A tariff classification has no claim to judicial deference under *Chevron U.S.A. Inc. v. Natural Resources Defense Council, Inc.*, 467 U.S. 837 (1984), because there is no indication that Congress intended such a ruling to carry the force of law; under *Skidmore v. Swift & Co.*, 323 U.S. 134 (1944), however, the ruling is eligible to claim respect according to its persuasiveness. Classification rulings, therefore, are best treated as interpretations contained in policy statements, agency manuals, and enforcement guidelines and do not require a *Chevron*-type deference; under *Skidmore*, however, the ruling is eligible to claim respect according to its persuasiveness. On the face of the statute, there is no congressional intent to give the Customs Service's classification rulings the force of law. There is in the agency's practice no indication that the Customs Service ever set out with a lawmaking pretense in mind when it undertook to make such classifications. The amendments to the statute do not reveal any new congressional objective of treating classification decisions generally as rulemaking with force of law. The authorization for classification rulings, and the Customs Service's practice in making them, present a case far removed not only from the notice and comment process but from any other circumstances reasonably suggesting that Congress ever thought of classification rulings as deserving the deference claimed for them here. The Customs Service's ruling at issue here fails to qualify for deference under *Chevron*, although the possibility that it deserves some deference under *Skidmore* means the case is to be vacated and remanded. Vacated and remanded.

ANALYSIS

This case demonstrates that the majority of the Court did not want to take an all-or-nothing approach in deferring to administrative agencies but preferred to support a variety of forms for such deference.

Barnhart v. Walton

Social Security Administration (D) v. Social Security applicant (P)

535 U.S. 212 (2002)

NATURE OF CASE: Suit challenging the denial of Social Security disability benefits.

FACT SUMMARY: Walton, a depressed, schizophrenic teacher lost his job because of his mental illness. The Social Security Administration denied his request for disability benefits because he was unable to engage in significant work for only 11 months instead of what the agency considered to be the statutorily required period of 12 months.

RULE OF LAW

The Social Security Act requires that applicants for disability benefits be unable to engage in substantial gainful activity for at least 12 months.

FACTS: Walton (P) developed a mental illness involving both schizophrenia and depression. He lost his teaching job because of his mental impairment, and the impairment then prevented him from engaging in "substantial gainful activity" for 11 months after he lost his teaching job. Walton (P) applied to the Social Security Administration (the Agency) (D) for disability benefits, but the Agency (D) denied his request. The Agency (D) reasoned that the statutory definition of disability required the plaintiff's inability to engage in substantial gainful activity to last at least 12 months. Walton (P) sued, and the trial court upheld the Agency's (D) denial of his request for benefits. The Fourth Circuit Court of Appeals reversed, concluding that the 12-month duration requirement applied to the underlying medical impairment itself, not to the period of inability to engage in substantial work that resulted from the impairment. The Agency (D) petitioned the United States Supreme Court for further review.

ISSUE: Does the Social Security Act require that applicants for disability benefits be unable to engage in substantial gainful activity for at least 12 months?

HOLDING AND DECISION: (Breyer, J.) Yes. The Social Security Act requires that applicants for disability benefits be unable to engage in substantial gainful activity for at least 12 months. The Social Security Act defines disability to require both an inability to perform substantial work and a medical impairment that causes the inability to work and lasts at least 12 months. The Social Security Administration (the Agency) (D) has promulgated a formal rule that extends the 12-month duration requirement to the "inability to engage in substantial gainful activity." The statute itself does not unambiguously foreclose the Agency's (D) interpretive regulation, and the Agency's (D) interpretation is permissible. Also, worth noting is the Agency's (D) interpretation is longstanding and has remained unaffected by several congressional amendments to the pertinent statutory provisions. Reversed.

ANALYSIS

Significant here is the Supreme Court's rejection of the "linguistic" reading of the statute used by the court of appeals. According to the strict letter of the statute, the 12-month duration requirement clearly modifies the word "impairment." Whether it also modifies the word "inability," however, is an ambiguous question. Under *Chevron U.S.A. Inc. v. Natural Resources Defense Council, Inc.*, 467 U.S. 837 (1984), that ambiguity justifies a permissible interpretation of whether the 12-month requirement also modifies "inability."

Kisor v. Wilkie

War veteran (P) v. Government official (D)

139 S. Ct. 2400 (2019)

NATURE OF CASE: Appeal from affirmance of judgment for defendant agency in action for disability benefits.

FACT SUMMARY: After Kisor's (P) second application for disability benefits was denied in part by the Department of Veterans Affairs (VA), and the VA's decision was affirmed by the federal courts pursuant to the deference accorded by *Auer v. Robbins*, 519 U.S. 452 (1997), to agency decisions regarding ambiguous rules, Kisor (P) asked the United States Supreme Court to overrule *Auer*.

RULE OF LAW

***Auer v. Robbins*, 519 U.S. 452 (1997), which requires judicial deference to an agency's construction of its own genuinely ambiguous regulation, should not be overruled.**

FACTS: Kisor (P), a war veteran, first applied for disability benefits from the Department of Veterans Affairs (the VA) in 1982, but his request was denied. Kisor (P) reapplied for such benefits in 2006, and although the benefits were granted, they were not retroactive to the date in 1982 of his first application, based on an agency rule governing such claims. The agency's decision was affirmed by the federal courts pursuant to the deference accorded agency decisions regarding ambiguous regulations under *Auer v. Robbins*, 519 U.S. 452 (1997), because the courts found that the regulation at issue was genuinely ambiguous. Under *Auer*, the agency's construction of its own regulation governs unless it is plainly erroneous or inconsistent with the agency's regulatory framework. Kisor (P) asked the United States Supreme Court to overrule *Auer*.

ISSUE: Should *Auer v. Robbins*, 519 U.S. 452 (1997), which requires judicial deference to an agency's construction of its own genuinely ambiguous regulation, be overruled?

HOLDING AND DECISION: (Kagan, J.) No. *Auer v. Robbins*, 519 U.S. 452 (1997), which requires judicial deference to an agency's construction of its own genuinely ambiguous regulation, should not be overruled. For various reasons, regulations may be genuinely ambiguous so that they can reasonably be interpreted in more than one way. *Auer* deference (as it is now called) is rooted in a presumption that Congress would generally want an agency to play the primary role in resolving regulatory ambiguities. In part, this is because it is believed that the agency that promulgated a rule is in the better position to reconstruct its original meaning. Additionally, resolving genuine regulatory ambiguities often entails the exercise of judgment grounded in policy concerns, and it is believed that agencies are better equipped than courts to make such policy judgments because of their expertise in a given area. Further, agencies are politically accountable, whereas courts are not. Finally, Congress prefers the resolution of interpretive issues by uniform administrative decision, rather than piecemeal by litigation, especially when such issues arise in the context of a complex and highly technical regulatory program. *Auer* deference thus serves to ensure consistency in federal regulatory law. Nonetheless, such deference is not appropriate for every interpretation of an agency's rules. First and foremost, a court should not afford *Auer* deference unless the regulation is genuinely ambiguous, and before concluding that a rule is genuinely ambiguous, a court must exhaust all the "traditional tools" of construction. Further, where genuine ambiguity remains, the agency's reading must still be "reasonable." Even so, a court must make an independent inquiry into whether the character and context of the agency interpretation entitles it to controlling weight. To begin with, the regulatory interpretation must be one actually made by the agency. In other words, it must be the agency's "authoritative" or "official position," rather than any m[e]re ad hoc statement not reflecting the agency's views. Additionally, the agency's interpretation must in some way implicate its substantive expertise. When the agency has no comparative expertise in resolving a regulatory ambiguity, Congress presumably would not grant it that authority. Finally, an agency's reading of a rule must reflect its fair and considered judgment. A court should decline to defer, for example, to a merely convenient litigating position or to a new interpretation that creates "unfair surprise" to regulated parties. The judgment below is vacated and remanded.

CONCURRENCE AND DISSENT: (Roberts, C.J.) The Court is correct not to overrule *Auer*, or its predecessor, *Bowles v. Seminole Rock & Sand Co.*, 325 U.S. 410 (1945), and the Court's delineation of the parameters of *Auer* deference is likewise correct.

CONCURRENCE AND DISSENT: (Gorsuch, J.) There are many good reasons to abandon *Auer*. In disputes involving the relationship between the government and the people, *Auer* requires judges to accept an executive agency's interpretation of its own regulations even when that interpretation doesn't represent the best and fairest

Continued on next page.

reading, thus creating a systematic judicial bias in favor of the federal government. Also, *Auer* is not well-reconciled with the Administrative Procedure Act (the APA) or the Constitution. Section 706 of the APA instructs reviewing courts to "decide all relevant questions of law" and "set aside agency action . . . found to be . . . not in accordance with law." The APA also directs courts to "determine the meaning" of any relevant "agency action," including any rule issued by the agency. The APA thus requires a reviewing court to resolve for itself any dispute over the proper interpretation of an agency regulation. A court that, in deference to an agency, adopts something other than the best reading of a regulation isn't "decid[ing]" the relevant "questio[n] of law" or "determin[ing] the meaning" of the regulation. Instead, it is allowing the agency to dictate the answer to that question. In doing so, the court is abdicating the duty Congress assigned to it in the APA. *Auer* is also incompatible with the APA's instructions in § 553. That provision requires agencies to follow notice-and-comment procedures when issuing or amending legally binding regulations (what the APA calls "substantive rules"), but not when offering mere interpretations of those regulations. Thus, *Auer* effectively nullifies the distinction Congress drew here. The majority suggests that if *Auer* cannot be squared with the text of the APA, it at least conforms to a reasonable "presumption about congressional intent." However, in the face of the APA's clear statutory commands, it makes little sense to presume that Congress wanted something other than what it legislated, i.e., that Congress secretly wanted courts to treat agency interpretations as binding. Not only is *Auer* incompatible with the APA, it also does not square well with the Constitution, which vests the power to interpret the laws in the courts. Despite the Court being clear that the judicial power under the Constitution should not be shared with the executive branch, that seems to be exactly what *Auer* requires. And, not even the most sensible policy argument can overcome the mandates of the APA and the Constitution. Justice Kagan suggests that determining the meaning of a regulation is largely a matter of figuring out what the "person who wrote it . . . intended." However, in interpreting binding laws, it is the words of the laws that should govern, not the intent of the authors who wrote the words. Moreover, if a court's goal in interpreting a regulation really were to determine what its author "intended," *Auer* would be an almost complete mismatch with the goal, because agency personnel change over time, and an agency's policy priorities may shift dramatically from one presidential administration to another. Yet, *Auer* tells courts that they must defer to the agency's current view of what the regulation ought to mean, which may or may not correspond to the views of those who actually wrote it. Justice Kagan also asserts that resolving ambiguities in a regulation is a task more suited to agency personnel than judges, but this contradicts the notion that we are governed by written laws whose meaning is fixed and ascertainable, rather than by bureaucrats. Justice Kagan's final policy argument is that *Auer* promotes "consistency" and "uniformity" in the interpretation of regulations. However, the judicial process is how we settle disputes about the meaning of written law, and our judicial system is more than capable of producing a single, uniform, and stable interpretation that will last until the regulation is amended or repealed. The majority's approach, in turning the *Auer* doctrine into a multi-step, multi-factor inquiry guarantees more uncertainty and much litigation. *Auer* should have been overruled, so courts could decide cases their independent judgment, and follow agencies' views only to the extent those views are persuasive.

ANALYSIS

Although Justice Kagan and Justice Gorsuch disagree as to the amount of deference courts should give agencies in interpreting their own ambiguous regulations, there is agreement that *Auer* deference will be denied when the regulation is merely a restatement of an enabling statute. Thus, an agency gets no "special authority to interpret its own words when, instead of using its expertise and experience to formulate a regulation, it has elected merely to paraphrase the statutory language." *Gonzales v. Oregon*, 546 U.S. 243, 257, 126 (2006). Justice Kavanagh, concurring in the judgment, expressed agreement that issues surrounding judicial deference to agency interpretations of their own regulations are distinct from those raised in connection with judicial deference to agency interpretations of statutes enacted by Congress, and that he did not regard the Court's decision in Kisor not to formally overrule *Auer* to touch upon the latter question.

CHAPTER 5

Reviewability

Quick Reference Rules of Law

Lujan v. Defenders of Wildlife

Secretary of Interior (D) v. Environmental group (P)

504 U.S. 555 (1992)

NATURE OF CASE: Appeal from denial of defense motion for summary judgment in action for injunctive relief.

FACT SUMMARY: In Defenders of Wildlife's (P) action against Lujan (D), the appellate court denied Lujan's (D) motion for summary judgment that challenged, on specificity grounds, the standing of this action.

RULE OF LAW

Standing is established when a plaintiff shows that he or she has suffered an actual and redressable injury that is fairly traceable to the challenged action of the defendant.

FACTS: Section 7(a)(2) of the Endangered Species Act (the ESA) of 1973 requires federal agencies to consult with the Secretary of the Interior to "insure that any action authorized, funded, or carried out by such agency . . . is not likely to jeopardize the continued existence of an endangered" or threatened species or to adversely modify its habitat. In lieu of the ESA requirement, the Secretary, Lujan (D), issued a regulation that limited the consultation requirement to agency action "in the United States or upon the high seas." As a result, Defenders of Wildlife (Defenders) (P) challenged this regulation in federal district court, averring that the regulation threatened the habitat of various endangered species abroad and caused injury to its cognizable interests. In rebuttal, Lujan (D) moved for summary judgment based on standing, on the grounds Defenders' (P) complaint failed to adequately specify the connection between the regulation and its alleged injuries. The district court granted the motion and the appellate court reversed. Lujan (D) appealed.

ISSUE: Is standing established when a plaintiff shows that he or she has suffered an actual and redressable injury that is fairly traceable to the challenged action of the defendant?

HOLDING AND DECISION: (Scalia, J.) Yes. Standing is established when a plaintiff shows that he or she has suffered an actual and redressable injury that is fairly traceable to the challenged action of the defendant. This rule represents the end result of common-law principles requiring, at a bare minimum, that a plaintiff establish the actuality, redressability, and traceability of an injury in order to have standing. In this vein, various stages of the litigative process require varying degrees of specificity for a plaintiff to establish standing; however, at the summary judgment stage, he or she must set forth, by evidence, specific facts, which for the purposes of the summary judgment motion will be taken as true. Even still, when this plaintiff asserts an injury arising from the government's allegedly unlawful action or inaction as affecting someone else, he or she must cross an even larger threshold to satisfy the necessary standing elements since, in this instance, causality and redressability issues become somewhat strained. In the instant case, since Defenders of Wildlife (Defenders) (P) failed to adequately demonstrate that any of its members suffered injury to a cognizable interest or, assuming injury, that relief would satisfactorily cushion this interest, Lujan's (D) motion to summarily dismiss Defenders' (P) injunctive action was wrongly denied. Reversed.

CONCURRENCE: (Kennedy, J.) Although the Court reached the correct result, the possibility that in different circumstances an ecosystem, animal, or vocational nexus theory might support a finding of standing should not be foreclosed. Also, the majority correctly notes that Congress may define injuries and specify chains of causation; Congress may exercise that power, though, only if it identifies the protected injury and relates it to the persons permitted to file suit. The citizen-suit provision at issue here fails these minimal conditions by failing to establish any injury in any person that results from any violation. Consistent with the case-or-controversy requirement of Article III, the person filing suit must have been injured in a concrete and personal way. Such a requirement is necessary to preserve the judiciary's limited role in our constitutional order.

CONCURRENCE: (Stevens, J.) Section 7(a)(2) of the Endangered Species Act (ESA) does not apply to occurrences in foreign countries, and the judgment of reversal is therefore correct on that basis. The plaintiffs here, however, do have standing because they have visited the affected habitat, have a professional interest in that habitat, and plan to visit that habitat again. Congress has recognized the very interests that the plaintiffs allege have been invaded by the interpretation of the ESA, and courts therefore have no power to ignore those interests. Accordingly, since the "imminence" of the injury here should depend on when the threatened harm is likely to occur, these plaintiffs do have standing to sue.

DISSENT: (Blackmun, J.) Under proper summary-judgment standards, the respondents (i.e., the original plaintiffs) have shown genuine issues of fact sufficient to survive summary judgment on the issues of injury and

Continued on next page.

redressability. As the majority itself notes, the respondents' affidavits do make it "questionable" whether the agency-funded projects threaten protected species. On the personal-injury element of standing, the Court today creates a pointless formality: the respondents still can simply buy airline tickets for their expected return trips. Likewise, the majority mistakenly rejects the theories of ecosystem nexus, vocational or professional injury, and procedural injury. Contrary to today's ruling, ecosystem nexus does not always depend on close proximity, and the distance of the site is irrelevant to a professional-injury analysis. Moreover, procedural injuries, as a class, are not automatically beyond judicial review. Frequently, procedural rights are so intertwined with substantive rights that courts cannot properly override the legislative decisions that link procedure with substance. The Court's broad language in denying procedural injury as a basis for standing is accordingly misplaced.

ANALYSIS

In *Japan Whaling Association v. American Cetacean Society*, 478 U.S. 221 (1986), the Society brought suit against the Secretary of Commerce to compel him to certify that Japan's whaling practices "diminish the effectiveness" of the International Convention for the Regulation of Whaling because Japan's annual harvest exceeded quotas established under the Convention. Such a certification would have required the President to impose economic sanctions against the offending nation. The Court raised the standing issue only in a footnote in the Solicitor General's Supreme Court brief, whereby it noted, in effect, that since the Society's right of action was expressly created by the Administrative Procedure Act (the APA), which states that "final agency action for which there is no other adequate remedy in court [is] subject to judicial review" (§ 704) at the behest of "[a] person . . . adversely affected or aggrieved by agency action," (§ 702) no separate indication of congressional intent to make agency action reviewable under the APA is necessary.

Quicknotes

ENDANGERED SPECIES ACT § 7 Provides that federal agencies insure that their actions do not threaten endangered species.

Monsanto Co. v. Geertson Seed Farms

Seed manufacturer (D) v. Farmer (P)

561 U.S. 139 (2010)

NATURE OF CASE: Certiorari review of entry of permanent injunction.

FACT SUMMARY: The Animal and Plant Health Inspection Service deregulated a variety of genetically engineered alfalfa manufactured by Monsanto Co. (D). Organic alfalfa farmers, such as Geertson Seed Farms (P), filed suit to enjoin almost all future planting of the genetically engineered alfalfa pending a detailed environmental assessment.

RULE OF LAW

Parties have standing to seek an injunction if they can demonstrate likelihood to suffer a constitutionally cognizable injury to themselves absent injunctive relief.

FACTS: The Animal and Plant Health Inspection Service (APHIS) deregulated a variety of genetically engineered alfalfa without first completing a detailed environmental assessment. Alfalfa farmers, such as Geertson Seed Farms (Geertson) (P) argued the deregulation violated the National Environmental Policy Act of 1969. The district court vacated the agency decision, ordered APHIS not to act on the deregulation until it completed a detailed environmental review, and enjoined almost all future planting of the genetically engineered alfalfa until completion of the review. The court of appeals affirmed the permanent injunction.

ISSUE: Do parties have standing to seek an injunction if they can demonstrate likelihood to suffer a constitutionally cognizable injury to themselves absent injunctive relief?

HOLDING AND DECISION: (Alito, J.) Yes. Parties have standing to seek an injunction if they can demonstrate likelihood to suffer a constitutionally cognizable injury to themselves absent injunctive relief. The case in chief involves the breadth of the injunctive relief. Monsanto (D), however, also argues Geertson Seed Farms (Geertson) (P) lacks standing to seek injunctive relief because it and the other respondents cannot demonstrate a constitutionally cognizable injury to themselves. Geertson (P) owner's affidavit states otherwise. He attests the planting of genetically engineered alfalfa within the compact area of alfalfa farms easily could result in contamination of the organic alfalfa with the genetically modified version because alfalfa is pollinated by bees and bees have a range of two to ten miles. Other affiants also swore the potential for contamination already increased their seed costs and would result in them having to raise prices and no longer be competitive in the market. Geertson (P) had to contract with growers outside the United States to ensure genetically pure alfalfa seed. The respondents (P) will suffer harm even if the Roundup Ready gene never actually infects the pure alfalfa and those harms are directly attributable to the Animal and Plant Health Inspection Service (APHIS) deregulation decision. The injunctive relief prohibiting the growth or sale of genetically engineered alfalfa minimizes or eliminates the risk of gene flow to conventional and organic crops. Reversed and remanded [on other grounds].

ANALYSIS

Parties seeking injunctive relief must demonstrate actual injury rather than speculative injury. Also, the injury must be to the parties seeking relief and not merely to those in similar circumstances.

Quicknotes

INJUNCTIVE RELIEF A court order issued as a remedy, requiring a person to do, or prohibiting that person from doing, a specific act.

Clapper v. Amnesty International USA

[Party not identified] (D) v. International human rights organization (P)

568 U.S. 398 (2013)

NATURE OF CASE: Certiorari review of standing in petition seeking injunctive relief.

FACT SUMMARY: Lawyers, human rights workers, and media (collectively, Respondents) (P) engage in electronic communications with foreign nationals who may be targets of the United States for surveillance under 50 U.S.C. § 1881(a). Respondents (P), as American citizens and agencies, sought to enjoin such surveillance because it necessarily could record their conversations.

RULE OF LAW

Article III standing requires a concrete, particularized, actual, or imminent injury certainly impending that is fairly traceable to the challenged action and redressable by a favorable ruling.

FACTS: The Attorney General and the Director of National Intelligence (the Government) (D) have authority pursuant to § 702 of the Foreign Intelligence Surveillance Act of 1978 (FISA), 50 U.S.C. § 1881(a) to surveil foreign nationals reasonably believed to be located outside the United States for the purpose of acquiring foreign intelligence information. Lawyers, human rights workers, and media (collectively, Respondents) (P) engage in sensitive conversations with persons who may be subject to the Government's (D) surveillance. Respondents (P) feared their communications would be collected by Government (D) even though Respondents (P) are not foreign nationals reasonably believed to be located outside the United States. Respondents (P) sought a declaratory judgment that § 1881(a) is unconstitutional and injunctive relief prohibiting § 1881(a)-authorized surveillance.

ISSUE: Does Article III standing require a concrete, particularized, actual, or imminent injury certainly impending that is fairly traceable to the challenged action and redressable by a favorable ruling?

HOLDING AND DECISION: (Alito, J.) Yes. Article III standing requires a concrete, particularized, actual, or imminent injury certainly impending that is fairly traceable to the challenged action and redressable by a favorable ruling. Respondents (P) assert standing based on injury in fact through an objectively reasonable likelihood their communications will be acquired under § 1881(a) in the future. Alternatively, Respondents (P) allege they have suffered a present injury because they have incurred costs to avoid possible collection of their communications. Section 1881(a) requires the Government (D) to obtain the Foreign Intelligence Surveillance Court's approval of procedures and certification attesting, in part, procedures are in place to limit the surveillance targets to the appropriate persons. First, Respondents' (P) claimed injury is not "certainly impending" because it is future, speculative, and rests on a highly attenuated chain of possibilities. Respondents (P) claim the surveillance "may" occur, and "might" be pursuant to § 1881(a) authority, and the Government (D) will be successful in obtaining their communications. Journalist Christopher Hedges (P) has to "assume" the Government (D) has targeted his contacts and he has to make choices based on that assumption. Attorney Scott McKay (P) states all must "assume" the Government (D) "may" be surveilling sensitive electronic communications. These are not specific facts, but mere allegations and speculation. Second, Respondents (P) fail to demonstrate their injury is fairly traceable to § 1881(a) because they can only speculate any surveillance would occur pursuant to that authority rather than some other authority, including older provisions of the Foreign Intelligence Surveillance Act of 1978 (FISA). Third, Respondents (D) are guessing if the Foreign Intelligence Surveillance Court will authorize the Government's (D) request. This Court has been reluctant to guess how independent decisionmakers will exercise discretion. This Court also finds a lack of standing when reaching the merits would extend the judiciary's role to determine whether an action taken by one of the other two branches is constitutional. Fourth, the Government (D) may not succeed in obtaining the communications even if so authorized. Fifth, Respondents (P) cannot know if their own communications would be incidentally acquired. Respondents' (P) alternative argument also falls. They cannot create standing by acting on a hypothetical fear even if that fear is not paranoid or otherwise unreasonable. This Court found similarly in *Laird v. Tatum*, 408 U.S. 1 (1972), when plaintiffs did not have standing based on allegations of a subjective "chill" to exercise of First Amendment rights without present objective harm or threat of a specific future harm. *Monsanto Co. v. Geertson Seed Farms*, 561 U.S. 139 (2010), is inapposite because that case rested on a "substantial risk" the harm will occur while this rests on mere conjecture. Respondents (P) lack Article III standing.

DISSENT: (Breyer, J.) The harm the Government (D) will intercept Respondents' (P) electronic communications is not "speculative" but is common-sense inference. The Government's (D) interception of a private

Continued on next page.

telephone or email communication is a concrete, particularized injury. The issue is whether the interception is "actual or imminent." Scott McKay (P) attests he is a lawyer representing Mr. Sami Omar Al-Hussayen and Khalid Sheik Mohammed and communicated with his clients, experts, investigators, and others located abroad while the Government (D) intercepted thousands of calls and emails prior to 2008. Sylvia Royce (P) attests she is an attorney representing Mohammedou Ould Salahi, a designated enemy combatant, and she receives occasional calls from Mr. Salahi's brother. Joanne Mariner (P) attests she is a human rights researcher and communicates with foreign nationals all over the world. There is a very high likelihood the Government (D), authorized by § 1881(a), will intercept Respondents' (P) communications. The Government (D) has a strong motive, has done so in the past, and it is part of the Government's (D) job. The Court previously has used "certainly" to emphasize rather than define the immediately following term "impending." In *Monsanto*, the Court found a reasonable probability of future injury accompanied with present injury in the form of mitigating threats provides standing. These are virtually identical circumstances here. The word "certainly" in "certainly impending" does not refer to absolute certainty but "reasonable probability" or "high probability." The standard is readily met in this case.

ANALYSIS

"Certainly impending" did not appear as a standing factor until *Clapper v. Amnesty International USA*, 561 U.S. 139 (2010), but it is unclear whether that is a distinct requirement to meet. This case also made standing difficult to obtain in any challenge to Foreign Intelligence Surveillance Act of 1978 (FISA) surveillance because individuals subject to secret governmental surveillance typically cannot demonstrate they themselves have had their communications intercepted or are looking at "certainly impending" interception. The FISA authorizations would have to be made public.

Quicknotes

ENJOIN The ordering of a party to cease the conduct of a specific activity.

INJUNCTIVE RELIEF A court order issued as a remedy, requiring a person to do, or prohibiting that person from doing, a specific act.

INJURY IN FACT An injury that gives rise to standing to sue.

REDRESSABILITY Requirement that in order for a court to hear a case there must be an injury that is redressable or capable of being remedied.

STANDING The right to commence suit against another party because of a personal stake in the resolution of the controversy.

Spokeo, Inc. v. Robins

Operator of online "people search engine" (D) v. Consumer (P)

578 U.S. 330 (2016)

NATURE OF CASE: Appeal from judgment that a consumer had Article III standing to bring suit under the Fair Credit Reporting Act of 1970 against an online "people search engine."

FACT SUMMARY: Spokeo, Inc. (D), an online "people search engine," contended that Robins (P) did not have Article III standing to bring suit against it under the Fair Credit Reporting Act of 1970 since, although he alleged particularized injury, he failed to allege concrete injury from Spokeo's (D) alleged erroneous information about Robins (P) that it disseminated.

RULE OF LAW

To satisfy the injury-in-fact requirement for Article III standing, a plaintiff must show concrete, de facto, injury in addition to particularized injury.

FACTS: The Fair Credit Reporting Act of 1970 (FCRA or the Act) requires consumer-reporting agencies to follow reasonable procedures to assure maximum possible accuracy of consumer reports, and it imposes liability on any person who willfully fails to comply with any requirement of the Act with respect to any individual. Spokeo, Inc. (D), an alleged consumer-reporting agency, operated a "people search engine," which searches a wide spectrum of databases to gather and provide personal information about individuals to a variety of users, including employers wanting to evaluate prospective employees. After Robins (P) discovered that his Spokeo (D)-generated profile contained inaccurate information, he filed a federal class-action complaint against Spokeo (D), alleging that the company willfully failed to comply with the FCRA's requirements. Specifically, his profile, he asserted, stated that he was married, had children, was in his fifties, had a job, was relatively affluent, and held a graduate degree. According to Robins's (P) complaint, all this information was incorrect. The district court dismissed Robins's (P) complaint, holding that he had not properly pleaded injury in fact as required by Article III. The court of appeals reversed. Based on Robins's (P) allegation that Spokeo (D) violated his statutory rights and the fact that Robins's (P) personal interests in the handling of his credit information were individualized, the court of appeals held that Robins (P) had adequately alleged an injury in fact. The United States Supreme Court granted certiorari.

ISSUE: To satisfy the injury-in-fact requirement for Article III standing, must a plaintiff show concrete, de facto, injury in addition to particularized injury?

HOLDING AND DECISION: (Alito, J.) Yes. To satisfy the injury-in-fact requirement for Article III standing, a plaintiff must show concrete, de facto, injury in addition to particularized injury. A plaintiff invoking federal jurisdiction bears the burden of establishing the irreducible constitutional minimum of standing by demonstrating (1) an injury in fact, (2) fairly traceable to the challenged conduct of the defendant, and (3) likely to be redressed by a favorable judicial decision. The injury-in-fact requirement requires a plaintiff to show that he or she suffered an invasion of a legally protected interest that is "concrete and particularized" and "actual or imminent, not conjectural or hypothetical." The Ninth Circuit Court of Appeals' injury-in-fact analysis elided the independent "concreteness" requirement. Both observations it made concerned only "particularization," i.e., the requirement that an injury affect the plaintiff in a personal and individual way, but an injury in fact must be both concrete and particularized. Concreteness is quite different from particularization and requires an injury to be "de facto," that is, actually exist. The appeals court concluded that Robins's (P) complaint alleged "concrete, de facto" injuries for essentially two reasons. First, the court noted that Robins (P) alleged that Spokeo (D) violated his statutory rights, not just the statutory rights of other people. Second, the court wrote that "Robins's (P) personal interests in the handling of his credit information are individualized rather than collective." Both of these observations, however, concerned particularization, not concreteness. A "concrete" injury need not be a "tangible" injury. To determine whether an intangible harm constitutes injury in fact, both history and the judgment of Congress are instructive. Congress is well positioned to identify intangible harms that meet minimum Article III requirements, but a plaintiff does not automatically satisfy the injury-in-fact requirement whenever a statute grants a right and purports to authorize a suit to vindicate it. Article III standing requires a concrete injury even in the context of a statutory violation. This does not mean, however, that the risk of real harm cannot satisfy that requirement. The violation of a procedural right granted by statute can be sufficient in some circumstances to constitute injury in fact; in such a case, a plaintiff need not allege any additional harm beyond the one identified by Congress. Although this decision takes no position on the correctness of the court of appeals' ultimate conclusion, these general principles demonstrate two things: that Congress

Continued on next page.

plainly sought to curb the dissemination of false information by adopting procedures designed to decrease that risk and that Robins (P) cannot satisfy the demands of Article III by alleging a bare procedural violation. Because the court of appeals failed to fully appreciate the distinction between concreteness and particularization, its standing analysis was incomplete. It did not address the question of whether the particular procedural violations alleged by Robins (P) entailed a degree of risk sufficient to meet the concreteness requirement. Vacated and remanded.

CONCURRENCE: (Thomas, J.) To understand the limits that the standing requirement imposes on federal courts, one must refer to the traditional, fundamental limitations upon the powers of common-law courts. Historically, common-law courts possessed broad power to adjudicate suits involving the alleged violation of private rights, which traditionally included rights of personal security (including security of reputation), property rights, and contract rights. In a suit for the violation of a private right, courts historically presumed that the plaintiff suffered a de facto injury merely from having his personal, legal rights invaded. Common-law courts, however, required a further showing of injury for violations of "public rights"—rights that involve duties owed to the whole community, considered as a community, in its social aggregate capacity. Generally, only the government had the authority to vindicate a harm borne by the public at large, such as the violation of the criminal laws. Even in limited cases where private plaintiffs could bring a claim for the violation of public rights, they had to allege that the violation caused them some extraordinary damage, beyond the rest of the community. These differences between legal claims brought by private plaintiffs for the violation of public and private rights underlie modern standing doctrine. Accordingly, the injury-in-fact requirement often stymies a private plaintiff's attempt to vindicate the infringement of public rights. The Court has repeatedly said that, when a plaintiff seeks to vindicate a public right, the plaintiff must allege that he has suffered a "concrete" injury particular to himself. This requirement applies with special force when a plaintiff files suit to require an executive agency to "follow the law"; at that point, the citizen must prove that he has sustained or is immediately in danger of sustaining a direct injury as a result of that challenged action, and it is not sufficient that he has merely a general interest common to all members of the public. On the other hand, the concrete-harm requirement does not apply as rigorously when a private plaintiff seeks to vindicate his own private rights, and contemporary decisions have not required a plaintiff to assert an actual injury beyond the violation of his personal legal rights to satisfy the "injury-in-fact" requirement. When Congress creates new private causes of action to vindicate private or public rights, these Article III principles circumscribe federal courts' power to adjudicate a suit alleging the violation of those new legal rights. Congress can create new private rights and authorize private plaintiffs to sue based simply on the violation of those private rights. A plaintiff seeking to vindicate such a statutorily created private right need not allege actual harm beyond the invasion of that private right. Nevertheless, a plaintiff seeking to vindicate a public right embodied in a federal statute must demonstrate that the violation of that public right has caused him a concrete, individual harm distinct from the general population. Thus, Congress cannot authorize private plaintiffs to enforce public rights in their own names, absent some showing that the plaintiff has suffered a concrete harm particular to him. Applying these principles to the case at bar, the majority is correct in vacating and remanding the case to the court of appeals. The Fair Credit Reporting Act of 1970 (the Act) creates a series of regulatory duties, and Robins (P) has no standing to sue Spokeo (D), in his own name, for violations of the duties that Spokeo (D) owes to the public collectively, absent some showing that he has suffered concrete and particular harm. However, a remand is required because one claim in Robins's (P) complaint rests on a statutory provision that could arguably establish a private cause of action to vindicate the violation of a privately held right, given that the Act requires Spokeo (D) to "follow reasonable procedures to assure maximum possible accuracy of the information concerning the individual about whom the report relates." If Congress has created a private duty owed personally to Robins (P) to protect his information, then the violation of the legal duty suffices for Article III injury in fact. If that provision, however, vests any and all consumers with the power to police the "reasonable procedures" of Spokeo (D), without more, then Robins (P) has no standing to sue for its violation absent an allegation that he has suffered individualized harm.

DISSENT: (Ginsburg, J.) There is no need to remand this case, because Robins (P) has adequately alleged concrete injury. The Court's decisions suggest that the particularity requirement bars complaints raising generalized grievances, seeking relief that no more benefits the plaintiff than it does the public at large. Robins's (P) claim does not present a question of that character. He seeks redress, not for harm to the citizenry, but for Spokeo's (D) spread of misinformation specifically about him. He complains of misinformation about his education, family situation, and economic status, inaccurate representations that could affect his fortune in the job market. These inaccuracies bear on Robins's (P) ability to find employment by creating the erroneous impression that he is overqualified for the work he is seeking, that he might be unwilling to relocate for a job due to family commitments, or that his salary demands would exceed what prospective employers were prepared to offer him. The procedural

Continued on next page.

requirements of the Fair Credit Reporting Act of 1970 aimed to prevent such harm. Therefore, no utility will be served in returning this case to the court of appeals to underscore what Robins's (P) complaint already conveys concretely: Spokeo's (D) misinformation caused actual harm to his employment prospects.

ANALYSIS

On remand, the Ninth Circuit considered the extent to which the violation of a statutory right can itself establish an injury sufficiently concrete for the purposes of Article III standing, *Robins v. Spokeo, Inc.*, 867 F.3d 1108 (2017). In evaluating Robins's (P) claim of harm, the court asked: (1) whether the statutory provisions of the Fair Credit Reporting Act of 1970 (FCRA) were established to protect his concrete interests (as opposed to purely procedural rights), and, if so, (2) whether the specific procedural violations he alleged actually harmed, or presented a material risk of harm to, such interests. As to the first question, the court agreed with Robins (P) that Congress established the FCRA provisions at issue to protect consumers' concrete interests. Given the ubiquity and importance of consumer reports in modern life—in employment decisions, in loan applications, in home purchases, and much more—the court concluded that the real-world implications of material inaccuracies in those reports are clear on their face. As to the second question, the Ninth Circuit concluded that Spokeo's (D) inaccurate reports on a broad range of material facts about Robins's (P) life could be deemed concrete harm. Finally, the court also rejected Spokeo's (D) suggestion that Robins's (P) allegations of harm were too speculative to establish a concrete injury. Accordingly, the court ruled that Robins (P) had standing to pursue his suit.

Quicknotes

INJURY IN FACT An injury that gives rise to standing to sue.

Abbott Laboratories v. Gardner

Pharmaceutical manufacturers and trade association (P) v. Commissioner of Food and Drugs (D)

387 U.S. 136 (1967)

NATURE OF CASE: Suit challenging regulations promulgated by the Commissioner of Food and Drugs (D).

FACT SUMMARY: Manufacturers of prescription drugs (P) brought suit against the Commissioner of Food and Drugs (D), challenging regulations requiring the manufacturers to include both their "established name" and the proprietary name of the drugs on all labels and in all advertisements.

RULE OF LAW

Only upon a showing of clear and convincing evidence of a contrary legislative intent should the courts restrict access to judicial review of final agency actions.

FACTS: In 1962 Congress amended the federal Food, Drug, and Cosmetic Act to require manufacturers of prescription drugs to print the "established name" corresponding to any proprietary name of the drug prominently on its labels. A similar rule was passed with respect to advertisements for such drugs. Thirty-seven individual drug manufacturers (P) and the Pharmaceutical Manufacturers Association (P) to which they belonged brought suit challenging the regulations on the basis that the Commissioner of Food and Drugs (D) exceeded his authority in promulgating the rule.

ISSUE: Should the courts restrict access to judicial review of final agency actions only upon a showing of clear and convincing evidence of a contrary legislative intent?

HOLDING AND DECISION: (Harlan, J.) Yes. Only upon a showing of clear and convincing evidence of a contrary legislative intent should the courts restrict access to judicial review of final agency actions. The issue here is whether Congress intended to forbid pre-enforcement review of this type of regulation promulgated by the Commissioner of Food and Drugs (D). Cases have held that judicial review of a final agency action by an aggrieved person will not be cut off unless it appears that that was Congress's intent. The Administrative Procedure Act (the Act) also provides for review of agency actions for which review is provided by statute or for which there is no other adequate legal remedy. The statutory scheme of the Act does not preclude judicial review of such actions as those taken in the present case, nor has the government demonstrated such an intent.

ANALYSIS

The Court notes that the intent to preclude judicial review must be gleaned from the statutory scheme as a whole. Furthermore, where a statute expressly provides that certain actions are reviewable, it should not be presumed that all other actions are not reviewable by the courts.

Quicknotes

CLEAR AND CONVINCING EVIDENCE An evidentiary standard requiring a demonstration that the fact sought to be proven is reasonably certain.

JUDICIAL REVIEW The authority of the courts to review decisions, actions, or omissions committed by another agency or branch of government.

Block v. Community Nutrition Institute

Government agency (D) v. Consumer group (P)

467 U.S. 340 (1984)

NATURE OF CASE: Appeal of a reversal of a dismissal of an action challenging certain milk pricing regulations.

FACT SUMMARY: The Community Nutrition Institute (P) challenged the Department of Agriculture (D) minimum milk price regulations.

RULE OF LAW

Consumers do not have standing to challenge regulations promulgated under the Agricultural Marketing Agreement Act of 1937.

FACTS: In 1937 Congress enacted the Agricultural Marketing Agreement Act, which provided, among other things, for extensive rulemaking authority in the Department of Agriculture (the Department) (D) to prevent dairy price collapses. Pursuant to this authority, the Department (D) promulgated rules fixing minimum prices on various classes of milk products. These rules were challenged by individual consumers, several milk handlers, and a consumer organization (the Community Nutrition Institute) (P). The district court dismissed for lack of standing and failure to exhaust administrative remedies. The court of appeals reversed as to the consumers, holding that the statutory scheme did not expressly prohibit consumer challenges.

ISSUE: Do consumers have standing to challenge regulations promulgated under the Agricultural Marketing Agreement Act of 1937?

HOLDING AND DECISION: (O'Connor, J.) No. Consumers do not have standing to challenge regulations promulgated under the Agricultural Marketing Agreement Act of 1937. The Administrative Procedure Act gives rise to a presumption of such standing, but it is only a presumption. Where such standing is contrary to the legislative scheme or expressly prohibited, it will not be found. Contrary to the holding of the court of appeals, an explicit prohibition on such standing need not be found. Here, Congress envisioned a complex administrative procedure, and to allow consumer suits would bypass this procedure. Reversed.

ANALYSIS

Prior to this decision some courts tended to hold, as the court of appeals did here, that congressional desire to prevent citizen standing in challenges to regulations had to be explicit. This was described as "clear and convincing evidence." The Supreme Court, in this opinion, quite clearly rejected this standard.

Quicknotes

ADMINISTRATIVE REMEDIES Relief that is sought before an administrative body as opposed to a court.

STANDING The right to commence suit against another party because of a personal stake in the resolution of the controversy.

Heckler v. Chaney

Food and Drug Administration director (D) v. Prison inmate (P)

470 U.S. 821 (1985)

NATURE OF CASE: Appeal of reversal of dismissal of action to compel Food and Drug Administration (D) enforcement proceedings.

FACT SUMMARY: Chaney (P) brought an action to compel the Food and Drug Administration (D) to stop the use of lethal drugs in executions.

RULE OF LAW

A decision by the Food and Drug Administration to refrain from enforcement proceedings is not subject to judicial review.

FACTS: The Food, Drug, and Cosmetic Act mandated that the Food and Drug Administration (the FDA) (D) take steps to prevent unauthorized or dangerous uses of approved drugs. Chaney (P), contending that use of approved drugs for execution by injection constituted an unauthorized and dangerous use of drugs, petitioned the FDA (D) to take steps to prevent such use. The FDA (D) declined. Chaney (P) brought an action to compel the FDA (D) to take such steps. The district court granted the FDA (D) summary judgment and dismissed, holding that such agency actions were unreviewable. The appellate court reversed, holding that such actions were reviewable, and further held the decision by the FDA (D) to be improper.

ISSUE: Is a decision by the Food and Drug Administration to refrain from enforcement proceedings subject to judicial review?

HOLDING AND DECISION: (Rehnquist, J.) No. A decision by the Food and Drug Administration to refrain from enforcement proceedings is not subject to judicial review. Traditionally, agency decisions to decline enforcement proceedings have been unreviewable. This is largely due to a respect for the greater knowledgeability that an agency will be presumed to have over a court. Another reason is that agency lack of enforcement generally does not involve coercive intrusion upon personal liberty, the protection of which is the main concern of the courts. As the Act in question gives no hint of an exception of this rule, the decision of the court of appeals must be reversed.

CONCURRENCE: (Brennan, J.) While Congress intended to afford administrative agencies broad discretion in making enforcement decisions, Congress did not intend administrative agencies to ignore clear jurisdictional, regulatory, statutory, or constitutional requirements.

ANALYSIS

Judicial unreviewability of agency inaction is often likened to prosecutorial discretion. In both instances, societal, not individual, interests are at stake. Justice Marshall takes issue with the analogy, contending that societal interests in criminal prosecutions are much more intangible than agency decisions.

Quicknotes

FEDERAL FOOD, DRUG, AND COSMETIC ACT Consumer-protection statute authorizing promulgation of rules governing food and drugs.

Webster v. Doe

CIA director (D) v. CIA employee (P)

486 U.S. 592 (1988)

NATURE OF CASE: Appeal from vacation of denial of claim for reinstatement.

FACT SUMMARY: When the Central Intelligence Agency (the CIA) (D) terminated Doe's (P) employment upon learning that he was homosexual, Doe (P) filed an action alleging statutory and constitutional violations by Webster (D), the CIA (D) director.

RULE OF LAW

Under § 102(c) of the National Security Act, employee termination decisions made by the Director of the Central Intelligence Agency are not judicially reviewable.

FACTS: After working for the Central Intelligence Agency (CIA) (D) for nine years, being promoted to a position as a covert electronics technician, and being consistently rated as an excellent or outstanding employee, John Doe's (P) employment was terminated after he revealed to the CIA (D) that he was a homosexual. Webster (D), director of the CIA (D), concluded that Doe's (P) homosexuality presented a security threat. Doe (P) submitted to a polygraph test concerning his homosexuality and possible security violations, denied having sexual relations with any foreign nationals, and maintained that he had not disclosed classified information to any of his sexual partners. The test results indicated he had answered all questions truthfully. When Doe (P) refused the CIA's (D) request that he resign, Webster (D) "deemed it necessary and advisable in the interests of the United States to terminate his employment." Doe (P) then filed an action, asserting a variety of statutory and constitutional claims against Webster (D), who moved for dismissal on the ground § 102(c) of the National Security Act precluded judicial review of his termination decisions under §§ 701, 702, and 706 of the Administrative Procedure Act (APA). The district court granted Doe's (P) motion for partial summary judgment and found that Doe (P) had been unlawfully discharged. The court of appeals vacated the district court's judgment and remanded the case for further proceedings, deciding first that judicial review of the CIA's (D) decision was not precluded under APA § 701(a)(1) or (a)(2) and second, that the CIA (D) regulations cited by Doe (P) did not limit Webster's (D) discretion in making termination decisions.

ISSUE: Under § 102(c) of the National Security Act, are employee termination decisions made by the Director of the Central Intelligence Agency judicially reviewable?

HOLDING AND DECISION: (Rehnquist, C.J.) No. Under § 102(c) of the National Security Act (the NSA), employee termination decisions made by the Director of the Central Intelligence Agency (the CIA) are not judicially reviewable. Section 701(a) of the Administrative Procedure Act (the APA) limits application of the entire APA to situations in which judicial review is not precluded by statute; subsection (a)(1) is concerned with whether Congress expressed an intent to prohibit judicial review, while subsection (a)(2) applies "in those rare instances where 'statutes are drawn in such broad terms that in a given case there is no law to apply.'" The standard set forth in § 102(c) of the NSA defers to the director and appears to foreclose the application of any meaningful judicial standard of review. Thus, the language and structure of § 102(c) indicate that Congress meant to commit individual employee discharges to the director's discretion and that § 701(a)(2) accordingly precludes judicial review of these decisions under the APA. However, nothing in § 102(c) demonstrates that Congress meant to preclude consideration of colorable constitutional claims arising out of the actions of the director pursuant to that section. Reversed as to judicial review of terminations under § 102(c).

DISSENT: (Scalia, J.) Congress can prescribe, at least within broad limits, that for certain jobs the dismissal decision will be unreviewable—that is, will be "committed to agency discretion by law." Further, it is entirely beyond doubt that if Congress intended to exclude judicial review of the President's decision (through the Director of Central Intelligence) to dismiss an officer of the Central Intelligence Agency (D), that disposition would be constitutionally permissible. Not the Constitution, our laws, or common sense gives an individual a right to come into court to litigate the reasons for his dismissal as an intelligence agent.

ANALYSIS

On remand, *Doe v. Webster*, 769 F. Supp. 1 (D.D.C. 1991), the district court concluded that Central Intelligence Agency (CIA) (D) regulations gave Doe (P) a post-probation property interest in his position and that his discharge without a statement of reasons why his homosexuality posed a security threat and an opportunity to respond to those reasons violated due process. Contrary

Continued on next page.

to the opinion expressed by both Justices O'Connor and Scalia that judicial review of constitutional claims is also precluded in this context, the majority's rejection of all arguments made on this point by Webster (D) sends a clear message that a legislative attempt to preclude review of constitutional claims would be unacceptable. Further, even where national security is concerned, methods exist to balance the need of the individual asserting constitutional claims against the extraordinary needs of the CIA (D) for confidentiality.

Quicknotes

NATIONAL SECURITY ACT § 102 Precludes judicial review of the Central Intelligence Agency director's employment decisions.

Department of Commerce v. New York

Federal agency (D) v. State (P)

139 S. Ct. 2551 (2019)

NATURE OF CASE: Appeal.

FACT SUMMARY: The Secretary of Commerce (D) sought to include in the 2020 census a citizenship question. The Secretary (D) contended that this decision was not reviewable under the Administrative Procedure Act.

RULE OF LAW

The Secretary of Commerce's decision to include a certain question in a census is reviewable under the Administrative Procedure Act.

FACTS: To apportion members of the House of Representatives among the states, the Constitution requires an "Enumeration" of the population every 10 years, to be made "in such Manner" as Congress "shall by Law direct." In the Census Act, Congress delegated to the Secretary of Commerce (D) the task of conducting the decennial census "in such form and content as he may determine." 13 U.S.C. § 141(a). The Secretary is aided in that task by the Census Bureau, a statistical agency housed within the Department of Commerce (D). The Secretary (D) decided to reinstate a citizenship question on the 2020 census questionnaire. Several states (P) and other parties challenged this decision in federal district court. The District Court set aside the Secretary's (D) decision on the grounds that the Secretary (D) acted arbitrarily and violated certain provisions of the Census Act. The Government (D) contested those rulings, but also argued that the Secretary's (D) decision was not judicially reviewable under the Administrative Procedure Act in the first place. The Government (D) appealed, and the United States Supreme Court granted certiorari.

ISSUE: Is the Secretary of Commerce's decision to include a certain question in a census reviewable under the Administrative Procedure Act?

HOLDING AND DECISION: (Roberts, C.J.) Yes. The Secretary of Commerce's decision to include a certain question in a census is reviewable under the Administrative Procedure Act (the APA). The APA instructs reviewing courts to set aside agency action that is "arbitrary, capricious, an abuse of discretion, or otherwise not in accordance with law," 5 U.S.C. § 706(2)(A), but it makes review unavailable "to the extent that" the agency action is "committed to agency discretion by law," § 701(a)(2). The Census Act confers broad authority on the Secretary (D), but it does not leave that discretion unbounded. The § 701(a)(2) exception is generally limited to certain categories of administrative decisions that courts traditionally have regarded as "committed to agency discretion." The taking of the census is not one of those areas. Nor is the statute drawn so that it furnishes no meaningful standard by which to judge the Secretary's (D) action, which is amenable to review for compliance with several Census Act provisions according to the general requirements of reasoned agency decisionmaking. Because this is not a case in which there is "no law to apply," the Secretary's (D) decision is subject to judicial review. [The Court ruled that the Secretary's (D) decision was arbitrary and capricious, finding that the Secretary's (D) explanation for the decision was pretextual.]

CONCURRENCE AND DISSENT: (Thomas, J.) The Secretary's (D) decision should have been upheld because it was improper to second-guess the Secretary's (D) basis for the decision.

CONCURRENCE AND DISSENT: (Alito, J.) The general presumption in favor of judicial review has been rebutted in this instance. The first factor for resolving this issue is whether the relevant statutory provisions provide any standard that courts can apply in reviewing the Secretary's (D) decision. Here, 13 U.S.C. § 141(a)—the statute that vests the Secretary (D) with authority to administer the decennial census—gives the Secretary (D) unfettered discretion to include on the census questions about basic demographic characteristics like citizenship. In this regard, the statutory language is so clear, that it is hard to imagine a clearer and less restricted conferral of discretion. Although two provisions are cited in support of reviewability, neither has anything to do with the issue of putting a citizenship question on the census, and so do not prove any meaningful judicial standard for reviewing the Secretary's (D) decision. Another factor is whether the agency action in question is a type that has traditionally been viewed as committed to agency discretion or whether it is instead one that federal courts regularly review. Here, there is no relevant record of judicial review, even though the taking of the census goes back over two centuries. In fact, until this case, the Court has never before encountered a direct challenge to a census question, and litigation in the lower courts about the census is sparse and generally of relatively recent vintage. It is argued that the Secretary's (D) decision is at least amenable to judicial review for consistency with the Administrative Procedure Act's reasoned-explanation requirement. This argument is that even if no statute sets out a standard that can be used in reviewing the particular

Continued on next page.

agency action in question, a court may review an agency's explanation of the reasons for its action and set it aside if the court finds those reasons to be arbitrary or irrational. This argument, however, would obliterate § 701(a)(2). Even if a statute expressly gave an agency absolute, unrestricted, unfettered, unlimited, and unqualified discretion with respect to a particular decision, a court could still review the agency's explanation of the reasons for its decision. That is not what § 701(a)(2) means, and the Court's precedents make clear that it is incorrect to suggest that if an agency gives a reviewable reason for otherwise unreviewable action, the action becomes reviewable.

ANALYSIS

Those challenging the Secretary's (D) decision also argued that the importance of the census provided a compelling reason to permit the Administrative Procedure Act review. Justice Alito countered this argument by noting that the Secretary (D) is accountable in other ways for census-related decisionmaking. Thus, if the Secretary (D) violates the Constitution or any applicable statutory provision related to the census, that action is reviewable. The Secretary (D) is also accountable to Congress with respect to the administration of the census since the Secretary (D) has that power only because Congress has found it appropriate to entrust it to the Secretary (D). Finally, the Secretary (D) is always answerable to the President, who is, in turn, accountable to the people. Justice Alito also contended that widespread judicial review of the Secretary's (D) conduct of the census would usher in an era of "disruptive practical consequences," which in his estimation also weighed against review.

Quicknotes

ADMINISTRATIVE PROCEDURE ACT (APA) Enacted in 1946 to govern practices and proceedings before federal administrative agencies.

JUDICIAL REVIEW The authority of the courts to review decisions, actions, or omissions committed by another agency or branch of government.

Lujan v. National Wildlife Federation

Government official (D) v. Environmental group (P)

497 U.S. 871 (1990)

NATURE OF CASE: Appeal of preliminary injunction against federal reclassification of wildlife lands.

FACT SUMMARY: Two members of the National Wildlife Federation (P) claimed an injury due to the reclassification of wildlife lands by Lujan (D), the Secretary of the Interior, because the two members had visited "in the vicinity" of the reclassified lands.

RULE OF LAW

A general allegation of visits "in the vicinity" of reclassified land is not sufficient to show "injury in fact" as a result of the reclassification.

FACTS: Lujan (D), the Secretary of the Interior, reclassified vast tracts of federal land in a way that the National Wildlife Federation (the NWF) (P) claimed opened those lands to various kinds of detrimental development, including mining. To establish standing and demonstrate an "injury in fact," the NWF (P) relied primarily upon affidavits from two members who asserted that they visited places "in the vicinity" of areas that two of Lujan's (D) land decisions had affected. The NWF (P) claimed that Lujan's (D) reclassification of the wildlife lands violated the National Environmental Policy Act and the Administrative Procedure Act, along with certain other land management statutes, by failing to follow various procedures and failing to pay proper attention to the environment. The NWF (P) appeared to be seeking improvement overall of the programs established by the Department of the Interior and the Bureau of Land Management. Lujan (D) filed a motion for summary judgment challenging NWF's (P) standing. The district court found for Lujan (D) and dismissed the action. The D.C. Circuit reversed, with the result that for two years a preliminary injunction prohibited Lujan (D) from making changes in the use classifications of millions of acres of public lands. The United States Supreme Court then reviewed the matter.

ISSUE: Is a general allegation of visits "in the vicinity" of reclassified land sufficient to show "injury in fact" as a result of the reclassification?

HOLDING AND DECISION: (Scalia, J.) No. A general allegation of visits "in the vicinity" of reclassified land is not sufficient to show "injury in fact" as a result of the reclassification. While there is some room for debate as to how "specific" the "specific facts" required for summary judgment under Fed. R. Civ. P. 56(e) must be in a particular case, the Rule is not satisfied by averments that state only that some National Wildlife Federation (NWF) (P) members use unspecified portions of an immense tract of territory, on some portions of which mining activity has occurred or probably will occur by virtue of the governmental action. Further, the overall programmatic improvements sought by NWF (P) are normally made by actions of the Interior Department or Congress, not through court decree. The NWF (P) cannot demand a general judicial review of the Department of the Interior's and the Bureau of Land Management's day-to-day operations.

DISSENT: (Blackmun, J.) The Court's hypothetical inquiry into the reviewability of the entire "land withdrawal review program" seems superfluous, given the ruling that the National Wildlife Federation (P) lacks standing. Even so, the Court's analysis of that issue is generally correct. Under 5 U.S.C § 702, a broad rule may be invalidated by one plaintiff who is injured by the rule; at the same time, a generally lawful rule may not be invalidated by one injured plaintiff if the injury arose only in one unlawful application of the rule. Thus, what matters in this case is whether the challenged actions are required by the agency plan or policy. If they are not, they may not be invalidated as to all applications of the agency action.

ANALYSIS

The Court distinguished its decision in *United States v. Students Challenging Regulatory Agency Procedures (SCRAP)*, 412 U.S. 669 (1973), on the ground *SCRAP* involved a Rule 12(b) motion to dismiss on the pleadings, not a Rule 56 motion for summary judgment. The Court stated that a Rule 12(b) motion presumes that general allegations embrace those specific facts that are necessary to support the claim, unlike a Rule 56 motion for summary judgment. However, the Court's decision in *SCRAP* represented a very expansive interpretation of what constitutes standing. Since *SCRAP*, the Court's decisions as to standing and the "injury in fact" requirement have been much less expansive, as demonstrated in the instant case.

Continued on next page.

Quicknotes

INJURY IN FACT An injury that gives rise to standing to sue.

JUDICIAL REVIEW The authority of the courts to review decisions, actions, or omissions committed by another agency or branch of government.

PRELIMINARY INJUNCTION A judicial mandate issued to require or restrain a party from certain conduct; used to preserve a trial's subject matter or to prevent threatened injury.

REDRESSABILITY Requirement that in order for a court to hear a case there must be an injury that is redressable or capable of being remedied.

STANDING The right to commence suit against another party because of a personal stake in the resolution of the controversy.

Norton v. Southern Utah Wilderness Alliance

Secretary of Interior (D) v. Environmental group (P)

542 U.S. 55 (2004)

NATURE OF CASE: Suit for declaratory and injunctive relief challenging federal management of potential wilderness areas.

FACT SUMMARY: The Bureau of Land Management (BLM) (D) permitted the use of off-road vehicles on federal lands in Utah. The Southern Utah Wilderness Alliance (P) sued the BLM (D) and others for an alleged failure to satisfy the BLM's (D) statutory mandate to manage such lands in a way that did not impair their suitability as wilderness.

RULE OF LAW

The Administrative Procedure Act, 5 U.S.C. § 706(1), does not provide a right of action for an agency's failure to take a general action that it is not required to take.

FACTS: The Bureau of Land Management (the BLM) (D) permitted users of potential wilderness areas on federal lands in Utah to operate off-road vehicles (ORVs) for recreational purposes on those lands. ORVs cause significant damage to the lands themselves, to wildlife, and to wilderness enthusiasts. To try to stop such detrimental impacts, the Southern Utah Wilderness Alliance (P) filed suit against the BLM (D) and others, requesting declaratory and injunctive relief requiring the BLM (D) to take action, by changing its management of the use of ORVs, in order to manage its Wilderness Study Areas in Utah "in a manner so as not to impair the suitability of such areas for preservation as wilderness." 43 U.S.C. § 1782(c). [The district court ordered dismissal on the claim challenging the BLM's (D) alleged failure to act, and the court of appeals reversed.] The BLM (D) petitioned the United States Supreme Court for further review.

ISSUE: Does the Administrative Procedure Act, 5 U.S.C. § 706(1), provide a right of action for an agency's failure to take a general action that it is not required to take?

HOLDING AND DECISION: (Scalia, J.) No. The Administrative Procedure Act (the APA), 5 U.S.C. § 706(1), does not provide a right of action for an agency's failure to take a general action that it is not required to take. Sections 702, 704, and 706(1) of the APA all require an "agency action" as the basis for suit, and the APA defines these litigable "agency actions" as discrete actions, not as general, amorphous goals or directives. Even where the APA permits suit for failures to act, the failures must be failures to take "agency actions," which are, by statute, necessarily discrete actions. Moreover, § 706(1) permits suit to compel agency action only when the action is required. Accordingly, there is no right of action even as against discrete agency action if the agency action is not required by law. The basis of the Southern Utah Wilderness Alliance's (P) claim against the Bureau of Land Management (the BLM) (D), 42 U.S.C. § 1782(c), does mandate a goal for the BLM (D), but it also grants a broad discretion to the BLM (D) for deciding how to achieve the mandated goal. The total exclusion of off-road vehicles, for example, certainly is not mandated by the non-impairment statute—at any rate, not with the clarity required by § 706(1). These limitations imposed by the APA serve the legislative purpose, as they do in this case, of prohibiting the courts from interfering with the discretion vested in administrative agencies. Reversed and remanded.

ANALYSIS

Principles of separation of powers and judicial restraint pervade administrative law. Here the Court defers to congressional requirements for reviewability, as established by 5 U.S.C. § 706(1), and the Administrative Procedure Act itself in turn exists largely to protect executive-branch agencies from what Justice Scalia calls "undue judicial interference with their lawful discretion." The Court was unanimous in *Southern Utah Wilderness Alliance*, which demonstrates how clearly those fundamental principles apply in this case.

Quicknotes

INJUNCTIVE RELIEF A court order issued as a remedy, requiring a person to do, or prohibiting that person from doing, a specific act.

Air Courier Conference of America v. American Postal Workers Union, AFL-CIO

Government agency (D) v. Union (P)

498 U.S. 517 (1991)

NATURE OF CASE: Appeal from refusal to dismiss action to reinstate suspended statutes.

FACT SUMMARY: In the American Postal Workers Union's (APWU's) (P) suit against Air Courier (D), challenging the Postal Service's suspension of the Private Express Statutes, the court of appeals, agreeing with the district court, found that the APWU (P) had standing to bring the suit.

RULE OF LAW

Plaintiffs have no standing to challenge the suspension of a statute unless they are within that statute's zone of interest.

FACTS: The American Postal Workers Union (APWU) (P) challenged the Postal Service's suspension of the Private Express Statutes, which prohibited private express carriers from competing with the Postal Service, by arguing that the suspension jeopardized postal worker job security. The court of appeals, agreeing with the district court, found that the APWU (P) had standing to bring the challenge since the revenue-protective purposes of the statutes plausibly related to the APWU's (P) interest in preventing the reduction of employment opportunities. Air Courier (D), a private express carrier, appealed.

ISSUE: Do plaintiffs have standing to challenge the suspension of a statute if they are outside that statute's zone of interest?

HOLDING AND DECISION: (Rehnquist, C.J.) No. Plaintiffs have no standing to challenge the suspension of a statute, unless they are within that statute's zone of interest. In respect to examining the legitimacy of the American Postal Workers Union's (APWU's) (P) standing to challenge the suspension of the Private Express Statutes, the express language and legislative purpose of these statutes shed light. First, their express language appears to be concerned not with opportunities for postal workers but with the receipt of necessary revenues for the Postal Service. Second, the legislative purpose behind the statutes is not to ensure employment for postal workers but to ensure that postal service is provided to the citizenry at large. Hence, postal unions are not within the Private Express Statutes' zone of interest. In the instant case, since APWU (P) is not within the Private Express Statutes' zone of interest, it lacks standing to challenge the Statutes' suspension by the Postal Service. Reversed.

ANALYSIS

Justice White was one of the justices to join the majority above. He also authored *Clarke v. Securities Industry Assn.* 479 U.S. 388 (1987), where he expansively read the zone-of-interests test. However, the remaining majority justices above did not join his reading of this test in *Clarke*. This raises the possibility that the Court may be retooling the doctrine, perhaps because of a changed understanding of the purposes to be served by deploying the injury-in-fact and zone-of-interests tests.

Quicknotes

INJURY IN FACT An injury that gives rise to standing to sue.

STANDING TO SUE Plaintiff must allege that he or she has a legally predictable interest at stake in the litigation.

ZONE OF INTERESTS The range or category of interests that a constitutional guarantee or statute is intended to protect.

Match-E-Be-Nash-She-Wish Band of Pottawatomi Indians v. Patchak

Native American tribe (D) v. Neighboring landowner (P)

567 U.S. 209 (2012)

NATURE OF CASE: Certiorari review of dismissal of petition for lack of standing.

FACT SUMMARY: The Match-E-Be-Nash-She-Wish Band of Pottawatomi Indians (the Band) (D) wanted to use the Bradley Property to build and operate a casino. The Secretary of the Interior acquired the Bradley Property in trust for the Band (D). Patchak (P) lives near the Bradley Property and believed a casino would destroy his use and enjoyment of his property.

RULE OF LAW

Plaintiffs seeking relief under the Administrative Procedure Act must fall within the "zone of interests" the allegedly violated statute seeks to protect to have standing to maintain the lawsuit.

FACTS: The Indian Reorganization Act (the IRA), 25 U.S.C. § 465, authorizes the Secretary of the Interior (the Secretary) to acquire property to provide land for Native Americans. The Match-E-Be-Nash-She-Wish Band of Pottawatomi Indians (the Band) resides in rural Michigan and was formally recognized by the Department of the Interior as a Native American tribe in 1999 although it had a much longer history. In 2001, the Band petitioned the Secretary to provide the Bradley Property, a tract of land in Michigan, for "gaming purposes." After significant administrative review, in 2005 the Secretary acquired the Bradley Property in trust for the Band. Patchak (P) lived "in close proximity" to the Bradley Property and believed the planned casino would destroy the rural character of his property. He filed suit under the Administrative Procedure Act against the Secretary for injunctive relief to prevent the Secretary from accepting title and argued the acquisition violated the IRA; the Band intervened. The district court dismissed the case for Patchak's (P) lack of prudential standing because his injuries fell outside § 465's "zone of interests." The Court of Appeals for the D.C. Circuit reversed, and the United States Supreme Court granted certiorari.

ISSUE: Must plaintiffs seeking relief under the Administrative Procedure Act fall within the "zone of interests" the allegedly violated statute seeks to protect to have standing to maintain the lawsuit?

HOLDING AND DECISION: (Kagan, J.) Yes. Plaintiffs seeking relief under the Administrative Procedure Act must fall within the "zone of interests" the allegedly violated statute seeks to protect to have standing to maintain the lawsuit. The merits of Patchak's (P) case are not before this Court nor does this Court consider the issue of the recognition of the Match-E-Be-Nash-She-Wish Band of Pottawatomi Indians (the Band) (D) as a tribe after the enactment of the Indian Reorganization Act (the IRA). Patchak (P) did not assert any ownership interest in the Bradley Property. Litigants suing under the APA must satisfy Article III standing requirements and the asserted interests must fall within the "zone of interests to be protected or regulated by the Statute" allegedly violated. Here, the Band (D) and Government argue § 465 is focused on land acquisition and Patchak's (P) interests are focused on the land's use. The prudential standing test "is not meant to be especially demanding." The benefit of the doubt goes to the plaintiff. Here, § 465 has more to do with land use than the Band (D) and Government will concede. The IRA intended land to provide a basis for the economic life of Native Americans. The Secretary must consider how the Native Americans will use the land they acquire. Here, the Band (D) petitioned for the land to be used in gaming, the Department of the Interior's notice of intent to take the land in trust informed it would be for gaming, and the Band (D) had to provide a plan for the land's use because the Bradley Property was an "off-reservation acquisition." The interests Patchak (P) raises arguably fall within the "zone of interests." Affirmed.

ANALYSIS

The "zone of interests" is to be broadly construed to permit more plaintiffs to have standing to seek redress from administrative actions than just those plaintiffs who are directly regulated by the agency regulation. Here, the Department of the Interior was not regulating Patchak (P) directly but he did claim to be affected by the agency action, so he would not have had recourse without the "zone of interests" test.

Quicknotes

ZONE OF INTERESTS The range or category of interests that a constitutional guarantee or statute is intended to protect.

Taylor-Callahan-Coleman Counties District Adult Probation Department v. Dole

Employer (P) v. Government agency (D)

948 F.2d 953 (5th Cir. 1991)

NATURE OF CASE: Appeal of challenge of opinion letters dismissed for lack of subject matter jurisdiction.

FACT SUMMARY: Employees (P) of the Taylor-Callahan-Coleman Counties District Adult Probation Department challenged opinion letters issued by the Department of Labor (D) because the letters had not gone through notice and comment.

RULE OF LAW

Where the action complained of was not final agency action, it is not subject to judicial review.

FACTS: Under the Fair Labor Standards Act of 1938 (FLSA), administrative and professional employees are exempt from overtime requirements. Taylor-Callahan-Coleman Counties District Adult Probation Department employees (Taylor-Callahan) (P) were advised that, under Department of Labor (DOL) regulations, they were exempt as administrative employees. When the DOL (D) later issued two opinion letters stating that probation officers were not exempt, based on the fact circumstances provided by the requesting parties, Taylor-Callahan (P) claimed that the opinion letters were legislative rules that were inconsistent with prior regulations and the statute and therefore should have gone through notice and comment. The district court dismissed the case for lack of subject matter jurisdiction. Taylor-Callahan (P) appealed.

ISSUE: Where the action complained of was not final agency action, is it subject to judicial review?

HOLDING AND DECISION: (Clark, C.J.) No. Where the action complained of was not final agency action, it is not subject to judicial review. Advisory opinions issued to guide the Department of Labor (the DOL) (D) in its operations are neither final nor binding. The letters at issue here did not constitute agency action that was broad or definitive. Rather, the letters were expressly limited to the factual situations provided by the requesting parties. They did not have the status of law and had no direct or immediate impact on the DOL (D). They were more in the nature of threshold determinations and did not constitute final agency action. Affirmed.

ANALYSIS

This was an action for declaratory judgment. The court found that a Fair Labor Standards Act of 1938 (FLSA) enforcement action could be brought instead. Informal advisory letters are necessary for the proper administration of FLSA.

Quicknotes

FAIR LABOR STANDARDS ACT (FLSA) Enacted in 1938, the statute establishes a minimum wage, overtime pay, recordkeeping, and youth employment standards applicable to all employees in the private sector and in federal, state, and local governments. Executive, administrative, and professional employees paid on a salary basis are exempt from the minimum wage and overtime provisions of the FLSA.

NOTICE AND COMMENT Informal rulemaking.

OPINION LETTER A letter that is drafted by an attorney for the benefit of the attorney's client, stating the attorney's knowledge of the law as applied to a particular set of facts.

SUBJECT MATTER JURISDICTION The authority of the court to hear and decide actions involving a particular type of issue or subject.

United States Army Corps of Engineers v. Hawkes Co., Inc.

Federal agency (D) v. Mining company (P)

578 U.S. 590 (2016)

NATURE OF CASE: Appeal from reversal of a decision dismissing a judicial challenge to an agency order on the ground it did not constitute final agency action.

FACT SUMMARY: The United States Army Corps of Engineers (D) contended that a revised approved jurisdictional determination (JD) it issued, concluding that certain property owned by mining companies (P) contained "waters of the United States," thus subjecting the property to the Clean Water Act, was not judicially reviewable final agency action, and that, even if the JD constituted final agency action, the mining companies had adequate alternatives to judicial review, so that the courts lacked jurisdiction to review the JD.

RULE OF LAW

An approved judicial determination (JD) issued by the Army Corps of Engineers, stating that property contains or does not contain "waters of the United States," is judicially reviewable final agency action.

FACTS: The Clean Water Act regulates the discharge of any pollutant into "the waters of the United States." When property contains such waters, landowners who discharge pollutants without a permit from the Army Corps of Engineers (the Corps) (D) risk substantial criminal and civil penalties, whereas those who do apply for a permit face a process that is often arduous, expensive, and long. It can be difficult to determine in the first place, however, whether "waters of the United States" are present. Because of that difficulty, the Corps (D) allows property owners to obtain a standalone "jurisdictional determination" (JD) specifying whether a particular property contains "waters of the United States." A JD may be either "preliminary," advising a property owner that such waters "may" be present, or "approved," definitively "stating the presence or absence" of such waters. An "approved" JD is considered an administratively appealable "final agency action," and is binding for five years on both the Corps (D) and the Environmental Protection Agency. Mining companies (P) sought a permit from the Corps (D) to discharge material onto wetlands located on property that they owned and hoped to mine. In connection with the permitting process, the mining companies (P) obtained an approved JD from the Corps (D) stating that the property contained "waters of the United States." After exhausting administrative remedies, the mining companies sought review of the approved JD, which the Corps (D) had affirmed in a revised approved JD, in federal district court under the Administrative Procedure Act, but the district court dismissed for want of jurisdiction, holding that the revised JD was not a final agency action for which there was no other adequate remedy in a court. The court of appeals reversed, and the United States Supreme Court granted certiorari.

ISSUE: Is an approved judicial determination (JD) issued by the Army Corps of Engineers, stating that property contains "waters of the United States," judicially reviewable final agency action?

HOLDING AND DECISION: (Roberts, C.J.) Yes. An approved judicial determination (JD) issued by the Army Corps of Engineers (the Corps), stating that property contains or does not contain "waters of the United States," is judicially reviewable final agency action. In general, two conditions must be satisfied for an agency action to be "final" under the Administrative Procedure Act (the APA). First, the action must mark the consummation of the agency's decision-making process, and second, the action must be one by which rights or obligations have been determined, or from which legal consequences will flow. It is undisputed that the first condition is satisfied, since the JD clearly marks the consummation of the Corps' (D) decision-making on the question whether a particular property does or does not contain "waters of the United States." The definitive nature of approved JDs also gives rise to direct and appreciable legal consequences, thereby satisfying the second condition as well. A "negative" JD, i.e., an approved JD stating that property does not contain jurisdictional waters, creates a five-year safe harbor from civil enforcement proceedings brought by the Government (D), and limits the potential liability a property owner faces for violating the Clean Water Act. Each of those effects is a legal consequence. It follows that an "affirmative" JD, like the one at bar, also has legal consequences, since it deprives property owners of the five-year safe harbor that "negative" JDs afford. This conclusion tracks the "pragmatic" approach the Court has long taken to finality. A "final" agency action is reviewable under the APA only if there are no adequate alternatives to APA review in court. The Corps (D) contends that the mining companies (P) have two such alternatives. First, they may proceed without a permit and argue in an enforcement action that a permit was not required, or they may complete the permit process and then seek judicial review, which, the Corps (D) suggests, is what Congress envisioned. However, contrary to the Corps' (D) argument, neither alternative is adequate. Parties

Continued on next page.

need not await enforcement proceedings before challenging final agency action where such proceedings carry the risk of "serious criminal and civil penalties." Additionally, the permitting process is not only costly and lengthy, but also irrelevant to the finality of the approved JD and its suitability for judicial review. Furthermore, because the Clean Water Act makes no reference to standalone jurisdictional determinations, there is little basis for inferring anything from it concerning their reviewability. Given the APA's presumption of reviewability for all final agency action, the mere fact that permitting decisions are reviewable is insufficient to imply exclusion as to other agency actions, such as approved JDs. Affirmed.

CONCURRENCE: (Kagan, J.) The memorandum of agreement between the Army Corps of Engineers (D) and the Environmental Protection Agency is central to the disposition of this case. That is because the memorandum of agreement establishes that judicial determinations (JDs) are binding on the Government (D) and represent the Government's (D) position in any subsequent federal action or litigation concerning that final determination.

CONCURRENCE IN PART AND IN THE JUDGMENT: (Ginsburg, J.) The majority erroneously relies upon the memorandum of agreement between the Army Corps of Engineers (D) and the Environmental Protection Agency. The Court received scant briefing about this memorandum, and the federal Government (D) does not share the Court's reading of it. Nonetheless, the judicial determination (JD) at issue is "definitive," not "informal" or "tentative," and has "an immediate and practical impact," and, therefore, the JD is final.

ANALYSIS

Justice Kennedy, concurring in the decision as a whole, observed the Clean Water Act's (Act's) reach is notoriously unclear, and the consequences to landowners even for inadvertent violations can be crushing, so an approved judicial determination (JD) gives a landowner at least some measure of predictability, so long as the agency's declaration can be relied upon. If, as the government (D) asserted, a JD has no legally binding effect on the Environmental Protection Agency's (EPA's) enforcement decisions and can be revoked or amended at the EPA's unfettered discretion, Justice Kennedy argues that the Act's ominous reach would again be unchecked by the limited relief the Court provided in this decision. In his view, even if, in an ordinary case, an agency's internal agreement with another agency cannot establish that its action is final, the Court is right to construe a JD as binding in light of the fact that in many instances it will have a significant bearing on whether the Act comports with due process—especially since the Act, without the JD procedure were the Government (D) permitted to foreclose it, continues to raise troubling questions regarding the Government's (D) power to cast doubt on the full use and enjoyment of private property throughout the country.

Quicknotes

ADMINISTRATIVE PROCEDURE ACT (APA) Enacted in 1946 to govern practices and proceedings before federal administrative agencies.

California Communities Against Toxics v. EPA

Environmental advocacy organization (P) v. Federal agency (D)

934 F.3d 627 (D.C. Cir. 2020)

NATURE OF CASE: Petition for preenforcement review of an agency directive.

FACT SUMMARY: The Environmental Protection Agency (the EPA) (D) issued a memorandum (the Wehrum Memo) that it was reversing course under the Clean Air Act regarding its treatment of major sources of air pollution. Environmental advocacy organizations (P) and the state of California (P) petitioned for preenforcement review of the Wehrum Memo, contending, inter alia, that it was final agency action. The EPA (D) countered that the court lacked subject matter jurisdiction over the Wehrum Memo because it was not final agency action.

RULE OF LAW

An agency action is not final and therefore reviewable, where, in the context of the statutes and regulations that govern the action at issue, the action marks the consummation of the agency's decisionmaking process but has no legal effect.

FACTS: Environmental advocacy organizations (P) and the state of California (P) petitioned for preenforcement review of an Environmental Protection Agency's (the EPA's) (D) memorandum from William Wehrum, the Assistant Administrator of the EPA's (D) Office of Air and Radiation. The memo (the Wehrum Memo) was issued to all Regional Air Division Directors, declaring that the plain language of § 112 of the Clean Air Act compelled the conclusion that a source of toxic emissions that had been classified as "major" could be reclassified as "area source," thereby easing its regulatory burden, at any time after the source limited its potential to emit to below the major source threshold. The Wehrum Memo stated that it superseded a prior 1995 EPA (D) memorandum (the Seitz Memo) issued by John Seitz, then Director of the EPA's (D) Office of Air Quality Planning and Standards, which interpreted § 112 to mean that once the EPA (D) classified a source as major, that source can never reclassify to area source status, even if it limits its potential to emit to below the major source threshold. The parties challenging the Wehrum Memo contended, inter alia, that it was judicially reviewable because it constituted final agency action and was prudentially ripe, and they made several arguments as to why the Wehrum Memo should be vacated. The EPA (D) countered that the court lacked subject matter jurisdiction over the Wehrum Memo because it was not final agency action. The court of appeals considered the petition for review.

ISSUE: Is an agency action final, and therefore reviewable, where, in the context of the statutes and regulations that govern the action at issue, the action marks the consummation of the agency's decisionmaking process but has no legal effect?

HOLDING AND DECISION: (Wilkins, J.) No. An agency action is not final, and therefore reviewable, where, in the context of the statutes and regulations that govern the action at issue, the action marks the consummation of the agency's decisionmaking process but has no legal effect. To answer the question of whether agency action is final for reviewability purposes, the action must be viewed in the context of the unique constellation of statutes and regulations that govern the action at issue. Here, those are the Clean Air Act (the CAA) provisions and Environmental Protection Agency (the EPA) (D) regulations that govern the Wehrum Memo. The CAA requires the EPA (D) to create a list of categories of sources of hazardous air pollutants. Also under the CAA, a major source means any source within a listed category that "emits or has the potential to emit considering controls, in the aggregate, 10 tons per year or more of any [listed hazardous air pollutant] or 25 tons per year or more of any combination of [listed hazardous air pollutants]." Area source means "any stationary source of [hazardous air pollutants] that is not a major source." For major sources, the CAA requires the EPA (D) to establish stringent emissions caps that result in "the maximum degree of reduction in emissions ... (including a prohibition on such emissions, where achievable)." These stringent limitations are known as "Maximum Achievable Control Technology" (MACT) standards. Although not required to set standards for area sources, if the EPA (D) chooses to, these are far less stringent than MACTs, and are known as "Generally Available Control Technology" (GACT) standards. To ensure compliance with these standards, the EPA (D) has in place a permitting scheme (Title V permitting) that relies on state permitting authorities. To address a state permitting authority's action on a permit application that a party believes contravenes the CAA, there is a detailed administrative process that dictates exactly when and how regulated sources and regulatory beneficiaries may seek EPA (D) review of a state permitting authority's action, and, ultimately, judicial review of EPA (D) action. The EPA (D) Administrator plays a role in the process, and if the Administrator does not object

Continued on next page.

in writing within a specified period of receiving a proposed permit, any person may, within a specified period, petition the Administrator to object. The Administrator must grant or deny such a petition within 60 days after it is filed. No objection to a state permitting authority's action is subject to judicial review until the Administrator takes final action to issue or deny a permit, and the Administrator's denial of a petition to object is also subject to judicial review. It is important to know this process in determining whether the Wehrum Memo is final agency action. In *United States Army Corps of Engineers v. Hawkes Co.*, 136 S. Ct. 1807 (2016), the Supreme Court affirmed that the two-prong test in *Bennett v. Spear,* 520 U.S. 154 (1997), remains finality's touchstone. Under the first prong, the agency action must mark the consummation of the agency's decisionmaking process, and under the second, the action must be one by which rights or obligations have been determined, or from which legal consequences will flow. As to the second prong, the inquiry focuses on whether the action at issue gives rise to direct and appreciable legal consequences. As to the first prong, it is undisputed that the Wehrum Memo marks the consummation of the EPA's (D) decisionmaking process. As to the second prong, however, those challenging the Memo (P) say that it creates a new right by allowing major sources unable to reclassify to area sources under the Seitz Memo to so reclassify, whereas the EPA (D) counters that the Wehrum Memo does not change the rights of regulated sources, since whether or not a regulated source has the right to reclassify is only determined within the permitting process. The EPA (D) has the better argument. The Wehrum Memo does not have concrete consequences in the context of the specific statutes and regulations that govern it. Notwithstanding that the Wehrum Memo unequivocally declares that major sources, at such time that they limit their potential to emit to below the major source threshold, "will no longer be" subject to MACT standards, viewed within the context of the CAA, the Wehrum Memo is all bark and no bite. Neither the EPA (D) nor any regulated source can rely on the Wehrum Memo within the permitting process or in any other proceeding. In other words, although the Wehrum Memo forecasts the EPA's (D) position as to § 112, it has no independent legal authority. In addition, under the CAA and EPA (D) regulations, a state permitting authority that refuses to comply with the Wehrum Memo faces no penalty or liability of any sort. Further still, the instant matter does not present a circumstance where the action at issue may be legally consequential because it binds agency staff, and affected parties have no means (outside of judicial review) by which to challenge it. To the contrary, the CAA contains clear provisions pursuant to which: (1) a state permitting authority can refuse to apply the Wehrum Memo and seek judicial review if the EPA (D) issues a permit over its refusal, and (2) a regulatory beneficiary can petition the EPA (D) to object to a state permitting authority's application of the Wehrum Memo and seek judicial review if the EPA (D) denies the petition. Major sources must comply with myriad permitting and reporting requirements, and the Wehrum Memo does not change those requirements or revoke or amend a single permit; it does not bind state permitting authorities or assure regulated entities of the ability to reclassify. For all these reasons, the Wehrum Memo is not final agency action, and, therefore, the court lacks subject matter jurisdiction to entertain the petition.

DISSENT: (Rogers, J.) The Clean Air Act (the CAA) provides that this court shall have jurisdiction to review nationally applicable "final action taken" by the Administrator of the Environmental Protection Agency (the EPA) (D). The term "final action" is synonymous with "final agency action" in the Administrative Procedure Act (the APA). The finality inquiry itself is governed by the two-prong test articulated in *Bennett*. This court has repeatedly held that judicial review is available pursuant to § 7607(b)(1) for guidance documents that bind EPA (D) officials on how to make Title V permitting decisions. Such guidance documents have reflected EPA (D) positions the agency planned to follow in reviewing state-issued permits, and that EPA (D) officials in the field were bound to apply. Such documents were viewed as having legal consequences for both enforcement officials and regulated entities and have been viewed as altering the legal regime. Like the guidance documents the court has previously reviewed, the Wehrum Memo states the law that EPA (D) officials must apply in Title V permitting; it reads like an edict, as it commands, orders, and dictates without caveats or disclaimers about the binding nature of its statutory interpretation. Under the statutory scheme, state permitting authorities are subject to the statutory interpretation announced in the Wehrum Memo, and those authorities are not free to ignore it. The CAA even contemplates that a state permitting authority can be sanctioned for not adequately administering and enforcing a program. In sum, by announcing an unequivocal interpretation of which federal standards apply to which sources under the CAA, the EPA (D) can expect states to fall in line. By publicly announcing an unequivocal statement that the plain text of the CAA "compels" its conclusion, the EPA (D) has given states their "marching orders" to allow reclassification of major sources. The Wehrum Memo is an action from which legal consequences *will* flow because it announces a binding change in the legal regime. To say—as does the EPA (D) and the majority—that the Wehrum Memo is not final because it has no immediate impact or direct legal consequences for specific sources, misstates the finality test, which is met if legal

Continued on next page.

consequences *will* flow from the action. The majority's suggestion that the Wehrum Memo is "all bark and no bite," ignores its plain text and the future-looking aspect of *Bennett's* second prong. With the EPA's (D) blessing, legal consequences will flow from the Wehrum Memo no later than when "major sources" take enforceable limits on their potential to emit below "major source" thresholds and obtain new or modified Title V permits. Additionally, the opportunity for judicial review at a later time has no direct bearing on the availability of pre-enforcement review of the Wehrum Memo. Although the CAA provides for judicial review an Administrator's objection or denial of a petition to object to a specific Title V permit for a specific source, the petitioners here are not challenging a source-specific objection. Instead, they seek review of a generally applicable guidance document pursuant to the CAA, which provides for judicial review of such a general guidance document that is a "final action." Irrelevant to the finality inquiry is the fact that the Wehrum Memo is deregulatory rather than regulatory. This is the fallacy underlying the court's efforts to distinguish the court's precedents on the basis that the Wehrum Memo does not require anyone to do anything. The focus must be on whether the legal regime has changed—and, as already explained—the Wehrum Memo effects such a change. Finally, the Wehrum Memo creates a safe harbor for "major sources" that will have a clear legal effect on regulated entities.

ANALYSIS

Judge Rogers, dissenting, argued, inter alia, that the Wehrum Memo is a legislative rule that failed to conform to the Administrative Procedures Act's (the APA's) notice-and-comment requirement and, hence, review and vacating the Wehrum Memo was required. Judge Rogers noted that the APA requires that a legislative rule, which carries the "force and effect of law," must be promulgated pursuant to notice-and-comment rulemaking, and that to determine whether agency action carries the force and effect of law, the court generally looks to the actual legal effect (or lack thereof) of the agency action, paying particular attention to the express words used in the document. A document that reads like an edict is likely to be binding, whereas one riddled with caveats is not. The court also considers whether the action was published in the Federal Register or the Code of Federal Regulations and whether the action has binding effects on the agency or private parties. An agency's adoption of a binding norm that could not be properly promulgated absent the notice-and-comment rulemaking required by the APA "obviously would reflect final agency action." When an agency action is final because it creates a binding norm that alters the legal regime, the question of whether the action is a legislative rule is clear. Because the Wehrum Memo satisfied the key criteria for a legislative rule but failed to satisfy the APA's notice-and-comment requirement, Judge Rogers would have granted the petition for review and vacated the Wehrum Memo. Although the majority did not reach this conclusion, it cautioned that although all legislative rules are final, not all final rules are legislative, and the finality analysis is therefore sui generis and separate and distinct from the test for whether an agency action is a legislative rule.

Quicknotes

NOTICE AND COMMENT Informal rulemaking.

RIPENESS A doctrine precluding a federal court from hearing or determining a matter unless it constitutes an actual and present controversy warranting a determination by the court.

SUBJECT MATTER JURISDICTION The authority of the court to hear and decide actions involving a particular type of issue or subject.

SUI GENERIS Peculiar to its own type or class.

McCarthy v. Madigan

Inmate (P) v. Prison employees (D)

503 U.S. 140 (1992)

NATURE OF CASE: Appeal from dismissal of action for damages for constitutional rights violations.

FACT SUMMARY: McCarthy (P), an inmate, contended that he should not have to resort to an internal grievance procedure before initiating suit against prison employees (D) for money damages.

RULE OF LAW

Exhaustion of administrative remedies is not required when the litigant's interests in immediate judicial review outweigh the government's interests in efficiency or administrative autonomy.

FACTS: McCarthy (P), an inmate in a federal prison, filed a complaint against four prison employees (D) for violating his constitutional rights under the Eighth Amendment. He sought money damages only. He chose not to pursue the grievance procedure set up by the Federal Bureau of Prisons, which requires an inmate to first seek informal resolution of his claim. If this fails, the inmate must file a written complaint within fifteen days, then appeal within thirty days to the Regional Director, and file a final appeal within an additional thirty days. The district court dismissed the complaint on the ground McCarthy (P) had failed to exhaust prison administrative remedies, and McCarthy (P) appealed.

ISSUE: Is exhaustion of administrative remedies required when the litigant's interests in immediate judicial review outweigh the government's interests in efficiency or administrative autonomy?

HOLDING AND DECISION: (Blackmun, J.) No. Exhaustion of administrative remedies is not required when the litigant's interests in immediate judicial review outweigh the government's interests in efficiency or administrative autonomy. The general rule is that exhaustion is required because it protects administrative agency authority and promotes judicial efficiency. However, the Court has recognized three sets of circumstances in which individual interests weigh against requiring exhaustion: (1) when exhaustion principles would unduly prejudice subsequent court action; (2) when an administrative agency is unable to grant effective relief; and (3) when an agency is shown to be biased. In this case, the prison grievance procedure imposes rapid filing deadlines that could penalize an inmate who is unable to comply with them. Furthermore, it does not authorize an award of monetary damages—the only relief requested by McCarthy (P). Therefore, given the type of claim raised by McCarthy (P) and the particular characteristics of the Bureau's grievance procedure, McCarthy's (P) individual interests outweigh institutional interests favoring exhaustion. McCarthy (P) is not required to exhaust the grievance procedure. Reversed.

CONCURRENCE: (Rehnquist, C.J.) A federal prisoner does not need to exhaust the Federal Bureau of Prisons' procedures, because the grievance procedure at issue here did not provide for any award of monetary damages. Where prisoners seek monetary relief, the remedy is not effective, and it is, therefore, improper to impose such a requirement.

ANALYSIS

In addition to those articulated in this case, courts have fashioned a number of exceptions to the doctrine of exhaustion. For example, exhaustion is not required when the administrative agency's decision is a foregone conclusion, according to *Orion Corp. v. State*, 693 P.2d 1369 (Wash. 1985). Nor is it required in instances where the agency's action would have a chilling effect on the plaintiff's First Amendment rights. See *Wolff v. Selective Serv. Local Bd.*, 372 F.2d 817 (2d Cir. 1967).

Quicknotes

ADMINISTRATIVE REMEDIES Relief that is sought before an administrative body as opposed to a court.

FIFTH AMENDMENT Provides that no person shall be compelled to serve as a witness against him- or herself, be subject to trial for the same offense twice, or be deprived of life, liberty, or property without due process of law.

Darby v. Cisneros

Real estate developer (P) v. Government department (D)

509 U.S. 137 (1993)

NATURE OF CASE: Appeal from dismissal of action to enjoin administrative sanctions.

FACT SUMMARY: Darby (P) and Garvin (P) argued that they should not be required to exhaust available administrative remedies prior to seeking judicial review after being barred from participating in Department of Housing and Urban Development (D) programs.

RULE OF LAW

A litigant seeking judicial review of a final agency action under the Administrative Procedure Act need not exhaust available administrative remedies, unless such exhaustion is expressly required by statute or agency rule.

FACTS: Darby (P), a South Carolina real estate developer, and Garvin (P), a mortgage banker, developed a plan to obtain single-family mortgage insurance from the Department of Housing and Urban Development (HUD) for multi-unit projects. The plan circumvented HUD (D) rules that prevented rental properties from receiving single-family mortgage insurance if the mortgagor had financial interests in seven or more similar rental properties in the same project. Darby (P) ultimately obtained financing for three separate multi-unit projects using this plan, but defaulted in 1988, making HUD (D) responsible for $6.6 million in insurance claims. Although HUD (D) had previously audited Garvin's (P) financing plan and concluded there was no wrongdoing, upon default, HUD (D) prohibited Darby (P) and Garvin (P) from participating in any South Carolina HUD (D) program for one year. Darby (P) and Garvin (P) sought administrative review of the decision. The administrative law judge (ALJ) conducted hearings and found that good cause existed to bar petitioners for 18 months. Instead of seeking further administrative review of the ALJ's decision, as permitted under HUD (D) regulations, Darby (P) and Garvin (P) filed suit in district court seeking injunctive relief. HUD (D) moved to dismiss the complaint for failure to seek review. The district court denied the motion and HUD (D) appealed. The court of appeals reversed, and the United States Supreme Court granted certiorari.

ISSUE: Must a litigant seeking judicial review of a final agency action under the APA exhaust all available administrative remedies?

HOLDING AND DECISION: (Blackmun, J.) No. A litigant seeking judicial review of a final agency action under the Administrative Procedure Act (the APA) need not exhaust available administrative remedies, unless such exhaustion is expressly required by statute or agency rule. APA § 10(a) grants individuals who are adversely affected by an administrative agency's action the general right to seek judicial review. However, APA § 10 establishes that such review is available only when the aggrieved party has exhausted all administrative remedies expressly prescribed by statute or agency rule. When both §§ 10(a) and (c) are satisfied, the agency action is final and therefore subject to review. As such, courts are not free to impose an additional exhaustion requirement where agency action has become final under APA § 10(c). Reversed.

ANALYSIS

Notice the Administrative Procedure Act provides a two-prong test: the agency decision must be final and the aggrieved party must have exhausted all administrative remedies if mandated to do so by statute or regulation. While finality is concerned with whether the decision-maker has reached a definitive position that inflicts an actual, concrete injury, exhaustion refers to the procedures by which an injured party may seek review of an adverse decision.

Quicknotes

APA § 10(a) Provides for a general right of judicial review.

APA § 10(c) Provides that judicial review is available for final agency actions.

INJUNCTION A court order requiring a person to do, or prohibiting that person from doing, a specific act.

Abbott Laboratories v. Gardner

Pharmaceuticals manufacturers and trade association (P) v. Government agency (D)

387 U.S. 136 (1967)

NATURE OF CASE: Review of suit seeking judicial review of agency rule.

FACT SUMMARY: Abbott Laboratories (P) claimed the Commissioner of Food and Drugs (D) had exceeded his authority in promulgating an order requiring all printed matter relating to prescription drugs to designate the name of the particular drug involved every time its trade name was used.

RULE OF LAW

Where the legal issue presented is fit for judicial resolution, and a regulation requires an immediate and significant change in plaintiffs' conduct with serious penalties attached to noncompliance, a controversy is ripe for review.

FACTS: When the Commissioner of Food and Drugs (D) promulgated rules requiring the manufacturers of prescription drugs to print the established name of the drug prominently on its labels, Abbott Laboratories (Abbott) (P) and almost all prescription drug manufacturers (P) challenged the regulations in court. The Commissioner (D) claimed pre-enforcement review was not possible since there were no issues ripe for judicial resolution. Both parties sought summary judgment. The United States Supreme Court granted certiorari.

ISSUE: Where the legal issue presented is fit for judicial resolution, and a regulation requires an immediate and significant change in plaintiffs' conduct with serious penalties attached to noncompliance, is a controversy ripe for review?

HOLDING AND DECISION: (Harlan, J.) Yes. Where the legal issue presented is fit for judicial resolution, and a regulation requires an immediate and significant change in plaintiffs' conduct with serious penalties attached to noncompliance, a controversy is ripe for review. The regulations in issue constitute final agency action. The impact of the regulations upon Abbott Laboratories (P) in its day-to-day operations is significant and costly. Serious criminal and civil penalties could result from the unlawful distribution of misbranded drugs. Access to the courts should be denied only if there is a statutory bar or other unusual circumstance, neither of which appears here. Such a pre-enforcement challenge by nearly all prescription drug manufacturers is calculated to speed enforcement and is in the public interest.

DISSENT: (Fortas, J.) The public interest in avoiding delay far outweighs the private interest here. A much stronger showing is necessary than the expense and trouble of compliance. Enforcement actions would be appropriate to test the regulations only in specific, concrete situations.

ANALYSIS

This case involved a petition for pre-enforcement review of an agency rule. In general, the test for ripeness involves two prongs. First, the issue must be fit for judicial decision. Second, the hardship to the parties is considered.

Quicknotes

JUDICIAL REVIEW The authority of the courts to review decisions, actions, or omissions committed by another agency or branch of government.

RIPENESS A doctrine precluding a federal court from hearing or determining a matter unless it constitutes an actual and present controversy warranting a determination by the court.

National Park Hospitality Assn. v. Dept. of Interior

Nonprofit trade association (P) v. Government department (D)

538 U.S. 803 (2003)

NATURE OF CASE: Certiorari review of challenge to agency regulation.

FACT SUMMARY: The National Park Service (D) issued final regulations defining "concession contract" as a contract that did not fall within the Contract Disputes Act of 1978 (CDA). This regulation conflicted with the Department of Interior's (D) Board of Contract Appeals (IBCA) determination that concession contracts do fall under the CDA. The National Park Hospitality Assn. (Petitioner) (P) sought to clarify the rule for those bidding on concession contracts in national parks.

RULE OF LAW

Determining whether administrative action is ripe for judicial review requires evaluation of (1) the fitness of the issues for judicial decision and (2) the hardship to the parties if court consideration is withheld.

FACTS: The National Parks Omnibus Management Act of 1998 (the Act) created a comprehensive concessional management program for national parks. The Secretary of the Interior delegated her authority to implement the Act to the National Park Service (NPS). After notice and comment rulemaking, NPS issued 36 CFR § 51.3 (2002) defining "concession contract" as one not falling under the Contract Disputes Act of 1978 (the CDA). The CDA establishes rules governing government contract disputes. The Department of the Interior's Board of Contract Appeals (IBCA), since 1989, treated concession contracts as falling within the CDA. The National Park Hospitality Assn. (Petitioner) (P) challenged the validity of § 51.3. The District Court for the District of Columbia applied deference under *Chevron U.S.A. Inc. v. Natural Resources Defense Council, Inc.*, 467 U.S. 837 (1984), to the NPS regulation and upheld the section. The Court of Appeals for the District of Columbia Circuit affirmed on different grounds finding NPS's reading of the CDA was consistent with the CDA and the Act. The United States Supreme Court granted certiorari to consider whether the CDA applies to park concession contracts; the Court requested additional briefing on ripeness.

ISSUE: Is administrative action ripe for judicial review if (1) the issues are fit for judicial decision and (2) there is hardship to the parties if court consideration is withheld?

HOLDING AND DECISION: (Thomas, J.) Yes. Determining whether administrative action is ripe for judicial review requires evaluation of (1) the fitness of the issues for judicial decision and (2) the hardship to the parties if court consideration is withheld. Ripeness is a justiciability doctrine preventing the courts' involvement in premature adjudication and abstract disagreements over administrative policies until those decisions are formalized and the effect on the parties' concrete. The Court may consider ripeness on its own motion. Here, the hardship element is not met because the National Park Service (NPS) is not empowered to administer the Contract Disputes Act of 1978 (the CDA) and thus § 51.3 is a "general statement of policy" about how NPS will treat concession contracts. It does not affect a concessioner's primary conduct. The Department of the Interior's Board of Contract Appeals still applies the CDA to certain concession contracts. Petitioner (P) seeks certainty so it can advise concessioners how to bid on potential contracts, but the courts cannot take away all legal uncertainty for business transactions. Resolution should wait for a concrete dispute about a specific concession contract. Judgment vacated as to validity of § 51.3 and remanded with instructions to dismiss the case.

CONCURRENCE: (Stevens, J.) Petitioner (P) failed to allege threshold requirement of injury. The issue of statutory interpretation of whether the Contract Disputes Act of 1978 applies to concession contracts with the National Park Service is fit for judicial decision. Petitioner (P), however, failed to allege sufficient injury even though it argued the issue was "important" and concessionaires "need to know now." The requested clarification is important but does not constitute an injury. Petitioner (P) has no standing.

DISSENT: (Breyer, J.) The case is ripe for adjudication because the issue is purely legal interpretation. This regulation is an "interpretive rule" rather than a "general statement of policy," but it is owed less deference because the National Park Service does not administer the Contract Disputes Act of 1978. The harm here, however, is immediate and particularized injury during the bidding process. There is no good reason to postpone review.

ANALYSIS

The majority, the concurring justices, and the dissenting justices all acknowledged the issue in *National Park Hospitality Assn.* was a purely legal interpretation of applicability of the Contract Disputes Act of 1978 (the CDA) to National Park Service (NPS) concession contracts. The only thing missing was someone actually having an NPS concession contract that was being handled pursuant to the CDA dispute resolution process. Advisory opinions where the court opines on possible results to transactions are disfavored in the judiciary.

CHAPTER 6

Agency Structure

Quick Reference Rules of Law

Stern v. Marshall

[Party not identified] (P) v. Millionaire's son (D)

564 U.S. 462 (2011)

NATURE OF CASE: Certiorari review of bankruptcy court judgment.

FACT SUMMARY: Anna Nicole Smith claimed half of her deceased husband's estate. The youngest son of her husband denied her interest in any of the estate. The two parties litigated in Texas and California state and federal courts. The California bankruptcy court entered judgment in Smith's favor on her non-bankruptcy-related counterclaim, but its authority to do so was questioned on appeal.

RULE OF LAW

Article III prohibits bankruptcy courts from finally adjudicating certain state-law claims even if the relevant statutory language designates them as "core" claims.

FACTS: Vickie Lynn Marshall, publicly known as Anna Nicole Smith (Smith), was the third wife of J. Howard Marshall, II (Marshall), who was believed to be one of the richest people in Texas. Anna Nicole Smith married Marshall approximately one year before his death. She was not included in his will, but she claimed he had intended to give her half his property. After he died, she filed a claim in Texas probate court asserting that his youngest son, Pierce Marshall (Pierce) (D), fraudulently prevented Marshall from including her in his living trust. Smith then filed a bankruptcy petition in California. Pierce (D) filed a complaint in the bankruptcy action alleging defamation based on the fraud allegations. Smith filed a counterclaim claiming Pierce (D) fraudulently seized control of his father's assets. The bankruptcy court granted Smith summary judgment on Pierce's (D) claim and entered judgment in her favor on her counterclaim. The Bankruptcy Court awarded Smith over $400 million in compensatory damages and $25 million in punitive damages. On appeal, the court of appeals held the Texas state court judgment controlled because the bankruptcy court lacked authority to enter final judgment on Smith's counterclaim. The United States Supreme Court granted certiorari review.

ISSUE: Does Article III prohibit bankruptcy courts from finally adjudicating certain state-law claims even if the relevant statutory language designates them as "core" claims?

HOLDING AND DECISION: (Roberts, C.J.) Yes. Article III prohibits bankruptcy courts from finally adjudicating certain state-law claims even if the relevant statutory language designates them as "core" claims. Article III of the Constitution defines the characteristics of the judiciary and is an "inseparable element of the constitutional system of checks and balances." Such checks and balances would not exist if the federal government could delegate judicial authority on entities outside Article III. This Court in *Northern Pipeline Construction Co. v. Marathon Pipe Line, Co.*, 458 U.S. 50 (1982), considered the authority of bankruptcy judges to decide a state-law contract claim not otherwise part of a bankruptcy proceeding and concluded such authority violates Article III. Here, Smith's claim is a state-law claim independent of federal bankruptcy law. *Murray's Lessee v. Hoboken Land & Improvement Co.*, 59 U.S. 272 (1856), recognized a public rights exception that includes matters capable of judicial determination, but Congress has deemed them otherwise. *Northern Pipeline* rejected restricting the public rights exception to only those cases involving the federal government as a party. The Court has recognized private disputes could be heard by a non-Article III tribunal but in limited circumstances and when the agency functions as a true "adjunct" of an Article III court. The only other bankruptcy-based case since *Northern Pipeline* has been *Granfinanciera, S.A. v. Nordberg*, 492 U.S. 33 (1989), in which this Court did not find a fraudulent conveyance action fell within the public rights exception because those claims are more accurately characterized as private rights of action. Smith's counterclaim does not fall within the public rights exception. This was a final judgment entered by a court on a common-law claim that neither derived from nor depended upon an agency regulatory regime. Such authority rests only with Article III courts. The bankruptcy court lacked constitutional authority to enter a final judgment on the state-law counterclaim that was not resolved in ruling on the creditor's proof of claim. Affirmed.

CONCURRENCE: (Scalia, J.) Public rights arise between the government and others.

DISSENT: (Breyer, J.) The delegation of adjudicatory authority is constitutional here. Bankruptcy courts often decide claims that resemble common-law actions. The judges are protected from undue influence and work under the supervision of Article III judges. Determinations may be appealed to federal district court where a federal district judge will review determinations of law *de novo*. The parties consented to the Bankruptcy Court's jurisdiction. Finally, a bankruptcy tribunal should have broad authority to resolve all matters in dispute and

Continued on next page.

restructure relationships. Jurisdictional ping-pong leads to inefficiency and needless additional suffering.

ANALYSIS

Anna Nicole Smith died during the litigation and Stern continued the litigation as the executor of her estate. Her estate did not receive a share of Marshall's estate. Since *Stern*, bankruptcy judges and attorneys have had to wrestle with what constitutes a proper claim for bankruptcy adjudication if it is tangentially but not directly related to the bankruptcy estate. In 2014, the Supreme Court decided *Executive Benefits Insurance Agency v. Arkison*, 573 U.S. 25 (2014), and somewhat clarified that a bankruptcy court does not have authority to decide a non-core *Stern* claim but may propose findings of fact and conclusions of law to the district court for *de novo* determination.

Quicknotes

DE NOVO The review of a lower court decision by an appellate court, which is hearing the case as if it had not been previously heard and as if no judgment had been rendered.

Immigration and Naturalization Service v. Chadha

Government agency (P) v. Deported immigrant (D)

462 U.S. 919 (1983)

NATURE OF CASE: Challenge to constitutionality of resolution procedure for overturning deportation suspension.

FACT SUMMARY: Chadha (D) challenged the constitutionality of an Immigration and Nationality Act provision allowing either the House of Representatives (P) or the Senate, acting individually, to overturn the Attorney General's suspension of deportation proceedings by passing a resolution stating in substance that the deportation suspension is not favored.

RULE OF LAW

Where the action of either house of Congress is legislative in nature, such action is subject to the presentment and bicameral requirements of Article I of the Constitution.

FACTS: Chadha (D), who was born in Kenya, remained in the United States after his visa expired. He was ordered deported, but the Attorney General suspended the deportation. Pursuant to an Immigration and Nationality Act (INA) provision allowing either house of Congress to overturn a deportation suspension by adopting a resolution to that effect, the House of Representatives (P) adopted a resolution overturning Chadha's (D) suspension, and he was ordered deported. There was no public hearing, report, or meaningful statement of reasons on the committee's recommendation favoring the resolution. Chadha (D) challenged the constitutionality of the House of Representatives' (P) action under the INA provision.

ISSUE: Where the action of either house of Congress is legislative in nature, is such action subject to the presentment and bicameral requirements of Article I of the Constitution?

HOLDING AND DECISION: (Burger, C.J.) Yes. Where the action of either house of Congress is legislative in nature, such action is subject to the presentment and bicameral requirements of Article I of the Constitution. The clear and unambiguous dictates of Article I of the Constitution require that, before any legislation is to take effect, it must have been passed with the concurrence of the prescribed majority of both houses of Congress and must be presented to the President for approval. Presentment of legislation to the President establishes a salutary check on the legislature and assures that a "national" perspective is grafted on the legislative process. The bicameral requirement assures that the legislative power will be exercised only after full study and debate in separate settings. The powers delegated to each branch of government are identifiable, and when any branch acts, it presumptively exercises the power delegated to it. The legislative character of the House of Representative's (the House's) (P) action in the present case is apparent, since it is conceded that, absent the Immigration and Nationality Act (INA) provision, Chadha's (D) deportation could only have been accomplished by legislation requiring deportation. The House's (P) action does not fall into one of the constitutionally prescribed exceptions to the bicameral requirement, and involves determinations of policy that should only be implemented by adhering to the presentment and bicameral requirements of Article I. The action taken by the House (P) pursuant to the INA provision was in violation of Article I of the Constitution.

DISSENT: (White, J.) If possible, this decision should have been decided on the narrower grounds of separation of powers and sounds a death knell for nearly 200 other statutes where Congress has reserved a legislative veto. The decision is inconsistent with the accepted practice of delegating lawmaking power to independent executive agencies and private persons and ignores the fact that the operation of the Immigration and Nationality Act provision at question satisfies the bicameral and presentment requirements of Article I.

ANALYSIS

It is not clear to what extent the "legislative veto" is dead. It is clear, however, that Congress can accomplish many of the legislative veto's objectives through use of traditional weapons in its legislative and political arsenal. Among others, Congress can tailor statutes more carefully, can provide that an agency's legislative power will expire after a given period of time, and perhaps most importantly, can control an agency's budget. Each of these alternatives has obvious drawbacks and can serve to greatly undermine an agency's effectiveness.

Quicknotes

BICAMERALISM The necessity of approval by a majority of both houses of Congress when ratifying legislation or approving other legislative action.

LEGISLATIVE VETO A statutory provision that contemplates the congressional ability to require the President

Continued on next page.

or another part of the executive branch to act or to refrain from taking action.

PRESENTMENT The act of bringing a congressional decision before the President for his approval or veto.

SEPARATION OF POWERS The division of government into the legislative, executive, and judicial branches, with each branch having specific duties upon with the other branches may not encroach.

Buckley v. Valeo

Member of Federal Election Commission (P) v. Opposing member (D)

424 U.S. 1 (1976)

NATURE OF CASE: Appeal of challenge to portions of the Federal Election Campaign Act of 1971.

FACT SUMMARY: Members of the Federal Election Commission were to be appointed by a method deviating from Article II, § 2 of the Constitution.

RULE OF LAW

Officers of the United States must be appointed in a manner consistent with Article II, § 2 of the Constitution.

FACTS: The Federal Election Campaign Act of 1971 (the Act) created the Federal Election Campaign Commission (the Commission), which was given broad sanctioning and investigative power with respect to elections. The Commission consisted of six voting members appointed by the President Pro Temp of the Senate, the Speaker of the House, and the President, who each selected two members of the Commission. The Secretary of the Senate and the Clerk of the House were nonvoting members. The Act was challenged on constitutional grounds. The court of appeals upheld the section dealing with the Commission.

ISSUE: Must officers of the United States be appointed in a manner consistent with Article II, § 2 of the Constitution?

HOLDING AND DECISION: (Per curiam) Yes. Officers of the United States must be appointed in a manner consistent with Article II, § 2 of the Constitution. The Constitution provides that no member of Congress will be appointed an officer of the United States during his term. This demonstrates that the Framers intended that strict separation be maintained between executive officers and legislative officials. Further, the Constitution mandates that all such executive officials shall be nominated by the President and confirmed by the Senate. The Commission in question exercises important executive functions, and, therefore, its members are officers of the United States. This being the case, they must be appointed per the constitutional requirements of Article II. Reversed.

ANALYSIS

In theory, the Court created a fairly simple standard to follow in this area. Congress may appoint officials who perform purely legislative acts but not officers who perform executive or judicial acts. Of course, the principle is much easier in theory than in practice, and uncertainty will always exist as to which sort of officials do not have to be appointed pursuant to Article II.

Quicknotes

FEDERAL ELECTION CAMPAIGN ACT Created a commission to investigate and administrate federal elections.

U.S. CONSTITUTION, ARTICLE II, § 2 Provides that the President shall nominate executive officials with the advice and consent of the Senate.

Morrison v. Olson

Independent prosecutor (P) v. Assistant Attorney General (D)

487 U.S. 654 (1988)

NATURE OF CASE: Appeal from order quashing subpoenas issued at behest of a special prosecutor.

FACT SUMMARY: Olson (P) alleged that a provision of the Ethics in Government Act impermissibly interfered with the President's exercise of his constitutionally appointed functions.

RULE OF LAW

The Constitution does not require that an independent counsel be terminable at will by the President.

FACTS: Olson (P) was under investigation for allegedly giving false and misleading testimony to a House Subcommittee when he was the Assistant Attorney General for the Office of Legal Counsel. Morrison (D), acting as independent counsel pursuant to the Ethics in Government Act, caused subpoenas to be issued and served on Olson (P). Olson (P) moved to quash the subpoenas, alleging that the provisions of the Act, restricting the Attorney General's power to remove the independent counsel only when good cause could be shown, were unconstitutional because they interfered with the President's absolute discretion to discharge purely executive officials at will.

ISSUE: Does the Constitution require that an independent counsel be terminable at will by the President?

HOLDING AND DECISION: (Rehnquist, C.J.) No. The Constitution does not require that an independent counsel be terminable at will by the President. The President's need to control the independent counsel's discretion is not so central to the functioning of the executive branch as to require, as a matter of constitutional law, the counsel be terminable at will. Imposition of the good cause standard for removal does not by itself unduly trammel on executive authority.

ANALYSIS

There was no dispute that the functions of the independent counsel were executive. The dissent argued that no standards were set to determine how the new test functioned. In the aftermath of Kenneth Starr's investigation of President Clinton, the independent counsel statute was allowed to expire.

Quicknotes

APPOINTMENTS CLAUSE Article II, § 2, cl. 2 of the U.S. Constitution conferring power upon the President to appoint ambassadors, public ministers and consuls, judges of the Supreme Court, and all other officers of the United States with the advice and consent of the Senate.

ETHICS IN GOVERNMENT ACT Allows for the appointment of special independent counsel to investigate high ranking government officials.

INDEPENDENT COUNSEL An officer, whose appointment is authorized by the Ethics in Government Act, who is charged with the investigation of possible criminal activity by high-level government officials.

SEPARATION OF POWERS The division of government into the legislative, executive, and judicial branches, with each branch having specific duties upon with the other branches may not encroach.

Freytag v. Commissioner of Internal Revenue

Taxpayer (P) v. Federal official (D)

501 U.S. 868 (1991)

NATURE OF CASE: Appeal in action seeking review of tax deficiency determinations.

FACT SUMMARY: Taxpayers (P) challenged as violating the Appointments Clause the appointment by the Chief Judge of the United States Tax Court of special trial judges, who were empowered to hear and prepare findings and opinions for all matters and cases in the court. The Taxpayers (P) contended that the special tax judges were "inferior officers" who had to be appointed according to the Appointment Clause and that the Chief Judge did not have the authority to appoint such "Officers."

RULE OF LAW

(1) Special trial judges of the United States Tax Court who are appointed by the Chief Judge of that Article I court and who may hear and prepare findings and opinions for any case or matter in that court are "inferior officers" whose appointment must conform to the Appointments Clause.

(2) A statute that permits the chief judge of an Article I court to appoint special trial judges of that court to hear and prepare findings and opinions for any case or matter does not violate the Appointments Clause, which limits congressional discretion to vest the appointment of "inferior officers" to the President, the heads of departments, and the courts of law.

FACTS: The United States Tax Court is an Article I court. The Chief Judge of the Tax Court, who is appointed by the President with the advice and consent of the Senate, is authorized by statute to appoint special trial judges and to assign to them certain specified proceedings and "any other proceeding which the chief judge may designate," 26 U.S.C. § 7443A(b)(4). As to subsection (b)(4) proceedings, the special trial judge may hear the case and prepare proposed findings and an opinion, but the actual decision is rendered by a Tax Court judge, who is appointed by the President with the advice and consent of the Senate. Taxpayers (P), whose case was heard by a special trial judge, contended that § 7443A(b)(4) violated the Appointments Clause of the Constitution, because a special trial judge is an "inferior officer" of the United States who must be appointed in compliance with the Appointments Clause, and that such appointment may be made only by the President, the heads of departments, and the courts. The Taxpayers (P) also contended that the Tax Court's Chief Judge did not fall into one of those three categories. If, on the other hand, special trial judges were deemed to be merely employees, as contended by the Commissioner (D) of the Internal Revenue Service, they would not need to be selected in compliance with the Appointments Clause. The United States Supreme Court granted certiorari in the case.

ISSUES:

(1) Are special trial judges of the United States Tax Court who are appointed by the Chief Judge of that Article I court and who may hear and prepare findings and opinions for any case or matter in that court "inferior officers" whose appointment must conform to the Appointments Clause?

(2) Does a statute that permits the chief judge of an Article I court to appoint special trial judges of that court to hear and prepare findings and opinions for any case or matter violate the Appointments Clause, which limits congressional discretion to vest the appointment of "inferior officers" to the President, the heads of departments, and the courts of law?

HOLDING AND DECISION: (Blackmun, J.)

(1) Yes. Special trial judges of the United States Tax Court who are appointed by the Chief Judge of that Article I court and who may hear and prepare findings and opinions for any case or matter in that court are "inferior officers" whose appointment must conform to the Appointments Clause. The Court's precedent establishes that any appointee exercising significant authority pursuant to the laws of the United States is an "Officer of the United States" and must, therefore, be appointed in the manner prescribed by the Appointments Clause. The Commissioner (D) argues that a special trial judge assigned under § 7443A(b)(4) acts only as an aide to the Tax Court judge responsible for deciding the case. The special trial judge, as the Commissioner (D) of the Internal Revenue Service characterizes that judge's work, does no more than assist the Tax Court judge in taking the evidence and preparing the proposed findings and opinion. Thus, the Commissioner (D) concludes, special trial judges acting pursuant to § 7443A(b)(4) are employees rather than "Officers of the United States." The Commissioner (D) reasons that special trial judges may be deemed employees in subsection (b)(4) cases because they lack authority to enter a final decision. But this argument ignores

Continued on next page.

the significance of the duties and discretion that special trial judges possess. Special trial judges perform more than ministerial tasks. They take testimony, conduct trials, rule on the admissibility of evidence, and have the power to enforce compliance with discovery orders. In the course of carrying out these important functions, the special trial judges exercise significant discretion. Additionally, they exercise independent authority under other sections of the statute and are concededly inferior officers for purposes of those sections. Special trial judges are not inferior officers for purposes of some of their duties under § 7443A, but mere employees with respect to other responsibilities. Merely because an inferior officer on occasion performs duties that may be performed by an employee not subject to the Appointments Clause does not transform their status under the Constitution. If a special trial judge is an inferior officer for purposes of subsections (b)(1), (2), and (3), he or she is an inferior officer within the meaning of the Appointments Clause and must be properly appointed.

(2) No. A statute that permits the chief judge of an Article I court to appoint special trial judges of that court to hear and prepare findings and opinions for any case or matter does not violate the Appointments Clause, which limits congressional discretion to vest the appointment of "inferior officers" to the President, the heads of departments, and the courts of law. It is beyond question that Congress did not intend to grant to the President the power to appoint special trial judges. Therefore, there are three remaining possibilities. First, as the Commissioner (D) urges, the Tax Court could be treated as a department with the Chief Judge as its head. Second, the Tax Court could be considered one of "the Courts of Law." Third, as argued by the taxpayers (P), the Tax Court is neither a "Departmen[t]" nor a "Cour[t] of Law." The most compelling of these is that although the Tax Court is not an Article III court, because its members do not hold their offices during good behavior, it is a court for purposes of the Appointments Clause because the text of the Clause does not limit "Court of Law" to those established under Article III, and because they operate for all intents and purposes as courts that exercise the judicial power of the United States. Therefore, because the Tax Court is a "Cour[t] of Law," the special trial judges were constitutionally appointed by that court's Chief Judge.

CONCURRENCE AND DISSENT: (Scalia, J.) The majority incorrectly concludes that the Tax Court is a "Court of Law" for purposes of the Appointments Clause. Any "Court of Law" must be an Article III court, because the Clause refers to "the" Courts of Law, not just "any" courts of law. Article III judges serve during good behavior with undiminishable salary, but Article I judges do not. Also, the Tax Court's predecessor was the United States Board of Tax Appeals, an independent agency in the executive branch of the government that exercises executive power, not judicial power. When the Tax Court was statutorily denominated an "Article I Court" in 1969, its judges did not magically acquire the judicial power. They still lack life tenure; their salaries may still be diminished; and they are still removable by the President for "inefficiency, neglect of duty, or malfeasance in office." For these reasons, the Tax Court is best viewed as a "department" under the Appointments Clause, because it is a separate organization within the executive branch. Nowhere in the text of the Constitution is a "department" required to be a "Cabinet." Also, modern practice as well as original practice refutes the distinction between Cabinet and non-Cabinet agencies. The Constitution does not define "department," but a number of factors support the proposition that "Heads of Departments" includes the heads of all agencies immediately below the President in the organizational structure of the executive branch. Thus, "Departments" means all independent executive establishments. Because the Tax Court is a "department" under this view, and the Chief Judge is the head of the department, the appointment of the special trial judges was constitutional.

ANALYSIS

Justice Scalia acknowledges that in the case of the Tax Court, as with some other independent establishments (notably, the so-called "independent regulatory agencies" such as the Federal Communications Commission) permitting appointment of inferior officers by the agency head may not ensure the high degree of insulation from congressional control that was the purpose of the Constitution's appointments scheme. Depending on how broadly one reads the President's power to dismiss "for cause," it may be that the President has no control over the appointment of inferior officers in such agencies; and, if those agencies are publicly regarded as beyond presidential control, it is arguable that the main purpose for permitting appointive power to be lodged in "Heads of Departments" does not exist with respect to the heads of these agencies, because they, in fact, will not be shored up by the President and are thus not resistant to congressional pressures. However, notwithstanding this possibility, according to Justice Scalia, the majority's position is even less tenable because, as he sees it, considering an Article I court as a "Court of Law" is even less resistant to such congressional pressures.

Continued on next page.

Quicknotes

APPOINTMENTS CLAUSE Article II, § 2, cl. 2 of the U.S. Constitution conferring power upon the President to appoint ambassadors, public ministers and consuls, judges of the Supreme Court, and all other officers of the United States with the advice and consent of the Senate.

INFERIOR OFFICERS Members of the executive branch having less power or authority in relation to others.

Edmond v. United States

[Party not identified] (P) v. Federal government (D)

520 U.S. 651 (1997)

NATURE OF CASE: Certiorari review of executive appointment of military judges

FACT SUMMARY: The Secretary of Transportation appointed two civilians to the Coast Guard Court of Criminal Appeals. Petitioners (P) were convicted by court-martial with the civilian judges participating in the decisions and appeals.

RULE OF LAW

The Secretary of Transportation's appointment of civilian members of the Coast Guard Court of Criminal Appeals is constitutional under the Appointments Clause of Article II because the civilian judges are "inferior officers" for purposes of the Appointments Clause.

FACTS: In *Weiss v. United States*, 510 U.S. 163 (1994), the United States Supreme Court held that military trial and appellate judges are officers of the United States and must be appointed pursuant to the Appointments Clause of Article II of the United States Constitution. In January 1993, considering the *Weiss* case, the Secretary of Transportation appointed two civilian judges to the Coast Guard Court of Criminal Appeals. One judge, Chief Judge Baum, participated in court-martial decisions, and the other judge, Judge Bridgman, participated in appeals involving two of the Petitioners (P).

ISSUE: Is the Secretary of Transportation's appointment of civilian members of the Coast Guard Court of Criminal Appeals constitutional under the Appointments Clause of Article II?

HOLDING AND DECISION: (Scalia, J.) Yes. The Secretary of Transportation's appointment of civilian members of the Coast Guard Court of Criminal Appeals is constitutional under the Appointments Clause of Article II because the civilian judges are "inferior officers" for purposes of the Appointments Clause. Petitioners (P) argue the civilian appointments are invalid because such judges are "principal" rather than "inferior officers" within the meaning of the Appointments Clause and thus the President must appoint with the advice and consent of the Senate. Article II vests the President with the exclusive power to select principal officers of the United States. The requirement of the "advice and consent of the Senate" curbs executive abuse of the appointment power and promotes judicious choice to fill positions. The manner of appointment for principal officers also is the default method for appointment for inferior officers. Congress, however, may vest appointment of inferior officers also in the courts or "Heads of Departments." This provision is sometimes called the "Excepting Clause." Its purpose obviously is administrative convenience. This Court's prior cases do not set forth exclusive criterion for distinguishing between principal and inferior officers. The finding in *Morrison v. Olson*, 487 U.S. 654 (1988), relied on several factors. Petitioners (P) are correct that two of those factors are not present here. They argue the military appeals judges bear important responsibilities, including resolution of constitutional challenges. Such responsibility is true of other officers we have found to be "inferior" for Appointments Clause purposes. The difference between an officer and a non-officer is the exercise of "significant authority pursuant to the laws of the United States" but that does not distinguish principal and inferior officers. Generally, an "inferior officer" is supervised at some level by Presidential appointees. Judges in the Court of Criminal Appeals are supervised by the Judge Advocate General and by the Court of Appeals for the Armed Forces. The Judge Advocate General exercises administrative oversight of the court and may remove a judge from his assignment without cause. The Judge Advocate General may not attempt to influence proceeding outcomes and may not reverse court decisions. The reversal power does lie with the Court of Appeals for the Armed Forces. The significance is that judges for the Court of Criminal Appeals do not render final decisions unless permitted to do so by other executive officers. *Freytag v. Commissioner*, 501 U.S. 868 (1991), does not control here because the Tax Court has no supervisory officer comparable to the Judge Advocate General and no executive tribunal similar to the Court of Appeals for the Armed Forces. The judicial appointments here are valid.

CONCURRENCE: (Souter, J.) The Court's opinion is appropriate to hold judges of the Coast Guard Court of Criminal Appeals to be inferior officers. Inferior officers have supervisors. The Court properly finds these judges have supervisors. The analysis should not stop there, however. The existence of a superior is not sufficient alone to establish inferior officer status. There should be a detailed look at the powers and duties of the judges to determine whether the factors weigh more heavily in favor of inferior officer status.

ANALYSIS

Administrative ease encourages finding a position is one for an "inferior officer" because political wrangling

Continued on next page.

can hold up principal officer appointments indefinitely. For example, President Obama appointed three members to the National Labor Relations Board during a three-day Senate recess after Senate's "advice and consent" had remained elusive. In ensuing litigation, *NLRB v. Noel Canning*, 573 U.S. 513 (2014), the United States Supreme Court held the recess appointments unconstitutional under the Appointments Clause.

Quicknotes

APPOINTMENTS CLAUSE Article II, § 2, cl. 2 of the U.S. Constitution conferring power upon the President to appoint ambassadors, public ministers and consuls, judges of the Supreme Court, and all other officers of the United States with the advice and consent of the Senate.

INFERIOR OFFICERS Members of the executive branch having less power or authority in relation to others.

United States v. Arthrex, Inc.

Federal government (P) v. Patent holder (D)

141 S. Ct. 1970 (2021)

NATURE OF CASE: Appeal from judgment for plaintiff holding that the review structure of the Patent Trial and Appeal Board was unconstitutional under the Appointments Clause, and appeal from remedy to address such unconstitutionality.

FACT SUMMARY: Arthrex, Inc. (D), a patent holder, contended that permitting Administrative Patent Judges (APJs), who were appointed as inferior officers to the Patent Trial and Appeal Board, to render final decisions without further review in inter partes review proceedings violated the Appointments Clause. The Federal Circuit agreed and ruled that the appropriate remedy was to invalidate the tenure protections for APJs, making them inferior officers instead of principal officers.

RULE OF LAW

(1) The unreviewable authority held by Administrative Patent Judges during inter partes review proceedings of the Patent Trial and Appeal Board is incompatible under the Appointments Clause with their appointment by the Secretary of Commerce to an inferior office.

(2) For a system of review in the Patent and Trademark Office (PTO) to be constitutional under the Appointments Clause, the PTO Director must be statutorily authorized to review final Patent Trial and Appeal Board (PTAB) decisions rendered by Administrative Patent Judges and, upon review, issue decisions on behalf of the PTAB.

FACTS: Administrative Patent Judges (APJs) conduct adversarial proceedings for challenging the validity of an existing patent before the Patent Trial and Appeal Board (the PTAB or the Board). Such proceedings are known as "inter partes review." During such proceedings, the PTAB sits in panels of at least three of its members, who are predominantly APJs. The Secretary of Commerce (the Secretary) appoints the APJs. Congress provided that APJs would be appointed as inferior officers. The PTAB is part of the Patent and Trademark Office (PTO), which is headed by a Director appointed by the President with the advice and consent of the Senate. The Director fixes the rate of pay for APJs, controls the decision whether to institute inter partes review, and selects the APJs to reconsider the validity of the patent. The Director also promulgates regulations governing inter partes review, issues prospective guidance on patentability issues, and designates past PTAB decisions as "precedential" for future panels. The Director is thus "the boss," except when it comes to reviewing APJ decisions. The PTAB's panels have the final say as to the validity of a challenged patent, and billions of dollars can turn on a single PTAB decision. When a patent held by Arthrex, Inc. (D) was held invalid by the PTAB as part of inter partes review filed by Arthrex's (D) competitor, Smith & Nephew, Inc. (P), Arthrex (D) challenged in the Federal Circuit the constitutionality under the Appointments Clause of permitting APJs to bind the executive branch with no further review, arguing that, based on APJs' responsibilities and lack of review of their decisions, APJs were, in fact, principal officers who had to be appointed by the President with the Senate's advice and consent. The Appointments Clause provides that only the President, with the advice and consent of the Senate, can appoint principal officers. With respect to inferior officers, the Appointments Clause permits Congress to vest appointment power in the President alone, in the courts, or in department heads. The Federal Circuit agreed with Arthrex (D) that APJs were principal officers, and, to fix this constitutional violation, the Federal Circuit invalidated the tenure protections for APJs. Making APJs removable at will by the Secretary, the Federal Circuit held, prospectively rendered them inferior rather than principal officers. The Federal Circuit vacated the PTAB's decision and remanded for a fresh hearing before a new panel of APJs, who would no longer enjoy protection against removal. The United States Supreme Court granted certiorari.

ISSUE:

(1) Is the unreviewable authority held by Administrative Patent Judges during inter partes review proceedings of the Patent Trial and Appeal Board incompatible under the Appointments Clause with their appointment by the Secretary of Commerce to an inferior office?

(2) For a system of review in the Patent and Trademark Office (PTO) to be constitutional under the Appointments Clause, must the PTO Director be statutorily authorized to review final Patent Trial and Appeal Board (PTAB) decisions rendered by Administrative Patent Judges and, upon review, issue decisions on behalf of the PTAB?

HOLDING AND DECISION: (Roberts, C.J.)

(1) Yes. The unreviewable authority held by Administrative Patent Judges (APJs) during inter partes review proceedings of the Patent Trial and Appeal

Continued on next page.

Board (PTAB or Board) is incompatible under the Appointments Clause with their appointment by the Secretary of Commerce (the Secretary) to an inferior office. To determine whether the nature of the APJs' responsibilities is inconsistent with their method of appointment, the Court looks to *Edmond v. United States*, 520 U.S. 651 (1997), where the Court held that whether one is an inferior officer depends on whether one has a superior other than the President. In other words, an inferior officer must be directed and supervised at some level by others who were appointed by presidential nomination with the advice and consent of the Senate. Although the Patent and Trademark Office Director (the PTO Director or the Director) possesses powers of administrative oversight, the Director lacks statutory authority to review the APJs' decisions. Thus, there is no principal officer at any level within the executive branch who directs and supervises the APJs' most important power—to render decisions as to patentability. This "diffusion of power carries with it a diffusion of accountability." The United States (P) and Smith & Nephew (P) contend that the Director has various ways to indirectly influence the course of inter partes review. The Director, for example, could designate APJs predisposed to decide a case in the Director's preferred manner or stack a rehearing panel, but such machinations are not the solution; they reflect the problem. To force such maneuvering blurs the lines of accountability demanded by the Appointments Clause and leaves the parties with neither an impartial decision by a panel of experts nor a transparent decision for which a politically accountable officer must take responsibility. The Director also could respond after the fact by removing an APJ from his or her judicial assignment without cause and refusing to designate that APJ on future PTAB panels. Even assuming that is true, reassigning an APJ to a different task going forward gives the Director no means of countermanding the final decision already on the books. Nor are APJs meaningfully controlled by the threat of removal from federal service entirely. Given the insulation of PTAB decisions from any executive review, the President can neither oversee the PTAB directly nor attribute the Board's failings to those whom the President can oversee. APJs accordingly exercise power that conflicts with the design of the Appointments Clause to preserve political accountability. Accordingly, the statutory review system currently in place is unconstitutional.

(2) Yes. For a system of review in the Patent and Trademark Office (PTO) to be constitutional under the Appointments Clause, the PTO Director (the Director) must be statutorily authorized to review final Patent Trial and Appeal Board (PTAB) decisions rendered by Administrative Patent Judges (APJs) and, upon review, issue decisions on behalf of the PTAB. In every respect save the insulation of their decisions from review within the executive branch, APJs appear to be inferior officers—an understanding consistent with their appointment in a manner permissible for inferior but not principal officers. Because Congress has vested the Director with the power and duties of the PTO, the Director has the authority to provide for a means of reviewing PTAB decisions, and accordingly may review final PTAB decisions and, upon review, may issue decisions on behalf of the Board. Notwithstanding that the Federal Circuit's remedy of at-will removal of APJs by the Secretary of Commerce might cure the constitutional problem, review by the Director better reflects the structure of supervision within the PTO and the nature of APJs' duties. Therefore, the appropriate remedy in this case is to remand to the Director, for the Director to decide whether to rehear the petition filed by Smith & Nephew (P). Vacated and remanded.

CONCURRENCE AND DISSENT: (Gorsuch, J.) The plurality is correct that the statutory review system is unconstitutional. However, it errs as to the appropriate remedy. It is not the Court's place to repair the unconstitutional statutory review system. Instead, the Court should have limited itself to identifying the constitutional violation, explain its reasoning, and set aside the Patent Trial and Appeal Board decision in the case at bar.

DISSENT: (Thomas, J.) There cannot be serious dispute that Administrative Patent Judges (APJs) in fact are inferior officers under the Constitution. They are lower in rank by two levels to the President; they serve below the Director of the Patent and Trademark Office (PTO) and to the Secretary of Commerce (the Secretary). Therefore, instead of rewriting the Director's statutory powers, the patent scheme Congress has created should be left intact. The Director already has the ability to influence individual proceedings, by deciding in the first instance whether to institute review, and then, if review is instituted, by either selecting the APJs that will hear the review, or, in the alternative, designating himself or herself and other higher-ups in the PTO hierarchy to review the case. In addition, the Director decides which of the thousands of decisions issued each year bind other panels as precedent, and no statute bars the Director from taking an active role to ensure the Board's decisions conform to the Director's policy direction. Moreover, if the administrative patent judges reach a result the Director does not like, the Director can add more members to the panel—including himself or herself—and order the case reheard. Further, if an APJ consistently fails to follow instructions, the Secretary has the authority to fire the APJ. What the

Continued on next page.

Director cannot do is singlehandedly reverse decisions. The plurality essentially agrees with this analysis but boils down "inferior-officer" status to the way Congress structured a particular agency's process for reviewing decisions, but there is no precedent for such an approach. A bigger problem is that interpreting the Appointments Clause to bar any nonprincipal officer from taking "final" action poses serious line-drawing problems that could lead to courts having to sort through lists of each officer's duties and categorize each one as principal or inferior. Finally, the plurality's remedy is unnecessary. If indeed the Appointments Clause inherently grants the Director power to reverse Board decisions, then another problem arises: No constitutional violation has occurred in this suit. The Board had the power to decide, and lawfully did decide, the dispute before it. The Board did not misinterpret its statutory authority or try to prevent direct review by the Director. Nor did the Director wrongfully decline to rehear the Board's decision. Without any constitutional violation in this suit to correct, the Court lacks the power to issue a remedy, and it should not have rewritten the statutory text to ensure that the Director can directly review Board decisions.

ANALYSIS

Justice Gorsuch emphasizes that the remedy chosen by the plurality—to strip away statutory constraints from the Patent and Trademark Office Director's review powers—is at odds with Congress's intent. Justice Gorsuch points out that the plurality believes that Congress would have wanted to render Patent Trial and Appeal Board (PTAB) decisions reviewable by the Director, since that regime is consistent with the "standard federal model" for agency adjudication. However, as he observes, it is clear that Congress rejected this familiar approach when it came to PTAB proceedings, apparently to ensure that Administrative Patent Judges (APJs) enjoy independence from superior executive officers and, therefore, are more impartial. In fact, the Court in prior cases noted that there was a possibility that permitting politically motivated executive officials to "cancel" patents might raise due process concerns, especially since for two centuries only courts could do so. Accordingly, Justice Gorsuch bemoans that allowing executive officials to assume a historic judicial function was always destined to invite familiar due process problems—like decisions favoring those with political clout, the powerful and the popular, given that those with power can amass armies of lobbyists and lawyers to influence (and even capture) politically accountable bureaucracies. To illustrate his point, Justice Gorsuch relates the tale of a "supposedly" independent APJ, who had formerly been a patent attorney at one of the world's largest technology companies who left the company to become an APJ, who then presided over dozens of inter partes reviews (IPRs) brought by his former company, in which the company prevailed in its efforts to cancel patents damaging to its private economic interests 96 percent of the time, and who, after six years of work, resigned, and returned to the company. "Without a hint of irony, that company has filed an amicus brief in this case to inform us, as a self-described 'frequent user of the IPR process,' about 'the benefits of the system.' Accordingly, Justice Gorsuch is grateful that at least the Court's decision avoided "investing the power to revoke an individual's property rights in some unaccountable fourth branch controlled by powerful companies seeking a competitive advantage."

Quicknotes

APPOINTMENTS CLAUSE Article II, § 2, cl. 2 of the U.S. Constitution conferring power upon the President to appoint ambassadors, public ministers and consuls, judges of the Supreme Court, and all other officers of the United States with the advice and consent of the Senate.

INTER PARTES REVIEW A process by which members of the Patent Trial and Appeal Board reconsider whether existing patents meet the novelty and nonobviousness requirements for inventions; inter partes review was established in 2011.

Bowsher v. Synar

Comptroller General (D) v. Congressman (P)

478 U.S. 714 (1986)

NATURE OF CASE: Appeal from declaratory judgment invalidating the Balanced Budget Act.

FACT SUMMARY: Synar (P) contended that the Balanced Budget Act violated separation of powers by providing strict requirements for appointment of an executive branch office.

RULE OF LAW

Congress cannot retain power to remove executive branch officers except by impeachment.

FACTS: Congress enacted the Balanced Budget Act, which invested in the Comptroller General the power to make broad budgetary decisions as a member of the executive branch. The President appointed the Comptroller General (D) from a list provided by Congress. Removal was obtained by a joint resolution of Congress. Synar (P) sued, contending the statute unconstitutionally violated the separation of powers doctrine. The district court invalidated the statute. The court of appeals affirmed, and the United States Supreme Court granted certiorari.

ISSUE: Can Congress retain power to remove executive branch officers?

HOLDING AND DECISION: (Burger, C.J.) No. Congress cannot retain power to remove executive branch officers except by impeachment. Any other removal power over executive officers imposes undue power over that branch and is inconsistent with separation of powers. Such a power would make the executive officer subservient to Congress and, in effect, allow Congress to execute the laws. The Comptroller General's (D) duties under the statute are not merely mechanical and ministerial, but they are indeed the very essence of executive functions. The statute requires the Comptroller General (D) to both interpret the Balanced Budget Act (the Act) and exercise judgment in how to apply the Act—functions usually committed to executive officers. As a result, the statute was unconstitutional. Affirmed.

ANALYSIS

The Comptroller General performs many functions that identify the office more closely with Congress than with the executive branch. The office settles all claims against the government and determines all accounts owed or owing. Despite this, the office was created under the executive branch.

Quicknotes

EXECUTIVE BRANCH The branch of government responsible for the administration of the laws.

LEGISLATIVE BRANCH The branch of government charged with the promulgation of laws.

SEPARATION OF POWERS The division of government into the legislative, executive, and judicial branches, with each branch having specific duties upon with the other branches may not encroach.

Free Enterprise Fund v. Public Accounting Oversight Board

Nonprofit organization (P) v. An SEC Board (D)

561 U.S. 477 (2010)

NATURE OF CASE: Certiorari review of constitutionality of governmental entity.

FACT SUMMARY: Every foreign and domestic accounting firm that participates in auditing public companies registers with the Public Accounting Oversight Board (the Board) (D) and must comply with its rules and oversight. Free Enterprise Fund (P), a nonprofit trade association representing firms who must register with the Board, asserted the Board's existence and regulations were unconstitutional.

RULE OF LAW

A removal restriction is unconstitutional when it limits presidential power of executive oversight and compliance.

FACTS: Congress enacted the Sarbanes-Oxley Act of 2002 (the Act), which introduced tighter regulation of the accounting industry through the creation of the Public Accounting Oversight Board (the Board) (D). Every foreign and domestic accounting firm that participates in auditing public companies registers with the Board (D) and must comply with its rules and oversight. The Securities and Exchange Commission (the Commission) appoints members to the Board (D) and those members are not considered government officers or employees for statutory purposes, but they do engage in executive branch governmental activity. The Commission may remove Board (D) members only for good cause. The Board (D) has expansive powers to govern the entire accounting industry. The Free Enterprise Fund (the Fund) (P) filed a complaint seeking a declaratory judgment that the Board is unconstitutional and an injunction prohibiting it from exercising its powers. [The United States Supreme Court granted certiorari review.]

ISSUE: Is a removal restriction unconstitutional when it limits presidential power of executive oversight and compliance?

HOLDING AND DECISION: (Roberts, C.J.) Yes. A removal restriction is unconstitutional when it limits presidential power of executive oversight and compliance. The Constitution vests the executive power in the President. Removal of officers was discussed and not expressly removed from the President's authority, so it remained with the President. Article II confers the authority for the President to have general administrative control of those executing the laws. If Congress vests appointment authority of inferior officers in the head of a department, then that head typically also has removal power. This Court has upheld limitations on the President's removal power and department head removal power. Here, only the Securities and Exchange Commission (the Commission) may remove members of the Public Accounting Oversight Board (the Board) upon good cause shown and the President has no ability to remove a commissioner without good cause. Therefore, Board members are not accountable to the President and the President cannot hold the Commission fully responsible for the Board's conduct. If the President believes a Board member is not discharging his or her duty, but the Commission disagrees, the President can do nothing. The President's executive powers are stripped. The Board has executive powers but no executive oversight. The dissent focuses on other civil service employees, but those employees do not enjoy the same significant and unusual protections as the Board members. Congress may not deprive the President of oversight and control over the primary law enforcement agency for a vital sector of this economy. The existence of the Board does not violate the separation of powers but the removal restrictions do. The Sarbanes-Oxley Act of 2002 remains fully operative but without the tenure restrictions. The remaining challenges to the Board under the Appointments Clause have no merit. The Board members are not principal officers as alleged but are inferior officers whose appointment rests with the Commission. The Commission is a freestanding executive branch component and constitutes a "department" for the Appointments Clause. Further, the "Head of a Department" may consist of a multimember body rather than the Commission Chairman alone. The Commission validly appointed the Board members.

DISSENT: (Breyer, J.) The Necessary and Proper Clause does not permit Congress the authority to free all executive branch officials from dismissal at will. The separation-of-powers principle does not permit the President to dismiss all executive branch officials at will. Congress may sometimes limit the President's power. The Constitution is completely silent on removal power so this Court cannot look to its language for guidance. History is not helpful because the subject is of much dispute. The Court's precedent does not clearly invalidate the removal restrictions at issue here. The Court is left to examine how the provision would function. The "for cause" provision here passed Congress nearly unanimously and the President signed the Sarbanes-Oxley Act of 2002. No one expressed a separation-of-powers

Continued on next page.

concern and the Court's proposed fix does not address the central issue. The President still cannot intervene if the Commission reasonably decides not to remove a Board member. Congress sought to protect Board members from removal for political reasons. When the "for cause" provision furthers a legitimate institutional need and does not restrict presidential power, its constitutionality is strongly supported. The Court also reads in a "for cause" provision for the Commissioners, so the multilayer protection is fabricated. The Court has created a constitutional defect in the Act and then relied on that defect to rule it unconstitutional.

ANALYSIS

There is no such thing as a truly independent government agency. Each agency member ultimately serves at the pleasure of the President or upon advice-and-consent of the Senate. While the President may not exercise power over the day-to-day operations of an agency and its employees, Congress can never constitutionally fully insulate agencies from oversight.

Quicknotes

NECESSARY AND PROPER CLAUSE Article I, § 8 of the U.S. Constitution, enables Congress to make all laws that may be "necessary and proper" to execute its other, enumerated powers.

SEPARATION OF POWERS The division of government into the legislative, executive, and judicial branches, with each branch having specific duties upon with the other branches may not encroach.

Seila Law LLC v. Consumer Financial Protection Bureau

Subject of agency investigation (D) v. Agency (P)

140 S. Ct. 2183 (2020)

NATURE OF CASE: Appeal from affirmance of judgment ordering compliance with an independent agency's investigative demand.

FACT SUMMARY: In response to an investigative demand made by the Consumer Financial Protection Bureau (CFPB) (P), Seila Law LLC (D) contended that the structure of the CFPB (P), an independent agency headed by a single Director appointed by the President and removable from office only for "inefficiency, neglect of duty, or malfeasance in office," violated the Constitution's separation of powers.

RULE OF LAW

(1) An independent agency's structure violates the Constitution's separation of powers where the agency is vested with significant executive power and is led by a single individual removable from office only for inefficiency, neglect, or malfeasance in office.

(2) Where Congress has violated the Constitution's separation of powers by creating an independent agency that is headed by a single individual leader who can be removed only for inefficiency, neglect, or malfeasance in office, the appropriate remedy is to sever those provisions of the act creating the agency that prevent the President from removing the agency head at will.

FACTS: In response to the Great Recession financial crisis, Congress in the Dodd-Frank Act (the Act) created the Consumer Financial Protection Bureau (CFPB) (P) as an independent financial regulatory agency tasked with ensuring that consumer debt products are fair, safe, competitive, and transparent. Congress gave the CFPB (P) extensive rulemaking, enforcement, and adjudicatory powers, including the authority to conduct investigations, issue subpoenas and civil investigative demands, initiate administrative adjudications, prosecute civil actions in federal court, and issue binding decisions in administrative proceedings. The CFPB (P) may seek restitution, disgorgement, injunctive relief, and significant civil penalties for violations of the 19 federal statutes under its purview. Unlike traditional independent agencies headed by multimember boards or commissions, the CFPB (P) is led by a single Director who is appointed by the President with the advice and consent of the Senate for a five-year term, during which the President may remove the Director only for "inefficiency, neglect of duty, or malfeasance in office." Unlike most other agencies, the CFPB does not rely on the annual appropriations process for funding. Instead, the CFPB receives funding directly from the Federal Reserve, which is itself funded outside the appropriations process through bank assessments. Seila Law LLC (D), which was being investigated by the CFPB (P), refused to comply with an investigation order to produce documents issued by the CFPB (P), contending that the CFPB's (P) structure violated the Constitution's separation of powers. The CFPB (P) declined to address the constitutional claim and sought to enforce its demand in federal District Court. Seila Law (D) renewed its constitutional defense, which the District Court rejected. The Court of Appeals affirmed, and the United States Supreme Court granted certiorari in the case.

ISSUE:

(1) Does an independent agency's structure violate the Constitution's separation of powers where the agency is vested with significant executive power and is led by a single individual removable from office only for inefficiency, neglect, or malfeasance in office?

(2) Where Congress has violated the Constitution's separation of powers by creating an independent agency that is headed by a single individual leader who can be removed only for inefficiency, neglect, or malfeasance in office, is the appropriate remedy to sever those provisions of the act creating the agency that prevent the President from removing the agency head at will?

HOLDING AND DECISION: (Roberts, C.J.)

(1) Yes. An independent agency's structure violates the Constitution's separation of powers where the agency is vested with significant executive power and is led by a single individual removable from office only for inefficiency, neglect, or malfeasance in office. Article II vests the entire executive power in the President alone, but the Constitution presumes that lesser executive officers will assist the President in discharging executive duties. The President's executive power generally includes the power to supervise—and, if necessary, remove—those who exercise the President's authority on the President's behalf. The President's removal power has long been confirmed by history and precedent. It was recognized by the First Congress in 1789, confirmed by the Court in *Myers v. United States*, 272 U.S. 52 (1926), and reiterated in *Free Enterprise Fund v. Public Company Accounting Oversight Bd.*, 561 U.S. 477 (2010), in which the Court left in place only two exceptions to the President's unrestricted removal

Continued on next page.

power. First, *Humphrey's Executor v. United States*, 295 U.S. 602 (1935), permitted Congress to give for-cause removal protection to the Commissioners of the Federal Trade Commission (FTC), a multimember body of experts who were balanced along partisan lines, appointed to staggered terms, performed only "quasi-legislative" and "quasi-judicial functions," and were said not to exercise any executive power. Second, *Morrison v. Olson*, 487 U.S. 654 (1988), approved good-cause tenure protection for an inferior officer—the independent counsel—who had limited duties and no policymaking or administrative authority. Neither *Humphrey's Executor* nor *Morrison* resolves whether the Consumer Financial Protection Bureau (CFPB) (P) Director's insulation from removal is constitutional. The New Deal–era FTC upheld in *Humphrey's Executor* bears little resemblance to the CFPB (P). Unlike the multiple Commissioners of the FTC, who were balanced along partisan lines and served staggered terms to ensure the accumulation of institutional knowledge, the CFPB (P) Director serves a five-year term that guarantees abrupt shifts in leadership and the loss of agency expertise. In addition, the Director cannot be dismissed as a mere legislative or judicial aid. Rather, the Director possesses significant administrative and enforcement authority, including the power to seek daunting monetary penalties against private parties in federal court—a quintessential executive power not considered in *Humphrey's Executor*. The logic of *Morrison* also does not apply. The independent counsel approved in *Morrison* was an inferior officer who lacked policymaking or administrative authority and exercised narrow authority to initiate criminal investigations and prosecutions of Governmental actors identified by others. By contrast, the CFPB (P) Director is a principal officer whose duties are far from limited. The question, therefore, is whether to extend the *Humphrey's Executor* and *Morrison* exceptions to a "new situation." Because the CFPB's (P) structure has no foothold in history or tradition and is incompatible with the Constitution's power structure, the Court declines to extend those precedents to the CFPB (P). First, an agency with a structure like that of the CFPB (P) is almost wholly unprecedented. Congress has provided removal protection to principal officers who alone wield power in only four isolated instances: the Comptroller of the Currency (for a one-year period during the Civil War); the Office of Special Counsel; the Administrator of the Social Security Administration (SSA); and the Director of the Federal Housing Finance Agency (FHFA). Aside from the one-year blip for the Comptroller of the Currency, these examples are modern and contested; and they do not involve regulatory or enforcement authority comparable to that exercised by the CFPB (P). As compared to these other agencies, the CFPB (P) is in an entirely different league. It acts as a mini legislature, prosecutor, and court, responsible for creating substantive rules for a wide swath of industries, prosecuting violations, and levying weighty penalties against private citizens, not to mention that it is the only agency of its kind run by a single Director. Second, the CFPB's (P) single-Director configuration is also incompatible with the structure of the Constitution, which—with the sole exception of the Presidency—scrupulously avoids concentrating power in the hands of any single individual. The Framers' constitutional strategy is straightforward: divide power everywhere except for the Presidency and render the President directly accountable to the people through regular elections. In that scheme, individual executive officials may wield significant authority, but that authority remains subject to the ongoing supervision and control of the elected President. The CFPB's (P) single-Director structure contravenes this carefully calibrated system by vesting significant governmental power in the hands of a single individual who is neither elected by the people nor meaningfully controlled (through the threat of removal) by someone who is. The Director may unilaterally, without meaningful supervision, issue final regulations, oversee adjudications, set enforcement priorities, initiate prosecutions, and determine what penalties to impose on private parties. Additionally, the Director may do so without even having to rely on Congress for appropriations. Although the CFPB's (P) independent, single-Director structure is sufficient to render the agency unconstitutional, the Director's five-year term and receipt of funds outside the appropriations process heighten the concern that the agency will "slip from the Executive's control, and thus from that of the people." Text, first principles, the First Congress's decision in 1789, *Myers*, and *Free Enterprise Fund* all establish that the President's removal power is the rule, not the exception. Amicus submits that the Court can cure any constitutional defect in the CFPB's (P) structure by interpreting the language "inefficiency, neglect of duty, or malfeasance in office," to reserve substantial discretion to the President. However, it is clear that with the CFPB (P), Congress intended to impose meaningful restrictions on the President's removal authority, and the Court cannot rewrite the statute Congress promulgated. For these reasons, the CFPB's (P) leadership by a single independent Director violates the separation of powers.

(2) Yes. Where Congress has violated the Constitution's separation of powers by creating an independent agency that is headed by a single individual leader who

Continued on next page.

can be removed only for inefficiency, neglect, or malfeasance in office, the appropriate remedy is to sever those provisions of the act creating the agency that prevent the President from removing the agency head at will. Generally, when confronting a constitutional flaw in a statute, the Court tries to limit the solution to the problem, severing any problematic portions while leaving the remainder intact. The only constitutional defect in the Consumer Financial Protection Bureau's (CFPB's) (P) structure is the Director's insulation from removal. If the Director were removable at will by the President, the constitutional violation would disappear. The Dodd-Frank Act (the Act) contains a severability clause, and severing the provisions that insulate the Director from removal from the Act will not affect the remaining provisions relating to the CFPB's (P) structure and duties, which will remain fully operative. Additionally, there is no indication in the legislative history or the Act's text that Congress would have preferred no CFPB (P) to one where the President can remove the Director at will. Therefore, the appropriate remedy is to sever and remove the Director tenure restrictions from the Act.

CONCURRENCE AND DISSENT: (Thomas, J.) Although the Court correctly decides the removability issue in this case, *Humphrey's Executor v. United States*, 295 U.S. 602 (1935), was erroneous and should be repudiated completely. Additionally, although the Court correctly resolved the merits of the question before it, the Court did not need to resort to severability to decide this case. The Court should have simply denied the Consumer Financial Protection Bureau's (P) petition to enforce its investigative demand. Finally, the Court's treatment of the history of severability is questionable.

CONCURRENCE AND DISSENT: (Kagan, J.) Until now, the Court has left most decisions about how to structure administrative agencies to the legislative and executive branches and has on numerous occasions upheld removal restrictions identical to those it now invalidates. The Court also should have left intact the Consumer Financial Protection Bureau's (CFPB's) (P) structure, and the Director removal restrictions, as a matter of historical practice and the Constitution's text. The Constitution grants to Congress the authority to organize all the institutions of American governance, provided only that those arrangements allow the President to perform the duties the Constitution assigns to the President, and, throughout the nation's history, Congress has created spheres of administration detached from direct presidential control, confident it could do so under the Constitution. The Court's differentiation of the CFPB (P) structure from the structure of agencies that the Court previously approved rests on flawed premises and distinctions, and so the Court fails to respect its proper role. The Court's distinction between multimember bodies and single directors does not at all respond to the constitutional values at stake. The issue should have been framed exclusively as whether the agency's structure so deprives the President of control over an official that it impedes the President's functions, and regardless whether there is a for-cause removal provision, the President has at least as much control over an individual as over a commission, and possibly more. The Constitution does not expressly mention separation of powers or the President's removal authority, and the Founders intended separation of powers to be flexible, not rigid as the majority seems to believe. The branches of government are interconnected, and must be, for government to work. The Constitution reflects that vision of adaptability and flexibility by giving Congress broad authority to establish and organize the executive branch. Article II presumes the existence of "Officer[s]" in "executive Departments." § 2, cl. 1. However, contrary to the majority's insinuation, it does not give the President authority to decide what kinds of officers—in what departments, with what responsibilities—the executive branch requires. Instead, Article I's Necessary and Proper Clause puts those decisions in Congress's hands. Similarly, the Appointments Clause reflects Congress's central role in structuring the executive branch. To construct the executive branch, the President must work his will through the legislative process. The majority rests its decision on the Vesting Clause, which says only that "[t]he executive Power shall be vested in a President." However, the general and open-ended language of the Vesting Clause cannot establish a constitutional violation when Congress has constrained the way the executive power is implemented, since that is exactly the power the Necessary and Proper Clause gives to Congress. Only "a specific historical understanding" can bar Congress from enacting a given constraint, and there is no such historical understanding that broadly prevents Congress from limiting the President's removal power. The Take Care Clause also does not support the majority's position, since that Clause, which says "he shall take Care that the Laws be faithfully executed," can be complied with using a removal provision like the one at issue. The majority's position fares no better when viewed through an accurate historical perspective. The Founders were deeply divided about the President's removal power, and eventually settled on wide latitude for Congress to create spheres of administrative independence. The First Congress also was deeply divided regarding the removal power, and the founding era closed without any agreement that Congress lacked the power to curb the President's removal authority. With time, the number of agencies increased, and the "floodgates opened." In 1887, for example, the growing power of the railroads over the American economy led Congress to

Continued on next page.

create the Interstate Commerce Commission. Under that legislation, the President could remove the five Commissioners only "for inefficiency, neglect of duty, or malfeasance in office"—the same standard Congress applied to the CFPB (P) Director. Many more independent agencies followed as administrative needs became greater and more complex, and many more for-cause removal provisions were enacted; the agencies now are "everywhere." Nowhere do the Court's precedents suggest what the majority announces in its decision: that the President has an "unrestricted removal power" subject to two bounded exceptions. Instead, the majority relies on *Myers v. United States*, 272 U.S. 52 (1926), ignoring the way the Court subsequently cabined that decision and limited it to its specific facts. The majority says *Myers* found an unrestrained removal power "essential to the [President's] execution of the laws." but the majority fails to acknowledge that within a decade the Court unanimously abandoned that view in *Humphrey's Executor v. United States*, 295 U.S. 602 (1935). What *Myers* decided as a matter of stare decisis is that the President could remove a postmaster of the first class without the advice and consent of the Senate, and that Congress cannot reserve to itself the power to remove executive officers. What *Humphrey's* decided was that a statute identical to the one here, providing that the President could remove FTC Commissioners for "inefficiency, neglect of duty, or malfeasance in office," was constitutional. Then, after another three decades, *Morrison* both extended *Humphrey's* domain and clarified the standard for addressing removal issues. The Court in *Morrison v. Olson*, 487 U.S. 654 (1988), over a one-Justice dissent, upheld for-cause protections afforded to an independent counsel with power to investigate and prosecute crimes committed by high-ranking officials. The key question in all the cases, *Morrison* saw, was whether such a restriction would impede the President's ability to perform the President's constitutional duty, and only if it did so would it fall outside Congress's power. Thus, caselaw joins text and history in establishing the general permissibility of for-cause provisions giving some independence to agencies. For almost a century, the Court has made clear that Congress has broad discretion to enact for-cause protections in pursuit of good governance. The CFPB (P) Director exercises the same powers, and receives the same removal protections, as the heads of other, constitutionally permissible independent agencies. Why, then, is the majority treating this case differently? The majority says it is because the CFPB (P) Director is singular, not plural. However, there is no precedential support for this position. There is no support for the proposition that the number of people at the apex of an agency matters to the constitutional issue. Instead, the majority made up this "exception." Neither is there support for the position that novelty is a constitutional test for structuring agencies—the only novelty here is in the majority's opinion. "Congress regulates in that sphere under the Necessary and Proper Clause, not (as the majority seems to think) a Rinse and Repeat Clause." The Framers understood that new times would often require new measures, and exigencies often demand innovation, and, in any event, the CFPB's single-director structure has a fair bit of precedent behind it. If, as the majority says, the problem is that an official will slip away from presidential control and supervision, its distinction between single and multiple agency heads cuts in favor of a single agency head. That is because, contrary to the majority's position, it is more difficult to control and to hold accountable multiple heads of an agency or commission than a single head. It's easier to get one person to do what you want than a gaggle, and, indeed, that is precisely why Congress so often resorts to "hydra-headed" agencies. Because it has no meaningful answer on this score, the majority slides to a different question: Assuming presidential control of any independent agency is vanishingly slim, is a single-head or a multi-head agency more capable of exercising power, and so of endangering liberty? The majority says a single head is the greater threat because a single head may wield power "unilaterally" and "[w]ith no colleagues to persuade." Thus, the CFPB (P) falls victim to what the majority sees as a constitutional anti-power-concentration principle (with an exception for the President). "If you've never heard of a statute being struck down on that ground, you're not alone."

ANALYSIS

Following the Court's decision in this case, the Court in *Collins v. Yellen*, 141 S. Ct. 1761 (2021), invalidated as an unconstitutional violation of separation of powers the structure of the Federal Housing Finance Agency (FHFA), "an independent agency" tasked with regulating Fannie Mae and Freddie Mac, two of the Nation's leading sources of mortgage financing. The FHFA, like the Consumer Financial Protection Bureau (CFPB) (P), was created in response to the financial crisis known as the Great Recession, and, as with the CFPB (P), was an agency led by a single Director, and the President's power to remove the FHFA head was restricted. The Court relied on its decision in *Seila Law*, saying that a straightforward application of *Seila Law's* reasoning dictated the result. The Court rejected distinctions drawn between the FHFA and the CFPB (P) as insufficient to justify a different result. The Court rejected the argument that Congress should have greater leeway to restrict the President's power to remove the FHFA Director because the FHFA's authority is more limited than that of the CFPB (P), saying that the nature and breadth of an agency's authority is not dispositive in determining whether Congress may limit the President's power to remove its head. The Court also rejected this distinction

Continued on next page.

on the grounds that Courts are not well-suited to weigh the relative importance of the regulatory and enforcement authority of disparate agencies. The Court likewise rejected the assertion that the FHFA's structure did not violate the separation of powers because the entities it regulated were government-sponsored enterprises that had federal charters, served public objectives, and received special privileges. This argument failed, the Court said, because the President's removal power serves important purposes regardless of whether the agency in question affects ordinary Americans by directly regulating them or by taking actions that have a profound but indirect effect on their lives. Finally, the Court rejected the contention that there was no constitutional problem, because the FHFA's head was given only "modest" tenure protection, saying that the Constitution prohibits even "modest restrictions" on the President's power to remove the head of an agency with a single top officer.

Quicknotes

NECESSARY AND PROPER CLAUSE Article I, § 8 of the U.S. Constitution, enables Congress to make all laws that may be "necessary and proper" to execute its other, enumerated powers.

SEPARATION OF POWERS The division of government into the legislative, executive, and judicial branches, with each branch having specific duties upon with the other branches may not encroach.

Clinton v. City of New York

U.S. President (D) v. City (P)

524 U.S. 417 (1998)

NATURE OF CASE: Challenge to the constitutionality of new Presidential powers.

FACT SUMMARY: The Line Item Veto Act of 1996 (the Act) allowed the President to cancel provisions that have been signed into law. Parties affected by President Clinton's cancellation of a provision of the Balanced Budget Act of 1997 challenged the constitutionality of the Act.

RULE OF LAW

The cancellation provisions authorized by the Line Item Veto Act are not constitutional.

FACTS: President Clinton used his authority under the Line Item Veto Act of 1996 to cancel a provision of the Balanced Budget Act of 1997. This forced New York to repay certain funds to the federal government under the Medicaid program and removed a tax benefit to food processors acquired by farmers' cooperatives. New York City and several private organizations challenged the constitutionality of the Medicaid cancellation, and the Snake River Potato Growers (a farmer's cooperative) challenged the food processors provision. The District Court held the cancellation provisions unconstitutional.

ISSUE: Are the cancellation provisions authorized by the Line Item Veto Act constitutional?

HOLDING AND DECISION: (Stevens, J.) No. The cancellation provisions authorized by the Line Item Veto Act are not constitutional. The Line Item Veto Act gives the President the power to "cancel in whole" three types of provisions that have already been signed into law: (1) any dollar amount of discretionary budget authority; (2) any item of new direct spending; or (3) any limited tax benefit. With respect to each cancellation, the President must determine that it will (i) reduce the federal budget deficit; (ii) not impair any essential government functions; and (iii) not harm the national interest. A cancellation takes effect upon receipt by Congress of the notification of the cancellation. However, a majority vote of both Houses is sufficient to make the cancellation null and void. Although the Constitution expressly authorizes the President to veto a bill under Article I, § 7, it is silent on the subject of unilateral Presidential action that repeals or amends parts of duly enacted statutes as authorized under the Line Item Veto Act. Constitutional silence should be construed as express prohibition. If there is to be a new role for the President in the procedure to determine the final text of a law, such a change must come through the amendment procedures and not by legislation. Affirmed.

CONCURRENCE: (Kennedy, J.) Separation of powers was designed to protect liberty, because the concentration of power in any single branch is a threat to liberty.

CONCURRENCE AND DISSENT: (Scalia, J.) If the Line Item Veto Act authorized the President to "decline to spend" any item of spending rather than "cancelling" it, it would have been constitutional. Given that there is only a technical difference between the two actions and that it is no different from what Congress has permitted the President to do since the formation of the Union, the Line Item Veto does not offend Article I, § 7.

DISSENT: (Breyer, J.) Given how complex our nation has become, Congress cannot divide bills into thousands or tens of thousands of separate appropriations bills, each of which the President would have to veto or sign separately. Therefore, the Line Item Veto may help representative government work better.

ANALYSIS

The majority did not comment on the wisdom of the Line Item Veto Act, because they found this step unnecessary given their finding that the Act was unconstitutional. Justice Kennedy did not let that stop him, since he felt that the Line Item Veto Act affected the separation of powers, which in turn threatened liberty.

Quicknotes

LINE ITEM VETO ACT Authorizes a government official to veto specified items in appropriation bills.

CHAPTER 7

Inspections, Reports, and Subpoenas

Quick Reference Rules of Law

Camara v. Municipal Court

Apartment owner (D) v. Court (P)

387 U.S. 523 (1967)

NATURE OF CASE: Appeal from conviction for not permitting a building inspection.

FACT SUMMARY: Camara (D) refused to let city building inspectors enter his apartment.

RULE OF LAW

Administrative searches are reasonable searches, but still require a warrant.

FACTS: San Francisco building inspectors sought to inspect Camara's (D) apartment pursuant to a general city ordinance. Camara (D) refused to allow the inspectors to enter his apartment without a warrant and was convicted of violating the municipal code. Camara (D) appealed, claiming that the proposed search violated the Fourth Amendment.

ISSUE: Are administrative searches reasonable searches requiring a warrant?

HOLDING AND DECISION: (White, J.) Yes. Administrative searches are reasonable searches, but still require a warrant. The Fourth Amendment was designed to safeguard the privacy and security of individuals against arbitrary invasions by governmental officials. Except in certain cases, a search of private property without proper consent is an unreasonable search, unless a warrant has authorized the search. Probable cause is the standard by which a decision to search is considered reasonable and constitutional. Administrative searches that cover an entire area to enforce community building standards have a long history of acceptance, are necessary to protect the public, and involve a limited invasion of privacy. Thus, an area inspection is reasonable as long as a warrant is issued prior to the inspection. A warrant does not need to consider a specific condition or knowledge about a particular dwelling. Without a warrant, a person is unable to verify the need for, or the appropriate limits of, the inspection. Accordingly, the city building inspectors should have obtained a warrant first, and Camara (D) should not have been charged with a crime for refusing to allow the inspection. Conviction reversed.

ANALYSIS

The Court acknowledged that some administrative searches might be justified by emergency situations. Obviously, this case did not provide that justification, since the inspectors tried on three different occasions to inspect Camara's (D) apartment. Subsequently, the Court made an exception to the warrant requirement for administrative searches of industries that had a long history of close government regulation.

Quicknotes

FOURTH AMENDMENT Provides that persons be secure as to their person and private belongings against unreasonable searches and seizures.

WARRANT An order issued by a court directing an officer to undertake a certain act (e.g., an arrest or search).

Trinity Industries, Inc. v. OSHRC

Manufacturer (D) v. Government agency (P)

16 F.3d 1455 (6th Cir. 1994)

NATURE OF CASE: Appeal from administrative penalties for safety violations.

FACT SUMMARY: Trinity Industries, Inc. (D) complained that the Occupational Safety and Health Administration's (P) inspection was broader than the scope of the complaint that prompted the inspection.

RULE OF LAW

An administrative inspection, based upon specific evidence of a violation, must bear a relation to that violation.

FACTS: Trinity Industries, Inc. (Trinity) (D) manufactures tanks and pressure vessels at its plant in Ohio. In 1988, an employee filed a complaint with the Occupational Safety and Health Administration (OSHA) (P) alleging multiple safety violations at the plant. Trinity (D) refused to permit an inspection, so OSHA (P) obtained an administrative inspection warrant. OSHA (P) ended up reviewing and inspecting Trinity records and sites that exceeded the allegations of the original complaint. Trinity (D) was charged with multiple violations and fined $33,000. Trinity (D) contested some of the citations based on that part of the inspection that went beyond the reach of the complaint, which enabled the warrant to be issued.

ISSUE: Must an administrative inspection, based upon specific evidence of a violation, bear a relation to that violation?

HOLDING AND DECISION: (Martin, J.) Yes. An administrative inspection, based upon specific evidence of a violation, must bear a relation to that violation. Warrants are required for administrative inspections. Probable cause justifying the issuance of a warrant for administrative purposes may be based on either specific evidence of an existing violation or on a showing that a specific business has been chosen for a search on the basis of a general administrative plan derived from neutral sources. Inspections done pursuant to a general administrative plan may properly extend to the entire workplace. However, warrants issued because of specific complaints have an increased danger of abuse of discretion and intrusiveness. Therefore, a complaint inspection must bear an appropriate relationship to the violation alleged in the complaint. In the present case, the Occupational Safety and Health Administration (OSHA) (P) used an employee complaint to trigger a full-scope inspection of Trinity (D) without the required showing of probable cause. However, OSHA (P) was entitled to review all the inspection records of Trinity (D), even if a comprehensive plant inspection was unauthorized.

ANALYSIS

The court noted that the Occupational Safety and Health Administration (OSHA) (P) should have reviewed Trinity Industries' (D) records first. Then, if the review of the injury and illness records led to further suspicions, OSHA (P) could have applied for a second warrant. This second warrant could have included a full and comprehensive inspection of the physical facility.

Quicknotes

COMPLAINT The initial pleading commencing litigation that sets forth a claim for relief.

WARRANT An order issued by a court directing an officer to undertake a certain act (e.g., an arrest or search).

In re Trinity Industries, Inc.

Manufacturers (D) v. Government agency (P)

876 F.2d 1485 (11th Cir. 1989)

NATURE OF CASE: Appeal of order to permit inspection.

FACT SUMMARY: Two industrial manufacturers, Trinity Industries, Inc. (D) and Mosher Steel Co. (D), claimed that warrant applications for Occupational Safety and Health Administration inspections of their plants were defective.

RULE OF LAW

A warrant application for an administrative search is valid if the plan is based on specific, neutral criteria and it adequately establishes that the particular company was selected pursuant to the neutral criteria.

FACTS: Occupational Safety and Health Administration (OSHA) regulations for safety and health inspections establish a ranking system for inspecting companies in high-hazard industries. The agency ranks employers based on lost workday injury rates, and companies that are below average are subject to placement on the inspection list. Companies that recently underwent inspections are taken off the list and higher priority is given to larger companies. Pursuant to this administrative search plan, OSHA obtained warrants for inspecting Trinity Industries, Inc. (Trinity) (D) and Mosher Steel Co. (Mosher) (D), two manufacturers. The companies refused to permit the inspections. Under threat of contempt, Mosher (D) permitted the inspection, but the court was forced to fine Trinity (D), who then appealed the court's order.

ISSUE: Is a warrant application for an administrative search valid if the plan is based on specific, neutral criteria and it adequately establishes that the particular company was selected pursuant to the neutral criteria?

HOLDING AND DECISION: (Cox, J.) Yes. A warrant application for an administrative search is valid if the plan is based on specific, neutral criteria and it adequately establishes that the particular company was selected pursuant to the neutral criteria. To satisfy the Fourth Amendment, a warrant for an administrative search must be obtained prior to the inspection. Probable cause for this warrant can be justified by a general administrative plan for the enforcement of the law as long as the criteria for picking the individuals who will be inspected is neutral. In making this determination, the court must apply a two-priority test: (1) whether the plan pursuant to which the warrant is to be issued is based on neutral criteria; and (2) whether the warrant application clearly and adequately established that the company was selected for inspection pursuant to the neutral criteria. In the present case, the Occupational Safety and Health Administration (OSHA) administrative plan is rational and neutral. It is intended and designed to protect the greatest number of employees who are exposed to the greatest risks. Although the plan may result in more frequent inspections of select portions of all industries, it seems eminently reasonable that OSHA has decided to allocate its resources in this manner. The warrant at issue in the present case contained a detailed description of the procedure used in selecting companies and a sworn affidavit that Trinity Industries, Inc. (D) and Mosher Steel Co. (D) were selected according to the procedure. This was sufficient for the magistrate to issue the warrant. Therefore, the district court was not in error in holding the companies in contempt for failing to allow the inspections. Affirmed.

ANALYSIS

The probable cause standard for an administrative warrant is obviously somewhat less than for a criminal-type search. Still, illegal searches do happen. Agencies and officials can be liable for civil penalties for violating the Fourth Amendment.

Quicknotes

FOURTH AMENDMENT Provides that persons be secure as to their person and private belongings against unreasonable searches and seizures.

PROBABLE CAUSE A reasonable basis for believing that a crime has been committed.

City of Los Angeles v. Patel

Municipality (D) v. Motel operator (P)

576 U.S. 409 (2015)

NATURE OF CASE: Appeal from reversal of judgment upholding the constitutionality of a municipal ordinance requiring administrative searches by lodging operators without providing them an opportunity for precompliance review.

FACT SUMMARY: The City of Los Angeles (D), which required lodging (e.g., motels, hotels) operators (P) to record and keep specific information about their guests on the premises for a 90-day period and to make that information available to any police officer for inspection upon demand—or face criminal penalties for noncompliance—contended that the ordinance was not facially invalid under the Fourth Amendment, notwithstanding that the ordinance did not provide lodging operators (P) with an opportunity for precompliance review by a neutral magistrate, because lodging operators (P) had a diminished expectation of privacy in their records, and because places of public accommodation are "closely regulated," and the ordinance came within the more relaxed standard that applies to searches of this such closely regulated industry.

RULE OF LAW

An ordinance that requires lodging (e.g., motels, hotels) operators to collect, retain, and make available for police inspection specified information about guests—or face criminal penalties for noncompliance—is facially unconstitutional under the Fourth Amendment where the ordinance fails to provide lodging operators with an opportunity for precompliance review by a neutral magistrate.

FACTS: The City of Los Angeles (the City) (D) required hotel operators to record and keep specific information about their guests on the premises for a 90-day period and to make that information available to any police officer for inspection upon demand. A hotel operator's failure to make the records available was a criminal misdemeanor. Motel operators (P) and others in the hotel business brought a facial challenge to the City's (D) ordinance on Fourth Amendment grounds seeking declaratory and injunctive relief. The district court entered judgment for the City (D), finding that the motel operators (P) lacked a reasonable expectation of privacy in their records. The court of appeals subsequently reversed, determining that inspections under the ordinance were Fourth Amendment searches, and that such searches were unreasonable under the Fourth Amendment because hotel owners were subjected to punishment for failure to turn over their records without first being afforded the opportunity for precompliance review. The United States Supreme Court granted certiorari.

ISSUE: Is an ordinance that requires lodging (e.g., motels, hotels) operators to collect, retain, and make available for police inspection specified information about guests—or face criminal penalties for noncompliance—facially unconstitutional under the Fourth Amendment where the ordinance fails to provide lodging operators with an opportunity for precompliance review by a neutral magistrate?

HOLDING AND DECISION: (Sotomayor, J.) Yes. An ordinance that requires lodging (e.g., motels, hotels) operators to collect, retain, and make available for police inspection specified information about guests—or face criminal penalties for noncompliance—is facially unconstitutional under the Fourth Amendment where the ordinance fails to provide lodging operators with an opportunity for precompliance review by a neutral magistrate. Searches conducted outside the judicial process are per se unreasonable under the Fourth Amendment—subject only to a few exceptions. One exception is administrative searches. To be constitutional, the subject of an administrative search must, among other things, be afforded an opportunity to obtain precompliance review before a neutral decisionmaker. Assuming the administrative search exception otherwise applies here, the challenged ordinance is facially invalid because it fails to afford hotel operators any opportunity for precompliance review. To be clear, a hotel owner must only be afforded an opportunity for precompliance review; actual review need occur only when a hotel operator objects to turning over the records. This opportunity can be provided without imposing onerous burdens on law enforcement. For instance, officers in the field can issue administrative subpoenas without probable cause that a regulation is being infringed. This narrow holding does not call into question those parts of the ordinance requiring hotel operators to keep records nor does it prevent police from obtaining access to those records where a hotel operator consents to the search, where the officer has a proper administrative warrant, or where some other exception to the warrant requirement applies. The City of Los Angeles (the City) (D) also maintains that the ordinance is facially valid under the more relaxed standard for closely regulated industries. This assertion is rejected, since over the last 45 years, the Court has only recognized four such industries (liquor sales, firearms dealing, mining, and running an automobile junkyard), and

Continued on next page.

nothing inherent in the operation of hotels poses a comparable clear and significant risk to the public welfare. Additionally, because the majority of regulations applicable to hotels apply to many businesses, to classify hotels as closely regulated would permit what has always been a narrow exception to swallow the rule. But even if hotels were closely regulated, the challenged ordinance would still contravene the Fourth Amendment as it fails to satisfy the additional criteria that must be met for searches of closely regulated industries to be reasonable. Those criteria are: (1) There must be a substantial government interest that informs the regulatory scheme pursuant to which the inspection is made; (2) warrantless inspections must be necessary to further the regulatory scheme; and (3) the statute's inspection program, in terms of the certainty and regularity of its application, must provide a constitutionally adequate substitute for a warrant. Even assuming that the City's (D) interest in ensuring that hotels maintain accurate and complete registries might fulfill the first of these requirements, the ordinance fails the second and third prongs of this test. The City (D) claims that affording hotel operators (P) any opportunity for precompliance review would fatally undermine the scheme's efficacy by giving them a chance to falsify their records. However, the Court has previously rejected this exact argument, which could be made regarding any recordkeeping requirement. Also, the ordinance is constitutionally deficient under the "certainty and regularity" prong of the closely regulated industries test because it fails sufficiently to constrain police officers' discretion as to which hotels to search and under what circumstances. Although the Court has upheld inspection schemes of closely regulated industries that called for searches at least four times a year, or on a "regular basis," the challenged ordinance imposes no comparable standard. Affirmed.

DISSENT: (Scalia, J.) In determining whether a business is closely regulated, this Court has looked to factors including the duration of the regulatory tradition; the comprehensiveness of the regulatory regime; and the imposition of similar regulations by other jurisdictions. At the time of the founding, searches—indeed, warrantless searches—of inns and similar places of public accommodation were commonplace. Government regulation of lodging operations has continued since then, and is longstanding and comprehensive. This is likewise true of the City of Los Angeles' (the City's) (D) lodging regulations. Since the Court concluded that warrantless searches of closely regulated businesses are reasonable, the Court has identified only one industry as not closely regulated, and the lower courts have identified many more businesses as closely regulated under the Court's test. The reason closely regulated industries may be searched without a warrant has nothing to do with the risk of harm they pose; rather, it has to do with the expectations of those who enter such a line of work. Further, the ordinance satisfies the three prongs of the test for searches of closely regulated industries to be reasonable: It furthers a substantial governmental interest, it is necessary to achieving that interest, and it provides an adequate substitute for a search warrant. First, the recordkeeping requirement operates by deterring crime by reducing criminals' use of public places of accommodation, since criminals who seek anonymity will, arguably, not want to produce their true identification to lodging operators. If searches were not warrantless, lodging operators who conspire with drug dealers and procurers could demand precompliance judicial review simply as a pretext to buy time for making fraudulent entries in their guest registers. The majority's suggestion that the police obtain either an administrative or an ex parte warrant is not workable since it is quite plausible that the costs of obtaining such warrants would be prohibitive for a police force in one of America's largest cities, juggling numerous law-enforcement priorities, and confronting more than 2,000 places of public accommodation within its jurisdiction. Moreover, the fact that obtaining a warrant might be costly will not by itself render a warrantless search reasonable under the Fourth Amendment. In any event, in the context of an administrative-search regime governing closely regulated businesses, such as motels and hotels, the administrative search need only be reasonable. Finally, the City's (D) ordinance provides an adequate substitute for a warrant. The purpose of a warrant is to advise the owner of the scope and objects of the search, beyond which limits the inspector is not expected to proceed, and thus to limit an inspector's unbridled discretion. Here, the ordinance limits warrantless police searches to the pages of a guest register in a public part of a motel, thus circumscribing police discretion in exacting terms.

ANALYSIS

One of the significant aspects of this decision is that it tightens the administrative exception to the warrant requirement for administrative searches. In so doing, the Court implicitly emphasized the importance of the Fourth Amendment in curtailing questionable government searches, whether conducted by the police or administrative agents. The Court explained that the subjects of administrative searches must be afforded an opportunity to obtain precompliance review before a neutral decisionmaker because such review alters the dynamic between police and lodging operators by reducing the "intolerable risk" that searches "will exceed statutory limits, or be used as a pretext to harass hotel operators and their guests." The majority also clarified, however, that there need only be an opportunity for precompliance review, and that, in its view, such opportunity would impose only de minimis burdens on

Continued on next page.

law enforcement. First, actual judicial review is required only in those cases when the subject of a search objects. Second, in the event that an officer reasonably suspects that a hotel operator may tamper with the registry while the precompliance review is pending, the officer can guard the registry until the required hearing can occur. The decision also strengthened the protections afforded to businesses under the administrative search doctrine by limiting the "closely regulated business" exception to "inherently dangerous" industries. The decision thus serves to provide businesses that are not inherently dangerous with a greater shield from police harassment and unreasonable searches.

Board of Education of Independent School District No. 92 of Pottawatomie County v. Earls

Public school district (D) v. Student (P)

536 U.S. 822 (2002)

NATURE OF CASE: Suit by students to invalidate public school district's drug-testing policy.

FACT SUMMARY: A public school district required all students who wanted to participate in any extracurricular activity to first pass a drug test and to consent to future drug tests.

RULE OF LAW

A public school's drug-testing policy for students is reasonable, as required by the Fourth Amendment, if the policy requires no individualized suspicion and is mandatory for participation in all extracurricular activities.

FACTS: The School District (the District) (D) implemented a drug-testing policy that conditioned student participation in any school-sponsored extracurricular activity upon a student's consent to drug testing. Despite this breadth in the policy, the District (D) applied the policy to competitive extracurricular activities, most of which were non-athletic activities. Specifically, the policy required students to consent to a drug test before they participated in an extracurricular activity, to consent to random testing while they participated in their activity, and to consent to random testing whenever reasonable suspicion justified a test. The tests revealed the presence of only illegal drugs and did not confirm the presence of any medical conditions or authorized medications. A student in the District (D), Lindsay Earls (P), participated in show choir, marching band, the Academic Team, and the National Honor Society. Another student in the District (D), Daniel James (P), wanted to participate in the Academic Team. The two students (P) sued the District (D) to invalidate the policy, and the trial court entered judgment for the District (D). The court of appeals reversed, and the District (D) petitioned the United States Supreme Court for further review.

ISSUE: Is a public school's drug-testing policy for students reasonable, as required by the Fourth Amendment, if the policy requires no individualized suspicion and is mandatory for participation in all extracurricular activities?

HOLDING AND DECISION: (Thomas, J.) Yes. A public school's drug-testing policy for students is reasonable, as required by the Fourth Amendment, if the policy requires no individualized suspicion and is mandatory for participation in all extracurricular activities. As the students (P) correctly agree, probable cause is not required for the tests here because these tests are not part of a criminal investigation. Contrary to the students' (P) position, however, not even individualized suspicion is required in the administrative context when "special needs," such as those inherent in the school setting, justify the search. The Court's upholding of suspicionless drug tests for high school athletes in *Vernonia School District 47J v. Acton*, 515 U.S. 646 (1995), requires the same result on the slightly different facts presented here. Even students engaged in extracurricular activities who are not athletes have only a limited expectation of privacy, considering the requisite travel for non-athletic activities and students' consent to various other rules and regulations. Further, compared to the policy in *Vernonia*, this policy's requirement that a faculty monitor wait outside a closed bathroom stall for a student's urine sample imposes a less-than-negligible intrusion upon students' privacy. The policy itself also requires that test results remain confidential, that they not be divulged to law-enforcement officials, and that they not be used for disciplinary action. Finally, the School District (the District) (D) faces immediate risks to students' health and safety because of the nationwide drug epidemic, and these risks have specifically appeared in the District (D). The policy at issue in this case, therefore, was entirely reasonable. The challenging students' (P) argument for requiring a "surpassing" safety risk is misplaced because drugs jeopardize the health and safety of all students. Similarly misplaced is the students' (P) argument for a presumption favoring individualized suspicion in such circumstances; the Fourth Amendment does not require government actors to use the least-intrusive methods. Reversed.

CONCURRENCE: (Breyer, J.) This policy discourages drug use by removing peer pressure; students can offer their peers a specific reason to decline to use drugs. Moreover, conscientious objectors still have an option, too—short of being expelled from school—though they must forego the privilege of participating in extracurricular activities if they exercise that option. Furthermore, in the school context, requiring individualized suspicion would only cause more problems than it solved because such a requirement would invite targeting students for improper reasons. The policy satisfies the Fourth Amendment.

Continued on next page.

DISSENT: (Ginsburg, J.) This policy is not only not reasonable; it is capricious and perverse, largely because the students targeted by this policy are the least likely to be at risk of using illegal drugs. *Vernonia School District 47J v. Acton*, 515 U.S. 646 (1995), does not control here: the communal undress required for the activity there, as well as the risk of physical injury there, dispositively distinguish *Vernonia* from this case. The school district in *Vernonia* faced a genuinely dangerous situation. The nature and immediacy of the School District's (the District's) (D) concern here, however, are lacking: the District (D) in this case has repeatedly reported to the federal government that drugs were not a major problem in the period leading up to the policy's adoption. This case is thus more like *Chandler v. Miller*, 520 U.S. 305 (1997), in which a suspicionless drug test was held to violate the Fourth Amendment. In this case, too, as in *Chandler*, the government's sole genuine benefit from using the policy is the image of itself that it wants to project. The District's (D) policy does not promote the "special needs" that exist in our schools.

ANALYSIS

In *Earls*, the majority's focus on the "special needs" present in schools effectively determined the outcome in the case. Justice Ginsburg, in dissent, concluded that the record evidence did not justify allowing the "special needs" rationale to trump what she saw as several other mitigating considerations, such as School District's (the District's) (D) repeatedly informing the federal government that drugs were not a problem in the District's (D) schools. Justice Thomas and the rest of the majority, however, placed special emphasis on the District's (D) "custodial and tutelary responsibility for children" and held for the school.

Quicknotes

FOURTH AMENDMENT Provides that persons be secure as to their person and private belongings against unreasonable searches and seizures.

Safford Unified School District #1 v. Redding

Public school district (D) v. Student (P)

557 U.S. 364 (2009)

NATURE OF CASE: Appeal of determination that student's Fourth Amendment rights were violated and that school district officials were not entitled to qualified immunity from liability.

FACT SUMMARY: School district officials (D) conducted a strip search of a 13-year-old female student (P) in an effort to uncover prohibited prescription and over-the-counter medications.

RULE OF LAW

Officials are protected from liability for a constitutional violation through qualified immunity when the basis for the constitutional right is insufficiently established.

FACTS: School district officials (D), acting on reasonable suspicion that middle school student Savana Redding (Savana) (P) was involved in the prohibited distribution of prescription-strength Ibuprofen and over-the-counter pain relievers at school, conducted a strip search of Savana (P). Two female employees of the school district (D) directed Savana (P) to remove her clothes to her underwear and required Savana (P) to pull her underpants and bra away from her body. The employees (P) viewed Savana's (P) exposed breasts and pelvic area but found nothing hidden on her person. Significantly, school district officials (D) understood prior to the search of Savana (P) that the contraband involved was of limited threat and quantity. Furthermore, the record reflects both that school district officials (D) had no reason to believe that Savana (P) was hiding the underlying medications in her underwear and that the preceding strip search of another female student suspected of receiving pills from Savana (P) yielded no contraband. It was never determined, in fact, at what time—whether the day of the strip search or in days prior—Savana (P) had distributed the prohibited pills.

ISSUE: Are officials protected from liability for a constitutional violation through qualified immunity when the basis for the constitutional right is insufficiently established?

HOLDING AND DECISION: (Souter, J.) Yes. Officials are protected from liability for a constitutional violation through qualified immunity when the basis for the constitutional right is insufficiently established. Here, the Fourth Amendment rights of a 13-year-old female student were violated when said student was subjected to a strip search on the basis of school district officials' reasonable suspicions that she possessed and had distributed forbidden prescription and over-the-counter drugs at school. The school district officials involved in the search, however, were protected from liability through qualified immunity because this Court insufficiently established her right to be free from this type of search. Pursuant to the Court's holding in *New Jersey v. T.L.O.*, 469 U.S. 325 (1985), in a school setting, searches by school officials require a modification of the level of suspicion of illicit activity needed to justify a search. As such, and in lieu of requiring probable cause to search, school officials need only have a reasonable suspicion of illegality to justify a search of a student. Nonetheless, a search of a student by school officials must be reasonably related to the objectives of the search and not excessively intrusive considering the age and sex of the student and the nature of the infraction. In light of the instant school district's (D) strict policy prohibiting the nonmedical use and possession of prescription or over-the-counter drugs, and on the strength of the suspicion that Savana Redding (Savana) (P) was involved in prohibited pill distribution, it is manifest that the school district (D) would be justified in searching Savana's (P) backpack and outer clothing. The record demonstrates, however, that the content of the suspicion of school district officials (D) did not support a strip search of a 13-year-old female student. There was simply no indication that Savana (P) possessed the kind or quantity of drug that would endanger other students, or that she concealed them in her underwear. Notwithstanding the Fourth Amendment violation at issue, school district officials (D) were entitled to qualified immunity in the execution of their professional judgment. Particularly because the lower courts have reached divergent conclusions regarding the application of the *T.L.O.* standard to student searches, it is doubtful that this Court was sufficiently clear in its articulation of the *T.L.O.* standard to withhold immunity here. Thus, school district officials (D), motivated here to eliminate drugs from the school and protect students from harm, are entitled to qualified immunity. The judgment of the Ninth Circuit Court of Appeals is affirmed in part and reversed in part.

CONCURRENCE AND DISSENT: (Stevens, J.) Because the law is clearly established, and because the conduct of the school official who authorized the

Continued on next page.

underlying search was clearly outrageous, qualified immunity is not justified.

CONCURRENCE AND DISSENT: (Ginsburg, J.) Upon the Fourth Amendment violation at issue here, qualified immunity is not justified.

CONCURRENCE AND DISSENT: (Thomas, J.) Courts should not be able to second-guess the measures school district officials take to ensure the health and safety of their students. As such, and because the search of Savana Redding (P) did not violate the Fourth Amendment, it was proper to extend immunity to school district officials.

ANALYSIS

While the Court in *Redding* cleared the actors of liability, it remanded the case on the issue of the whether immunity extended to the School District itself, as a government entity. In support of its remand, the Court cited *Monell v. New York City Department of Social Services*, 436 U.S. 658, 694 (1978), which held that a local government cannot be sued for injury inflicted solely by an employee, but only if the employee acted in execution of the government's policy. See also, 42 U.S.C. § 1983. Accordingly, it may be that the *Redding* Court opened the door for redress of the student's Fourth Amendment violations.

Quicknotes

FOURTH AMENDMENT Provides that persons be secure as to their person and private belongings against unreasonable searches and seizures.

IMMUNITY Exemption from a legal obligation.

QUALIFIED IMMUNITY An affirmative defense relieving officials from civil liability for the performance of activities within their discretion so long as such conduct is not in violation of an individual's rights pursuant to law as determined by a reasonable person standard.

REASONABLE EXPECTATION OF PRIVACY In order to invoke the Fourth Amendment's protection against unreasonable searches and seizures, an individual must have a reasonable expectation of privacy in respect to the location searched or thing seized.

United States v. Flores-Montano

Federal government (P) v. Indicted drug smuggler (D)

541 U.S. 149 (2004)

NATURE OF CASE: Appeal from affirmance of grant of motion to suppress in federal criminal prosecution for drug smuggling.

FACT SUMMARY: Flores-Montano (D) contended that reasonable suspicion was needed to justify the removal, disassembly, and search of his vehicle's gas tank that were conducted upon his entry into the country at its border, and, accordingly, he moved to suppress the 37 kilograms of marijuana that were seized from the gas tank.

RULE OF LAW

The government's authority to conduct suspicionless inspections at the border includes the authority to remove, disassemble, and reassemble a vehicle's fuel tank in the absence of reasonable suspicion.

FACTS: When Flores-Montano (D) and his vehicle entered the country at the international border, customs officials seized 37 kilograms of marijuana from the vehicle's gas tank by removing and disassembling the tank, which subsequently was reassembled. After Flores-Montano (D) was indicted on federal drug smuggling charges, he moved to suppress the drugs recovered from the gas tank on the grounds that the Fourth Amendment required reasonable suspicion for the search. The District Court granted the motion to suppress, and the Ninth Circuit Court of Appeals affirmed. The United States Supreme Court granted certiorari.

ISSUE: Does the government's authority to conduct suspicionless inspections at the border include the authority to remove, disassemble, and reassemble a vehicle's fuel tank in the absence of reasonable suspicion?

HOLDING AND DECISION: (Rehnquist, C.J.) Yes. The government's authority to conduct suspicionless inspections at the border includes the authority to remove, disassemble, and reassemble a vehicle's fuel tank in the absence of reasonable suspicion. Complex balancing tests to determine what is a "routine" vehicle search, as opposed to a more "intrusive" search of a person, have no place in border searches of vehicles. The Government's (P) interest in preventing the entry of unwanted persons and effects is at its zenith at the international border. Congress has always granted the executive branch plenary authority to conduct routine searches and seizures at the border, without probable cause or a warrant, in order to regulate the collection of duties and to prevent the introduction of contraband into this country. Flores-Montano's (D) assertion that he has a privacy interest in his fuel tank and that the suspicionless disassembly of his tank is an invasion of his privacy is rejected, as the privacy expectation is less at the border than it is in the interior, and the Court has long recognized that automobiles seeking entry into this country may be searched. Although the Fourth Amendment protects property as well as privacy, the interference with a motorist's possessory interest in the motorist's gas tank is justified by the Government's (P) paramount interest in protecting the border. Thus, the Government's (P) authority to conduct suspicionless inspections at the border includes the authority to remove, disassemble, and reassemble a vehicle's fuel tank. Reversed and remanded.

CONCURRENCE: (Breyer, J.) Customs keeps track of the border searches its agents conduct, including the reasons for the searches; this administrative process should help minimize concerns that gas tank searches might be undertaken in an abusive manner.

ANALYSIS

In support of its point that it is axiomatic that the United States, as sovereign, has the inherent authority to protect, and a paramount interest in protecting, its territorial integrity, the Court noted that the statute that authorized the search in this case, 19 U.S.C. § 1581(a), derived from a statute passed by the First Congress in 1790. Thus, the Government's (P) power and interest in conducting suspicionless searches at the nation's international borders has an impressive historical pedigree.

Quicknotes

PRIVACY RIGHT Those personal liberties or relationships that are protected against unwarranted governmental interference.

United States v. Ickes

Federal government (P) v. Convicted child pornography transporter (D)

393 F.3d 501 (4th Cir. 2005)

NATURE OF CASE: Appeal of denial of motion to suppress evidence in a criminal proceeding.

FACT SUMMARY: John Ickes (D) arrived at the United States–Canada border transporting marijuana seeds and pipes and child pornography. While he was in custody but prior to interrogation, border agents searched his van and confiscated his computer and disks. The computer and disks contained more child pornography. Ickes (D) was charged with transporting child pornography and moved to suppress the warrantless search of his computer and disks.

RULE OF LAW

The border search doctrine is not subject to a First Amendment exception.

FACTS: John Ickes (D) drove to the United States–Canadian border near Detroit, Michigan. His packed van aroused suspicion and the U.S. Customs Inspector referred Ickes (D) to a second inspector for a routine inspection of Ickes's (D) van. The second inspector found a video camera with a taped tennis match that focused excessively on a young ball boy. Agents then found marijuana seeds, marijuana pipes, a copy of a Virginia warrant for Ickes's (D) arrest, and several photo albums containing photographs of young nude or semi-nude boys. The agents placed Ickes (D) under arrest and detained him. The agents conducted a more thorough search of Ickes's (D) van and confiscated his computer and 75 disks. The disks later revealed child pornography. Ickes (D) was charged with transportation of child pornography. Ickes (D) filed a motion to suppress the warrantless search of his computer and disks. The district court denied the motion and later found Ickes (D) guilty. Ickes (D) appealed his conviction based on the denial of his suppression motion.

ISSUE: Is the border search doctrine subject to a First Amendment exception?

HOLDING AND DECISION: (Wilkinson, J.) No. The border search doctrine is not subject to a First Amendment exception. It is long-standing doctrine that border searches without probable cause or warrant are reasonable based on the United States' inherent authority to protect its territorial integrity. The potential entrant has less expectation of privacy when the port of entry is not his home while the government has a great interest at the border. Ickes (D) seeks a First Amendment exception to the broad border search doctrine based on "expressive" content. Permitting such an exception would undermine the very purpose of broad border searches because anything could be determined "expressive," including terrorist communications. Ickes's (D) argument that every computer of every traveler could be searched by customs agents is far-fetched. The agents search only when circumstances dictate further examination is necessary. Agents had already discovered Ickes's (D) marijuana paraphernalia, photographs, and outstanding warrant when they searched the contents of his computer. The United States Supreme Court has already been reluctant to extend a First Amendment exception for expressive materials in warrant applications, so it is unlikely to do so here. Affirmed.

ANALYSIS

United States Customs officials do not have unfettered authority, but the authorization to search and seize at borders is quite broad compared with usual restrictions under the First and Fourth Amendments. In 2008, the Ninth Circuit joined the Fourth Circuit in holding a cursory border search of a laptop does not require reasonable suspicion. Travelers entering the United States have very limited privacy expectations.

Quicknotes

EXPECTATION OF PRIVACY Requirement that in order to invoke the Fourth Amendment's protection against unreasonable searches and seizures, the individual must have a reasonable expectation of privacy in respect to the location searched or thing seized.

United States v. Cotterman

Federal government (P) v. Convicted child pornographer (D)

709 F.3d 952 (9th Cir. 2012) (en banc)

NATURE OF CASE: Appeal from reversal of grant of motion to suppress evidence in a criminal prosecution.

FACT SUMMARY: Howard Cotterman (D) was a known child molester and suspected of participating in child sex trafficking. He and his wife returned to the United States from Mexico and were searched at the border. His computer revealed password-protected files, which were later opened during a warrantless forensic examination of the computer long after Cotterman (D) and his wife re-entered the United States.

RULE OF LAW

Forensic examination of an entrant's electronic data during a border search requires reasonable suspicion.

FACTS: Cotterman (D) and his wife approached the Lukeville, Arizona, border entry from Mexico. In a primary inspection by a border agent, the Treasury Enforcement Communication System (TECS) returned a hit for Cotterman (D) as a convicted sex offender and child molester suspected of involvement in child sex tourism. Cotterman (D) and his wife were referred to a secondary investigator who followed up on the TECS hit and confiscated Cotterman's (D) laptop computers and digital cameras. The investigator found several password-protected files. Additional follow-up revealed the TECS alert was part of Operation Angel Watch, which aimed to combat child sex tourism. Customs agents permitted Cotterman (D) and his wife to leave the border crossing but detained the laptops for forensic examination. Cotterman (D) offered to assist with access, but the agents declined out of fear Cotterman (D) would delete files. The laptops and cameras were delivered 170 miles from Lukeville to the Tucson, Arizona, office of the Immigration and Customs Enforcement (ICE). An ICE agent forensically examined the laptops and found dozens of images of child pornography. Over the next couple of days, the agent discovered hundreds of images of a girl aged 7–10 over a 2–3 year period; Cotterman (D) was molesting her in many of the images. The agent uncovered hundreds more photographs, videos, and images depicting child pornography. A grand jury indicted Cotterman (D) on many charges related to child pornography. Cotterman (D) moved to suppress the evidence from the laptops and the fruits of that evidence. The district court granted the motion; a divided panel of the Court of Appeals reversed. The full Court of Appeals requested additional briefing on the reasonableness of the border search.

ISSUE: Does forensic examination of an entrant's electronic data during a border search require reasonable suspicion?

HOLDING AND DECISION: (McKeown, J.) Yes. Forensic examination of an entrant's electronic data during a border search requires reasonable suspicion. A traveler has a diminished expectation of privacy at the border because of the country's right to protect itself from those entering and bringing property over the border. This diminished privacy expectation is balanced against Fourth Amendment reasonableness requirements concerning the scope and nature of the search. This case illustrates the unique aspect of electronic data because it can contain the most intimate details of a person's life almost like a personal diary. The Founders had a deep concern with safeguarding citizens' private thoughts from invasion by the government. That does not mean all electronic information is free from border searches. The issue is reasonableness of the search based on the item being searched. An exhaustive forensic search of an electronic device is more intrusive than a cursory inspection of a gas tank. Suspicionless searches are permitted, but more forensic searches require reasonable suspicion. Travelers can anticipate border searches but do not necessarily expect to be deprived of property for days while agents mine every last piece of data from that property. Here, reasonable suspicion existed. The agents knew of the alert about Cotterman (D), found password-protected files on his electronic devices, and Cotterman (D) was returning from a country known to be associated with child sex tourism. The reasonable suspicion justified the more intrusive search. Reversed.

DISSENT: (Smith, J.) This is the first time federal courts have not upheld suspicionless border searches of electronic devices.

CONCURRENCE AND DISSENT: (Callahan, J.) It is the government's right and duty to exclude offensive, threatening, or otherwise unwanted people and things from entering the country. Just because electronic devices can store large amounts of private information does not make a forensic search "particularly offensive." The United States Supreme Court has only once required reasonable suspicion in the 125 years it has reviewed border searches.

Continued on next page.

ANALYSIS

In 2014, the United States Supreme Court denied Cotterman's (D) writ for certiorari review and his petition for reconsideration of the denial. This case stands as one of the only limitations to the Fourth Amendment exception for border searches.

Freese v. Federal Deposit Insurance Corp.

Former bank officer (P) v. Government agency (D)

837 F. Supp. 22 (D.N.H. 1993)

NATURE OF CASE: Motion to quash subpoena seeking personal financial records.

FACT SUMMARY: The Federal Deposit Insurance Corporation (D) sought to examine the personal records of former bank officers (P) to see if they had any potential claims against them.

RULE OF LAW

Government agencies may not use their subpoena powers for improper purposes.

FACTS: In 1991, the Federal Deposit Insurance Corporation (FDIC) (D) was appointed receiver and liquidating agent for the New Hampshire Savings Bank. The following year, the FDIC (D) wanted to investigate whether there were any valid claims against the former officers (P) of the bank. In connection with this investigation, the FDIC (D) issued administrative subpoenas to the officers and directors seeking extensive personal financial information for the previous five years. Among the purposes for seeking the information claimed by the FDIC (D) were to see if there was enough money to satisfy any potential claims and to determine whether a suit would be cost effective. The officers (P) claimed that the subpoenas were issued in violation of the Fourth Amendment and challenged their legality.

ISSUE: May government agencies use their subpoena powers for improper purposes?

HOLDING AND DECISION: (Loughlin, Sr. J.) No. Government agencies may not use their subpoena powers for improper purposes. Agency subpoenas are enforceable if for a proper purpose and adequately determined in the subpoena, the information sought is relevant to that purpose, and the statutory procedures have been followed. A determination of whether a civil suit is cost effective against a potential defendant is not a proper purpose to issue a subpoena. It is impermissible to peruse a person's financial records to check their ability to satisfy a judgment. The potential liability of a person, however, could form the basis of a valid subpoena. However, in the present case, the Federal Deposit Insurance Corporation (FDIC) (D) has not asserted any suspicion of wrongdoing on the part of the former officers (P). With no basis for potential liability, the FDIC (D) merely wants to go on a fishing expedition in the hope that some wrongdoing will surface. This is a violation of fundamental constitutional rights.

ANALYSIS

The decision fell short of requiring that the agency make a showing of probable cause before a subpoena can be issued. However, the court came down hard on the Federal Deposit Insurance Corporation (FDIC) (D) in this case. They acknowledged that the records in question were sealed and never given to the agency but noted the former officers (P) had nonetheless been forced to incur legal expenses and anxiety.

Adams v. Federal Trade Commission

Dairy company (D) v. Government agency (P)

296 F.2d 861 (8th Cir. 1961)

NATURE OF CASE: Appeal of decision to deny enforcement of administrative subpoenas.

FACT SUMMARY: The Federal Trade Commission (P) issued a series of subpoenas covering an extensive amount of information pursuant to an investigation into whether Adams (D) had engaged in fixing prices.

RULE OF LAW

Subpoenas are not too broad as long as the information sought is reasonably relevant.

FACTS: The Federal Trade Commission (FTC) (P) issued a complaint against Adams Dairy Company (D) alleging that the company was involved in a conspiracy to fix prices. A hearing examiner issued several administrative subpoenas for various documents of Adams (D). Among those documents sought were product sales records from 1940 to 1959, the names of all companies that Adams did business with since its incorporation and all writings to these companies, and all types of corporate records. The FTC (P) was forced to seek judicial enforcement when Adams (D) refused to comply. The district court decided to deny enforcement of many of the aspects of the subpoenas based on the fact they were too broad in scope. The FTC (P) appealed.

ISSUE: Can subpoenas be too broad if the information sought is reasonably relevant?

HOLDING AND DECISION: (Matthes, J.) No. Subpoenas are not too broad as long as the information sought is reasonably relevant. The critical issue in the validity of an administrative subpoena is the relevance of the requested information to the charges and allegations that the agency is making. In the present case, the Federal Trade Commission (FTC) (P) is alleging a sweeping conspiracy involving many companies over a long period of time. Accordingly, the agency has wide latitude in seeking documents that pertain to the alleged conspiracy. Therefore, the district court's denial of enforcement of many of the subpoenas on the ground they were too burdensome and broad is overruled. Where the district court found that the documents sought were not relevant because they dated back past 1954, denial in part of the scope of those administrative subpoenas was appropriate. Reversed in part, affirmed in part.

ANALYSIS

The court had to look at each of the subpoena specifications individually to determine their relevance. This decision does indicate that claims of burden will not go far in quashing administrative subpoenas. This decision might also lead agencies to expand the scope of their allegations so that they have access to a fuller document record.

Quicknotes

CONSPIRACY Concerted action by two or more persons to accomplish some unlawful purpose.

Braswell v. United States

Business proprietor (D) v. Federal government (P)

487 U.S. 99 (1988)

NATURE OF CASE: Appeal from denial of motion to quash.

FACT SUMMARY: Braswell (D) contended he was not bound, as the custodian of corporate records, to comply with a subpoena for such records because the act of production would incriminate him in violation of his Fifth Amendment rights.

RULE OF LAW
The custodian of corporate records cannot resist a subpoena on the grounds such production would violate his or her Fifth Amendment rights against self-incrimination.

FACTS: Braswell (D) conducted business as a sole proprietor. He subsequently incorporated the business by forming two separate corporations. He, as president of each, was served with a subpoena by a federal grand jury ordering him to produce company records. He moved to quash the subpoena on the grounds the act of production constituted testimony that could be used against him. Thus, he argued, the subpoena violated his right against self-incrimination. The district court refused to quash the subpoena. The Fifth Circuit Court of Appeals affirmed, and the United States Supreme Court granted review.

ISSUE: Can the custodian of corporate records avoid a subpoena for such records on the grounds production would constitute self-incrimination?

HOLDING AND DECISION: (Rehnquist, C.J.) No. The custodian of corporate records cannot resist a subpoena on the grounds production of the records would constitute self-incrimination. Corporations are treated differently under the self-incrimination analysis. The collective entity rule, which applies to corporate defendants, dictates that custodians of corporate records hold them in a representative capacity, not a personal capacity. Thus, production is a fulfillment of corporate duties and is not a personal testimonial act. Thus, no Fifth Amendment violation would occur when compelling a corporate act. Affirmed.

ANALYSIS

The Court recognized that a different result in this case would simply hinder any prosecution of "white collar crime." All an individual would have to do to avoid turning over incriminating documents would be to make sure they were created in a corporate capacity. If in this case the business had remained a sole proprietorship, the subpoena might have been quashed because the custodian would hold the documents in a personal capacity.

Quicknotes

FIFTH AMENDMENT Provides that no person shall be compelled to serve as a witness against him- or herself, be subject to trial for the same offense twice, or be deprived of life, liberty, or property without due process of law.

Smith v. Richert

Alleged tax delinquent (D) v. Indiana Department of Revenue (P)

35 F.3d 300 (7th Cir. 1994)

NATURE OF CASE: Appeal from conviction for failing to permit an examination of records.

FACT SUMMARY: Smith (D) did not file income tax returns and refused to comply with a subpoena commanding production of income records.

RULE OF LAW

The required records doctrine with respect to self-incrimination does not apply to general records needed to determine tax liability.

FACTS: Smith (D) did not file Indiana tax returns for several years and the state's Department of Revenue (P) served him with a subpoena demanding the production of records necessary to determine his tax liability. An Indiana statute provided that any person subject to tax was required to keep records for purposes of determining their taxes. Smith (D) refused to comply with the subpoena on the ground it violated his right against self-incrimination. He was convicted for failing to permit the examination of records required by the state. The conviction was affirmed. The court ruled that the records sought by the subpoena were required records and, thus, not self-incriminating. Smith (D) appealed.

ISSUE: Does the required records doctrine with respect to self-incrimination apply to general records needed to determine tax liability?

HOLDING AND DECISION: (Posner, C.J.) No. The required records doctrine with respect to self-incrimination does not apply to general records needed to determine tax liability. The Fifth Amendment protects the rights of individuals not to testify against themselves. The required records doctrine developed as an exception in the cases where a document was required to be kept as part of a regulated industry. Its only applicability now is when the act of production itself is testimonial and would be protected by the Fifth Amendment. In such instances, a person cannot resist the subpoena because compliance shows only acknowledgment that the regulatory program applies. However, this required records doctrine should only be used where an industry is closely regulated by the government. A statute that requires taxpayers to maintain general records is far too broad; taxpayers do not voluntarily enter into any implicit agreement to maintain documents for the government. Furthermore, production by Smith (D) of certain tax forms in this case would be testimonial and incriminating in that it would foreclose a defense that he omitted income because he had no record of it. Therefore, the district court should not have affirmed the conviction on the basis that the documents sought by the subpoena were required records. Reversed and remanded.

ANALYSIS

The court pointed out that Indiana (P) could have agreed not to disclose at a prosecuting trial for willful nonpayment of taxes that Smith (D) had provided the documents that established his tax liability. This immunity-like use of the information would have protected Smith's (D) Fifth Amendment rights while still allowing the subpoena to go forward. The required records doctrine hasn't been used much since 1984, when the United States Supreme Court ruled that the compelled surrender of a self-incriminating document was not barred by the Fifth Amendment.

Quicknotes

FIFTH AMENDMENT Provides that no person shall be compelled to serve as a witness against him- or herself, be subject to trial for the same offense twice, or be deprived of life, liberty, or property without due process of law.

Securities and Exchange Commission v. Dresser Industries, Inc.

Federal agency (P) v. Corporation (D)

628 F.2d 1368 (D.C. Cir. 1980)

NATURE OF CASE: Appeal from decision to enforce subpoena.

FACT SUMMARY: Dresser (D) claimed that a Securities and Exchange Commission (P) subpoena should not be enforced because of a parallel criminal investigation into the same facts.

RULE OF LAW

In the absence of substantial prejudice to the rights of the parties involved, parallel civil and criminal proceedings are unobjectionable.

FACTS: In face of allegations that some U.S. companies had used corporate funds to bribe foreign officials, the Securities and Exchange Commission (SEC) (P) investigated whether Dresser (D) had falsified its financial records to hide such payments. The Department of Justice was also conducting investigation into possible criminal violations arising from illegal foreign payments. Both the SEC (P) and a grand jury issued subpoenas seeking information from Dresser (D). Dresser (D) appealed the district court's decision to enforce the SEC (P) subpoena.

ISSUE: In the absence of substantial prejudice to the rights of the parties involved, are parallel civil and criminal proceedings unobjectionable?

HOLDING AND DECISION: (Wright, C.J.) Yes. In the absence of substantial prejudice to the rights of the parties involved, parallel civil and criminal proceedings are unobjectionable. Only where the nature of the proceedings demonstrably prejudices substantial rights of the investigated party or of the government, may parallel investigations be blocked. Here, no indictment has been returned, no Fifth Amendment privilege has been threatened, and the Securities and Exchange Commission (SEC) (P) subpoena does not require Dresser (D) to reveal the basis for its defense. The SEC (P) and Justice should be able to investigate possible violations simultaneously. Affirmed.

ANALYSIS

Federal civil and regulatory laws frequently overlap with criminal laws. A stay of civil proceedings pending the outcome of the criminal charges is not usually required. Only where bad faith or malicious prosecution may exist, is such a stay mandatory.

Quicknotes

FIFTH AMENDMENT Provides that no person shall be compelled to serve as a witness against him- or herself, be subject to trial for the same offense twice, or be deprived of life, liberty, or property without due process of law.

STAY An order by a court requiring a party to refrain from a specific activity until the happening of an event or upon further action by the court.

United States v. Kordel

Federal government (P) v. Corporate officers (D)

397 U.S. 1 (1970)

NATURE OF CASE: Appeal from reversal of convictions for violations of the Federal Food, Drug, and Cosmetic Act.

FACT SUMMARY: Kordel (D), a corporate officer, was convicted of criminal offenses after being required to respond to civil interrogatories from the Food and Drug Administration.

RULE OF LAW

Agencies do not have to choose between criminal and civil proceedings or delay civil proceedings pending the outcome of a criminal trial.

FACTS: In June 1960, the Food and Drug Administration (FDA) filed a suit against Detroit Vital Foods (Vital Foods), alleging that two of its products violated the Food, Drug, and Cosmetic Act (the Act). The company was served with interrogatories from the FDA. The Government (P) then notified Vital Foods that it would begin a criminal prosecution. Vital Foods asked the district court to stay the FDA civil proceedings or delay the interrogatories until after the criminal trial was finished. However, Vital Foods did not raise the issue of self-incrimination and the court denied their request. Kordel (D), a corporate officer, and other officers answered the interrogatories and subsequently were convicted of violating the Act. The court of appeals reversed their convictions on the ground the Government's (P) use of the interrogatory responses in a nearly contemporaneous civil proceeding to obtain evidence was a violation of the right against self-incrimination. The Government (P) appealed.

ISSUE: Do agencies have to choose between criminal and civil proceedings or delay civil proceedings pending the outcome of a criminal trial?

HOLDING AND DECISION: (Stewart, J.) No. Agencies do not have to choose between criminal and civil proceedings or delay civil proceedings pending the outcome of a criminal trial. In the present case, the court of appeals found that the interrogatory responses were involuntary after the district court's order. However, the privilege of self-incrimination is a personal right. The individuals at Vital Foods could have invoked their privilege even though the corporation itself had no such right. Although it is possible that there would have been no one at Vital Foods who could have answered without subjecting himself to the risk of self-incrimination, and in such a case, a protective order might have been warranted. However, the record before us does not present this question. Additionally, it cannot be said that the government's conduct was so unfair as to require reversal. It would stultify the enforcement of federal law to require an agency to choose between giving up criminal prosecutions or deferring civil proceedings pending the outcome of a criminal trial. Often the decision of whether to proceed criminally against those responsible depends on having a full civil record. Therefore, Kordel (D) and the other officers' convictions are reinstated. Reversed.

ANALYSIS

The Court seemed concerned with the public interest in having the Food and Drug Administration remove offending products as soon as possible without having to worry about the implications for later criminal proceedings. The Court went out of its way to suggest that the attorneys for Vital Foods could have explored other options after the district court insisted that the interrogatories be answered. The Court did note that a company could elude answering discovery by assigning the responsibility to someone who would invoke the Fifth Amendment.

Quicknotes

FIFTH AMENDMENT Provides that no person shall be compelled to serve as a witness against him- or herself, be subject to trial for the same offense twice, or be deprived of life, liberty, or property without due process of law.

FEDERAL FOOD, DRUG, AND COSMETIC ACT Consumer-protection statute authorizing promulgation of rules governing food, drugs, and cosmetics. It gives the U.S. Food and Drug Administration (FDA) authority to oversee the safety of food, drugs, medical devices, and cosmetics.

PROTECTIVE ORDER Court order protecting a party against potential abusive treatment through use of the legal process.

STAY An order by a court requiring a party to refrain from a specific activity until the happening of an event or upon further action by the court.

United States v. LaSalle National Bank

Internal Revenue Service (P) v. Taxpayer's bank (D)

437 U.S. 298 (1978)

NATURE OF CASE: Appeal from denial of enforcement of administrative subpoena.

FACT SUMMARY: LaSalle (D) refused to comply with a subpoena for a customer's bank records from the Internal Revenue Service (P).

RULE OF LAW

An Internal Revenue Service summons must be enforced if it is issued in good faith before a recommendation for criminal prosecution.

FACTS: The Internal Revenue Service (IRS) (P) assigned Olivero, a special agent, to investigate the tax liability of Gattuso. Olivero issued summons for Gattuso's records at two banks, including LaSalle National Bank (D). The banks (D) refused to comply and the IRS (P) sought enforcement in district court. Olivero and other IRS (P) officials testified that there had been no decision or recommendation as to whether criminal charges were justified at the time of the summons. But Gattuso insisted that the investigation was purely criminal, and the district court agreed that Olivero's motivation seemed to be for criminal proceedings. The court refused to enforce the administrative subpoenas and the court of appeals affirmed. The IRS (P) appealed.

ISSUE: Must an Internal Revenue Service summons be enforced if it is issued in good faith before a recommendation for criminal prosecution?

HOLDING AND DECISION: (Blackmun, J.) Yes. An Internal Revenue Service (IRS) summons must be enforced if it is issued in good faith before a recommendation for criminal prosecution. The legislative history of the Internal Revenue Code shows that Congress intended to design a system with interrelated civil and criminal elements. Thus, tax fraud investigations were not categorized and any limitation on an IRS (P) summons should reflect this. The criminal and civil aspects of tax fraud cases diverge only when a recommendation for prosecution is sent from the IRS (P) to the Department of Justice. It would be an improper use of the summons power for the IRS (P) to gather evidence solely for a criminal investigation. Otherwise, the IRS (P) may issue summons as long as it is done in good faith for a legitimate purpose. The determination of whether an improper purpose was behind a summons is not dependent on the motivation of one agent but depends on institutional good faith. There are layers of review built into the IRS (P) administration that temper against the motivations of one agent. In the present case, LaSalle National Bank (D) has not demonstrated anything that goes against good faith other than that agent Olivero may have already possessed the information sought in the summons. Therefore, the summons should have been enforced. Reversed.

DISSENT: (Stewart, J.) The "institutional good faith" of the Internal Revenue Service (IRS) (P) will be just as, if not more, difficult to decide as the purpose of an individual agent.

ANALYSIS

The Court stated that the good faith standard does not permit the Internal Revenue Service (P) to become an information-gathering agency for other agencies, regardless of the status of the criminal case involved. This decision reflects a trend in the cases where most parallel proceedings are allowed. The Court noted that bad faith will rarely be found in cases of this type.

Quicknotes

GOOD FAITH An honest intention to abstain from taking advantage of another.

SUBPOENA A mandate issued by a court to compel a witness to appear at trial.

CHAPTER 8

Public Access to Agency Processes

Quick Reference Rules of Law

The Bureau of National Affairs, Inc. v. United States Department of Justice

Publisher (P) v. Government agency (D)

742 F.2d 1484 (D.C. Cir. 1984)

NATURE OF CASE: Appeal from a denial of disclosure of requested documents under the Freedom of Information Act (FOIA).

FACT SUMMARY: The Bureau of National Affairs (P) sought disclosure of appointment records and calendars of an assistant Attorney General under the Freedom of Information Act (FOIA).

RULE OF LAW

Only documents classified as agency records are subject to disclosure under the Freedom of Information Act (FOIA).

FACTS: The Bureau of National Affairs (BNA) (P) sued to compel disclosure of daily agendas and appointment calendars of an assistant Attorney General. The daily agendas were prepared so that the individual's staff would know where to reach him and were distributed to the staff daily. The appointment calendars were created for his personal convenience. The Department of Justice (D) contended the documents were not "agency records" and thus not subject to disclosure. The district court refused to compel production and the BNA (P) appealed.

ISSUE: Are only documents classified as agency records subject to disclosure under the Freedom of Information Act (FOIA)?

HOLDING AND DECISION: (Mikva, J.) Yes. Only documents classified as agency records are subject to disclosure under the Freedom of Information Act (FOIA). Here, the telephone message slips clearly are not agency records because they contained no substantive information, they were used only by the official for whom they were taken, and distinguishing between personal and business purposes for the calls was often impossible. The daily agendas were agency records because they were generated on agency time primarily for the use of agency personnel for agency business. The calendars, however, were not agency records because they were kept for the personal convenience of the officials. The Bureau of National Affairs' (P) request for daily agendas is granted, its other requests are denied.

ANALYSIS

The court in this case recognizes an absence of legislative and judicial guidance in defining the scope of "agency records." Some guidelines have been suggested such as how the records were generated, by whom, for what purpose, and under whose direction. Also, whether the agency possesses the documentation is a factor.

Quicknotes

FREEDOM OF INFORMATION ACT (FOIA), § 552 Expressly defines records that must be made available to the public.

United States Department of Justice v. Tax Analysts

Government agency (D) v. Publisher (P)

492 U.S. 136 (1989)

NATURE OF CASE: Appeal from order to comply with a Freedom of Information Act (FOIA) records request.

FACT SUMMARY: In July 1979, Tax Analysts (P) filed a Freedom of Information Act (FOIA) request asking the U.S. Department of Justice (the Department) (D) to make available all district court tax opinions and final orders received by the Tax Division earlier that month, but the Department (D) denied the request.

RULE OF LAW

The Freedom of Information Act (FOIA) confers jurisdiction on the district courts to enjoin an agency from withholding agency records and to order the production of any agency records improperly withheld.

FACTS: The Tax Division of the U.S. Department of Justice (the Department) (D) represents parties in litigation, receives copies of all opinions and orders issued by the courts in such cases, and makes copies of these decisions for the Tax Division's staff attorneys. The original documents are sent to the official files kept by the Department (D). In July 1979, Tax Analysts (P), publisher of a weekly magazine that reports on legislative, judicial, and regulatory developments in the field of federal taxation to a readership largely composed of tax attorneys, accountants, and economists, filed a request under the Freedom of Information Act (FOIA) asking the Department (D) to make available all district court tax opinions and final orders received by the Tax Division earlier that month. The Department (D) denied the request on the grounds these decisions were not Tax Division records. The Department (D) appealed a lower court order to comply with the request.

ISSUE: Does the Freedom of Information Act (FOIA) confer jurisdiction on the district courts to enjoin an agency from withholding agency records and to order the production of any agency records improperly withheld?

HOLDING AND DECISION: (Marshall, J.) Yes. The Freedom of Information Act (FOIA) confers jurisdiction on the district courts to enjoin an agency from withholding agency records and to order the production of any agency records improperly withheld. Under the FOIA, "federal jurisdiction is dependent on a showing that an agency had (1) 'improperly' (2) 'withheld' (3) 'agency records.'" Each of these criteria must be met before a district court will have jurisdiction to devise remedies to force an agency to comply with the FOIA's disclosure requirements. The test as to whether requested materials qualify as "agency records" requires two steps. First, the requested materials must have been either "created or obtained" by an agency, and second, the agency must have been in control of the requested materials at the time the FOIA request was made. Under these two tests, the requested district court decisions constituted "agency records." Congress used the word "withheld" only in its usual sense. When a document is under an agency's control, and that agency denies an otherwise valid request for its production, the agency has "withheld" the document, despite public availability of the document outside of the agency. Finally, Congress sought "to insulate its product from judicial tampering and to preserve the emphasis on disclosure by admonishing that the 'availability of records to the public' is not limited, 'except as specifically stated.'" It follows from the exclusive nature of the exemption scheme in § 552(b) that agency records that do not fall within one of the exemptions are "improperly" withheld. None of the § 552(b) enumerated exemptions protect the district court decisions sought by Tax Analysts (P). Thus, the documents requested by Tax Analysts (P) were agency records improperly withheld by the Tax Division of the U.S. Department of Justice (the Department) (D), which must comply with the request for production made under the FOIA by Tax Analysts (P).

DISSENT: (Blackmun, J.) Tax Analysts (P) is in the business of selling summaries of these opinions and supplies full texts to major electronic databases. The result of this litigation is to impose the cost of obtaining the court orders and opinions upon the government and thus upon taxpayers generally, rather than on the requesting party.

ANALYSIS

According to the dissent, the public—as taxpayers—is being asked to pay the cost of providing information to a commercial enterprise. It would appear Justice Blackmun's fears of the taxpayers bearing the expense of responding to Freedom of Information Act (FOIA) requests is not unfounded, since even though the FOIA stipulates that each agency shall promulgate regulations specifying a uniform schedule of fees applicable to all document search and duplication, oftentimes these fees are waived. In his hornbook on Administrative Law, Professor William F. Fox, Jr., reveals that because—in addition to the many agencies that waive fees—fee schedules rarely reflect the actual costs of searching

Continued on next page.

and retrieval, congressional inquiries indicate that the FOIA is costing agencies millions of dollars each year in processing expenses.

Quicknotes

FREEDOM OF INFORMATION ACT (FOIA), § 552 Expressly defines records that must be made available to the public.

Center for Constitutional Rights v. Central Intelligence Agency

FOIA requester (P) v. Federal agency (D)

765 F.3d 161 (2d Cir. 2014)

NATURE OF CASE: Appeal in action seeking the release of government records pursuant to the Freedom of Information Act (FOIA).

FACT SUMMARY: Pursuant to the Freedom of Information Act (FOIA), the Center for Constitutional Rights (P) sought disclosure of certain videos and photographs of a high-profile Guantanamo Bay detainee, Mohammed al-Qahtani, who was believed to be the so-called "20th hijacker" in the September 11, 2001, terrorist attacks on the United States. The Government (D) refused on the grounds that the records were exempt from disclosure pursuant to FOIA Exemption 1, which authorizes nondisclosure of records that are properly authorized by Executive Order to be kept secret in the interest of "national defense or foreign policy."

RULE OF LAW

The government meets its burden of showing that a record requested to be disclosed pursuant to the Freedom of Information Act (FOIA) falls within a FOIA exemption that implicates national security where the government's justification for invoking the exemption is reasonably detailed and appears logical or plausible.

FACTS: Mohammed al-Qahtani, a Saudi national, has been held at Guantanamo Bay from 2002 to the present day on suspicion that he had planned to act as the 20th hijacker of the planes used in the September 11, 2001 (9/11) terrorist attacks on the United States, but was prevented from entering the United States in August 2001. In 2010, the Center for Constitutional Rights (CCR) (P) sought disclosure, pursuant to the Freedom of Information Act (FOIA), by the Government (D) of certain videos, photographs, and other records of al-Qahtani at Guantanamo. Apart from his notable profile, al-Qahtani was unusual because a significant Government (D) official had publicly opined that the interrogation methods used on him met the legal definition of torture. The Government (D) identified records that were responsive to CCR's (P) requests (the Responsive Records) but claimed the right to withhold the records under FOIA Exemption 1, which authorizes nondisclosure of records that are properly authorized by Executive order to be kept secret in the interest of "national defense or foreign policy." Specifically, the Government (D) justified the invocation of Exemption 1 by declaring that the records were properly classified under Executive Order 13,526, which pertains, in relevant part, to: (1) "military plans . . . or operations"; (2) "intelligence activities (including covert action), intelligence sources or methods, or cryptology"; and (3) "foreign relations or foreign activities of the United States, including confidential sources." Major General Karl Horst made a public declaration (the Horst Declaration) that asserted, inter alia, that the disclosure of the Responsive Records could reasonably be expected to harm national security by endangering the lives and physical safety of U.S. military personnel, diplomats, and aid workers and by aiding in the recruitment and financing of extremist and insurgent groups because enemy forces had previously used videos and photographs, particularly of U.S. forces interacting with detainees, out of context to incite the civilian population and influence government officials. In the declaration, General Horst cited specific incidences where this had occurred. CCR (P) brought suit to compel disclosure of the Responsive Records; the Second Circuit Court of Appeals granted review in the case. [The procedural posture of the case is not presented in the casebook extract.]

ISSUE: Does the government meet its burden of showing that a record requested to be disclosed pursuant to the Freedom of Information Act (FOIA) falls within a FOIA exemption that implicates national security where the government's justification for invoking the exemption is reasonably detailed and appears logical or plausible?

HOLDING AND DECISION: (Cabranes, J.) Yes. The government meets its burden of showing that a record requested to be disclosed pursuant to the Freedom of Information Act (FOIA) falls within a FOIA exemption that implicates national security where the government's justification for invoking the exemption is reasonably detailed and appears logical or plausible. The Government (D) bears the burden of demonstrating that an exemption applies to each item of information it seeks to withhold; all doubts as to the applicability of the exemption must be resolved in favor of disclosure. An agency may carry its burden by submitting declarations "giving reasonably detailed explanations why any withheld documents fall within an exemption," and such declarations "are accorded a presumption of good faith. When such declarations are not controverted by either contrary evidence in the record nor by evidence of agency bad faith, summary judgment for the Government (D) is warranted. Notwithstanding the presumption in favor of disclosure, when the claimed exemption implicates national security, an agency's justification for invoking a FOIA exemption is sufficient if it appears logical or plausible. Here, the parties dispute whether the Responsive

Continued on next page.

Records satisfied the prerequisites for classification under Executive Order 13,526—specifically, whether the unauthorized disclosure of the Responsive Records reasonably could be expected to result in damage to national security—defined as harm to the national defense or foreign relations of the United States—taking into consideration such aspects of the information as the sensitivity, value, utility, and provenance of that information. The Government's (D) central argument, supported by the Horst Declaration, is that release of the Responsive Records logically and plausibly could serve as propaganda for extremists and incite anti-American violence, which, in turn, could reasonably be expected to result in damage to national security. In response, the Center for Constitutional Rights (CCR) (P) argues that accepting the "propaganda" justification would stymie FOIA's aims by permitting the Government (D) to disregard the people's right to a transparent government whenever there is a distant risk that someone, somewhere could respond with violence. CCR (P) also warns that this justification would, perversely, be most forceful where the information was most controversial and, accordingly, of greatest interest to the public. Finally, CCR (P) claimed that General Horst's justifications were too general and failed to explain how particular records would provoke the United States' enemies. In the particular circumstances of this case, surrounding al-Qahtani, the record establishes, at a minimum, a reasonable possibility that the Government's (D) release of the Responsive Records of al-Qahtani, in the context of what is already publicly known about him, would be singularly susceptible to use by extremist groups to incite anti-American hostility. That, in turn, could reasonably be expected to damage the national security of the United States. Accordingly, the Responsive Records were properly classified under Executive Order 13,526 and are therefore exempt from disclosure pursuant to FOIA Exemption 1.

ANALYSIS

In addressing the Center for Constitutional Rights' (P) "propaganda" argument, the court acknowledged that, if invoked reflexively by the government and accepted unquestioningly by reviewing courts the "propaganda" justification could shield a broad range of documents of significant public interest, in contravention of the Freedom of Information Act's (FOIA's) central purpose. However, the court also observed that the mere possibility that a particular justification might be abused does not render it meritless in all circumstances, since whether the government's justifications for withholding information in the name of national security go too far is a question that must be evaluated by a court in the context of the particular circumstances presented by each case. The court also emphasized that, as in every FOIA action, a court's holding is limited to the particular facts and circumstances of that case.

Quicknotes

EXECUTIVE ORDER An order issued by the President, or on behalf of the President, that has the force of law.

Avila v. U.S. Department of State

FOIA requester (P) v. Federal executive department (D)

2022 WL 2104483 [D.D.C. June 10, 2022]

NATURE OF CASE: Action under the Freedom of Information Act (FOIA) challenging the non-disclosure by the government of certain responsive records.

FACT SUMMARY: After Victor Avila, Jr. (P), a former federal agent, was ambushed and seriously wounded by members of a Mexican cartel, he requested, pursuant to the Freedom of Information Act (FOIA), the disclosure by the Department of State (State Department) (D) of all records concerning himself. The State Department (D) withheld in full or in part the majority of responsive records it located, on the basis of FOIA exemptions. Avila (P) challenged the applicability of Exemption 1, dealing with national security, to eight of the records.

RULE OF LAW

Where the government's assertion of an exemption from disclosure under the Freedom of Information Act (FOIA) is conclusory, so that a court has insufficient information to determine whether the document is properly withheld, the court has the discretion to afford the government an opportunity to discharge its burden by providing greater specificity as to what information is being withheld pursuant to which asserted privileges; to provide factual matter sufficient to establish the necessary elements for those privileges; and to assess whether factual matter can be segregated and disclosed.

FACTS: Victor Avila, Jr. (P), a former federal agent who worked for U.S. Immigration and Customs Enforcement (ICE), a federal law enforcement agency under the Department of Homeland Security (DHS), was ambushed and seriously wounded by members of a Mexican cartel when Avila (P) and another agent were transporting equipment to Mexico City. In the aftermath of the ambush, Avila (P), along with Judicial Watch, Inc. (P), a nonprofit organization, jointly submitted a Freedom of Information Act (FOIA) request to the Department of State (State Department) (D) seeking "records concerning Victor Avila, Jr," including those between the State Department (D) and ICE and/or DHS. It was not until Avila (P) and Judicial Watch (P) brought suit that the State Department (D) began to disclose records responsive to the FOIA request. The State Department (D) withheld in full or in part the majority of responsive records it located, on the basis of FOIA exemptions, and, in particular, Exemption 1, which exempts records "specifically authorized under criteria established by an Executive order to be kept secret in the interest of national defense or foreign policy and [which] are in fact properly classified pursuant to such Executive order." The State Department (D) asserted that Executive Order (E.O.) No. 13,526, which protected from disclosure information reasonably expected to cause some degree of harm to national security, was applicable to the records it withheld under Exemption 1. Avila (P) and Judicial Watch (P) disputed the exemption as to eight documents.

ISSUE: Where the government's assertion of an exemption from disclosure under the Freedom of Information Act (FOIA) is conclusory, so that a court has insufficient information to determine whether the document is properly withheld, does the court have the discretion to afford the government an opportunity to discharge its burden by providing greater specificity as to what information is being withheld pursuant to which asserted privileges; to provide factual matter sufficient to establish the necessary elements for those privileges; and to assess whether factual matter can be segregated and disclosed?

HOLDING AND DECISION: [Conteras, J.] Yes. Where the government's assertion of an exemption from disclosure under the Freedom of Information Act (FOIA) is conclusory, so that a court has insufficient information to determine whether the document is properly withheld, the court has the discretion to afford the government an opportunity to discharge its burden by providing greater specificity as to what information is being withheld pursuant to which asserted privileges; to provide factual matter sufficient to establish the necessary elements for those privileges; and to assess whether factual matter can be segregated and disclosed. When assessing nondisclosure decisions in a FOIA action, the court may rely solely on affidavits or declarations if they describe the justifications for nondisclosure with reasonably specific detail, demonstrate that the information withheld logically falls within the claimed exemption, and are not controverted by either contrary evidence in the record or by evidence of agency bad faith. Ultimately, an agency's justification for invoking a FOIA exemption is sufficient if it appears "logical" or "plausible." However, exemptions are to be narrowly construed, and conclusory and generalized allegations of exemptions are unacceptable. When an agency invokes an exemption, it must submit affidavits that provide the kind of detailed, scrupulous description of the withheld documents that enables a court to perform a de novo review. Notably, even if a FOIA exemption applies, an agency cannot withhold information unless it also reasonably foresees that disclosure would harm an interest

Continued on next page.

protected by the exemption. Further, when an agency asserts Exemption 1 as justification for nondisclosure, courts defer to the executive's prediction that disclosure of responsive records would harm national security and accord substantial weight to an agency's assertions concerning the details of the classified status of the disputed record. Here, the State Department (D) confirmed that the withheld information in the disputed documents continued to meet the classification criteria of Executive Order (E.O.) 13,526, and that the information in these withheld records was properly classified because it involved "foreign government information," "intelligence activities, sources, or methods," and "foreign relations or foreign activities of the United States," the disclosure of which would damage national security. In two of the disputed documents (Documents 18 and 115) the Government (D) failed to offer descriptions of what it withheld or how much it withheld under each section of E.O. 13,526; its blanket reference to what it described only as "information" was conclusory. Therefore, with respect to these two documents, the court lacks enough information to decide whether withholding is proper. As to the remaining six disputed documents, the Government (D) provided greater specificity and sufficient details to meet the Government's (D) light burden of showing how the information contained in the documents might harm national security. In the latter six documents, the Government (D) indicated that the documents included assessments, evaluations, and deliberations regarding Mexican policy and governance, regional security, foreign officials, security incidents, Government (D) personnel, and similar matters. Thus, with respect to these six documents, the court is satisfied that withholding is permitted. As to the two documents where the State Department (D) has failed to affirmatively establish each of the essential elements of the claimed privilege, the court has the discretion to order disclosure or to afford the agency an additional opportunity to fully discharge its burden. Here, the court will give the State Department (D) a second opportunity to: (1) conduct an adequate search using more than just Avila's (P) name as a search term, focusing on the attack that severely wounded him; and (2) describe with more specificity what information is being withheld pursuant to which asserted privileges, provide factual matter sufficient to establish the necessary elements for those privileges, and assess whether factual matter can be segregated and disclosed.

ANALYSIS

Although Avila (P) and Judicial Watch (P) asked the court to conduct in camera review of records over which the State Department (D) claimed Exemption 1, the court explained that a court should not undertake in camera review of withheld documents as a substitute for requiring an agency's explanation of its claimed exemptions. Accordingly, the court declined to conduct in camera review, because the court was affording the State Department (D) a second opportunity to explain its claimed exemptions in more detail when necessary.

Quicknotes

DE NOVO The review of a lower court decision by an appellate court, which is hearing the case as if it had not been previously heard and as if no judgment had been rendered.

IN CAMERA In the judge's private chambers.

United States Fish and Wildlife Service v. Sierra Club, Inc.

Federal agency (D) v. FOIA requester (P)

141 S. Ct. 777 (2021)

NATURE OF CASE: Appeal in Freedom of Information Act (FOIA) action challenging the nondisclosure of responsive records pursuant to the deliberative process privilege.

FACT SUMMARY: Sierra Club (P), Inc. an environmental organization, requested records, pursuant to the Freedom of Information Act (FOIA), of consultations between the U.S. Fish and Wildlife Service (FWS) (D) and the National Marine Fisheries Service (NMFS) (D) (together, the Services) (D), and the Environmental Protection Agency (EPA) regarding the EPA's proposed rule regarding cooling water intake structures used for cooling industrial equipment. Although the Services (D) turned over thousands of documents, the Services (D) invoked the deliberative process privilege under the fifth exemption to FOIA to prevent disclosure of certain draft biological opinions analyzing the EPA's proposed rule. Sierra Club (P) challenged the non-disclosure of these draft biological opinions.

RULE OF LAW

The deliberative process privilege protects from disclosure under the Freedom of Information Act (FOIA) in-house draft biological opinions prepared by an agency that are both predecisional and deliberative, notwithstanding that the drafts reflect the agency's last views about a proposal.

FACTS: The Environmental Protection Agency (EPA) proposed a rule in 2011 regarding "cooling water intake structures" used to cool industrial equipment. Because aquatic wildlife can become trapped in these intake structures and die, the Endangered Species Act of 1973 required the EPA to consult with the U.S. Fish and Wildlife Service (FWS) (D) and the National Marine Fisheries Service (NMFS) (D) (together, the Services) (D) before proceeding. Following this required consultation, the Services prepare an official "biological opinion" (known as a "jeopardy" or "no jeopardy" biological opinion) addressing whether the agency's proposal would jeopardize the existence of threatened or endangered species. Issuance of a "jeopardy" biological opinion here would require the EPA either to implement certain alternatives proposed by the Services (D), to terminate the action altogether, or to seek an exemption. After informally consulting with the Services (D), the EPA made changes to its proposed rule, and the Services received the revised version in November 2013. Staff members at NMFS (D) and FWS (D) soon completed draft biological opinions concluding that the November 2013 proposed rule was likely to jeopardize certain species. Staff members sent these drafts to the relevant decisionmakers within each agency, but decisionmakers at the Services (D) neither approved the drafts nor sent them to the EPA. The Services (D) instead shelved the draft opinions and agreed with the EPA to extend the period of consultation because it was agreed that more work needed to be done. After these continued consultation discussions, the EPA sent the Services (D) a revised proposed rule in March 2014 that differed significantly from the 2013 version. Satisfied that the revised rule was unlikely to harm any protected species, the Services (D) issued a joint final "no jeopardy" biological opinion. The EPA issued its final rule that same day. Sierra Club (P), an environmental organization, submitted requests under the Freedom of Information Act (FOIA) for records related to the Services' consultations with the EPA. Although the Services (D) turned over thousands of documents, the Services (D) invoked the deliberative process privilege under the fifth exemption to FOIA to prevent disclosure of the draft biological opinions analyzing the EPA's 2013 proposed rule. Sierra Club (P) sued to obtain these withheld documents. The United States Supreme Court granted certiorari in the case.

ISSUE: Does the deliberative process privilege protect from disclosure under the Freedom of Information Act (FOIA) in-house draft biological opinions prepared by an agency that are both predecisional and deliberative, notwithstanding that the drafts reflect the agency's last views about a proposal?

HOLDING AND DECISION: (Barrett, J.) Yes. The deliberative process privilege protects from disclosure under the Freedom of Information Act (FOIA) in-house draft biological opinions prepared by an agency that are both predecisional and deliberative, notwithstanding that the drafts reflect the agency's last views about a proposal. FOIA mandates the disclosure of documents held by a federal agency unless the documents fall within certain exceptions. One of those exceptions, the deliberative process privilege, shields from disclosure documents reflecting advisory opinions and deliberations comprising the process by which the government formulates decisions and policies. The privilege aims to improve agency decisionmaking by encouraging candor and blunting the chilling effect that accompanies the prospect of disclosure. The privilege distinguishes between predecisional, deliberative documents, which are exempt from disclosure, and documents reflecting a

Continued on next page.

final agency decision and the reasons supporting it, which are not. A document does not represent an agency's final decision solely because nothing follows it; sometimes a proposal dies on the vine or languishes. What matters is if the agency treats the document as its final view and concludes the deliberative process by which governmental decisions and policies are formulated, giving the document "real operative effect." Sierra Club (P) contends that notwithstanding that the documents were called "drafts," they had "operative effect" because they caused the Environmental Protection Agency (EPA) to revise its proposed rule. This contention, however, misunderstands the meaning of "real operative effect." That reference is to the legal, not practical, consequences that flow from an agency's actions. In this regulatory scheme, a final biological opinion leads to direct and appreciable legal consequences because it alters the legal regime to which the action agency is subject, authorizing it to take action affecting an endangered species if (but only if) it complies with the prescribed conditions. That is not true of a draft biological opinion. The deliberative process privilege protects the draft biological opinions at issue from disclosure because they reflect a preliminary view—not a final decision—about the EPA's proposed 2013 rule. The administrative context confirms that the draft opinions were subject to change and had no direct legal consequences. Because the decisionnmakers of the U.S. Fish and Wildlife Service (FWS) (D) and the National Marine Fisheries Service (NMFS) (D) (together, the Services) (D) neither approved the drafts nor sent them to the EPA, they are best described not as draft biological opinions but as drafts of draft biological opinions. Although the drafts may have had the practical effect of provoking the EPA to revise its rule, the privilege applies because the Services (D) did not treat the drafts as final. Reversed and remanded.

DISSENT: (Breyer, J.) A Final Biological Opinion embodies a final decision by the U.S. Fish and Wildlife Service (FWS) (D) and the National Marine Fisheries Service (NMFS) (D) (together, the Services) (D) that a proposed Environmental Protection Agency (EPA) action will jeopardize an endangered species. A Final Biological Opinion is not deliberative, so Freedom of Information Act (FOIA) Exemption 5 does not protect it from disclosure. On the other hand, a Draft of a Draft Biological Opinion normally is not final. It normally is deliberative, and Exemption 5 normally protects it from disclosure. However, it is not clear whether a Draft Biological Opinion is protected under Exemption 5. Whether a document is "final" or "deliberative" primarily depends upon its function within an agency's decision-making process. Here, the Services' (D) Draft Biological Opinions reflect "final" decisions regarding the "jeopardy" the EPA's then-proposed actions would have caused. Hence, they would normally fall outside, not within, Exemption 5. Five features of the Draft Biological Opinion lead to this conclusion. First, a Draft Biological Opinion is a "final" document with respect to its content. That is in fact the key difference between a Draft Biological Opinion and a Draft of a Draft Biological Opinion. Second, a Final Biological Opinion and a Draft Biological Opinion finding jeopardy serve the same functions within the formal administrative process. Both explain the Services' (D) findings, and both set forth "reasonable and prudent" modifications or alternatives Also, both have substantially the same effect on the EPA. In response to both documents, the EPA has essentially four options: It can drop the proposed action; it can accept the proposed modifications; it can take the proposed action and potentially expose itself to considerable penalties; or it can seek a Cabinet-level exemption. Transmitting the Draft Biological Opinion to the EPA simply allows the EPA to make its choice before a Final Biological Opinion issues. Third, agency practice shows that the Draft Biological Opinion, not the Final Biological Opinion, is the document that informs the EPA of the Services' (D) conclusions about jeopardy and alternatives, and triggers within the EPA the process of deciding what to do about those conclusions. In fact, the Services (D) very rarely issue Final Biological Opinions: out of 6,829 formal consultations between 2008 and 2015, the FSW (D) issued a Final Biological Opinion finding jeopardy only twice. Thus, if a Final Biological Opinion is discoverable under FOIA, why would a Draft Biological Opinion, embodying the same Service (D) conclusions (and leaving the EPA with the same four choices), not be? Fourth, permitting discovery of Draft Biological Opinions under FOIA is unlikely to chill frank discussion within a Service, because the Service's (D) staff are already aware that these Drafts may well be made public. When a private party prompts the agency action under review, for example, by seeking an EPA permit, regulations require the Service to make the Draft Biological Opinion available to the private applicant, removing the Draft Biological Opinion from Exemption 5's protection. Fifth, legal consequences flow from the Services' (D) completion of a Draft Biological Opinion. The Services' (D) regulations state that "[i]f requested, the Service shall make available to the Federal agency [i.e., the EPA] the draft biological opinion for the purpose of analyzing the reasonable and prudent alternatives." Once the Draft Biological Opinion is under review at the EPA, the Services (D) may not issue a Final Biological Opinion prior to the specified deadline. Moreover, Draft Biological Opinions, like Final Biological Opinions, limit the EPA's set of available options. For these reasons and given that the same consequences flow from Draft Biological Opinions as Final Biological Opinions, it is difficult to understand why Draft Biological Opinions should not fall outside Exemption 5's protection. The factual question

Continued on next page.

remains in this case whether the particular documents at issue are Draft Biological Opinions or Drafts of Draft Biological Opinions. As the majority points out, there are reasons to believe some of them may be the latter. The NMFS's (D) documents contain highlighting and editing marks reflective of a work-in-progress, whereas the FWS (D) documents do not, and they may have been complete but for a final signature. Given the fact-intensive nature of this question, the case should be remanded for a determination as to just how much work was left to be done. If the court determines that the documents are merely Drafts of Draft Biological Opinions, only then would a segregability analysis be appropriate.

ANALYSIS

Sierra Club (P) warned that ruling against it would permit the U.S. Fish and Wildlife Service (FWS) (D) and the National Marine Fisheries Service (NMFS) (D) (together, the Services) (D) to stamp every document "draft," thereby protecting even final agency decisions and creating "secret" agency law. In response to this contention, Justice Barrett, while acknowledging that a draft document will typically be predecisional because calling something a draft communicates that it is not yet final, also emphasized that determining whether an agency's position is final for purposes of the deliberative process privilege is a functional, rather than formal, inquiry. Thus, if the evidence establishes that an agency has hidden a functionally final decision in draft form, the deliberative process privilege will not apply. In this case, however, the record did not support a finding that the Services (D) engaged in such "a charade."

Chrysler Corporation v. Brown

Auto manufacturer (P) v. Labor department (D)

441 U.S. 281 (1979)

NATURE OF CASE: Appeal of court order mandating disclosure of certain documents.

FACT SUMMARY: Chrysler Corporation (P) contended that certain documents pertaining to it held by the government fell outside the Freedom of Information Act (FOIA) and, therefore, could not be disclosed pursuant to unrelated regulations.

RULE OF LAW

The Freedom of Information Act (FOIA) does not give rise to a private right to prevent disclosure of documents pursuant to unrelated regulations.

FACTS: Pursuant to Executive Order, Chrysler Corporation (P) had to prepare certain reports giving the status of Chrysler's (P) compliance with federal affirmative action programs. The Executive Order and Regulations of the Department of Labor (D) allowed for public inspection of these records. The Department of Labor (D) informed Chrysler (P) that a request for some of these records had been made. Chrysler (P) argued that the records contained trade secrets and, therefore, fell under Exemption 4 of the Freedom of Information Act (FOIA). The court of appeals held the documents subject to disclosure.

ISSUE: Does the Freedom of Information Act (FOIA) give rise to a private right to prevent disclosure of documents pursuant to unrelated regulations?

HOLDING AND DECISION: (Rehnquist, J.) No. The Freedom of Information Act (FOIA) does not give rise to a private right to prevent disclosure of documents pursuant to unrelated regulations. The FOIA, by its terms, is exclusively a disclosure statute. This is borne out by its provisions for judicial review, which allow a court to order disclosure but say nothing about withholding disclosure. Also, legislative history makes it clear that the FOIA was designed to create an avenue for disclosure pursuant to other laws. The Court went on to hold that the Trade Secrets Act may prevent disclosure and remanded to the court of appeals for consideration of this issue.

ANALYSIS

This case was what had been labeled a "reverse- FOIA" suit. Suppliers of information to the government had argued, as did Chrysler (P), that disclosure broader than that allowed by the FOIA was impermissible. The argument was that the FOIA had superseded all other disclosure rules. This decision put that argument to rest.

Quicknotes

FREEDOM OF INFORMATION ACT (FOIA), EXEMPTION 4 Exempts trade secrets and privileges or confidential financial information from disclosure.

TRADE SECRET Consists of any formula, pattern, plan, process, or device known only to its owner and business that gives an advantage over competitors; a secret formula used in the manufacture of a particular product that is not known to the general public.

Public Citizen v. U.S. Department of Justice

Lobby group (P) v. Government agency (D)

491 U.S. 440 (1989)

NATURE OF CASE: Suit alleging violation of the Federal Advisory Committee Act.

FACT SUMMARY: Public Citizen (P) alleged that the American Bar Association's Committee that reviewed the nominations for federal judgeships fell under rules of the Federal Advisory Committee Act.

RULE OF LAW

The Federal Advisory Committee Act was not meant to apply to the American Bar Association's review of judicial nominees.

FACTS: The Federal Advisory Committee Act (FACA) was passed by Congress to provide public access and accountability to committees that advise the executive branch. According to FACA, it is to be applied to "any committee, board, commission . . . established or utilized by one or more agencies in the interest of obtaining advice or recommendations for the President." For many years prior to FACA, the American Bar Association (ABA) had reviewed potential nominees for appointment as federal judges and reported whether the nominee was qualified. These recommendations were very influential in the appointment process. Public Citizen (P), a public interest lobbying group, filed suit claiming that these ABA Committee meetings should be open to the public since they fell within the purview of FACA. The issue reached the United States Supreme Court.

ISSUE: Was the Federal Advisory Committee Act meant to apply to the American Bar Association's review of judicial nominees?

HOLDING AND DECISION: (Brennan, J.) No. The Federal Advisory Committee Act (FACA) was not meant to apply to the American Bar Association's (ABA's) review of judicial nominees. According to a straightforward reading of FACA, it is clear the ABA Committee on judicial nominees are "utilized" by the executive branch. However, it does not seem that Congress could have intended that any group of two or more people from which the President seeks advice would have to meet FACA requirements. The principal purpose of FACA was to enhance public accountability of advisory committees that were actually established by the executive branch. This could be done without expanding FACA's coverage to privately organized groups such as the ABA. The legislative history of FACA demonstrates that neither the House nor the Senate intended to bring all private advisory committees within FACA. Given its prominence, it is telling that it was omitted from a list of groups that would be covered by FACA. The words "or utilized" appear to have been added to the final statute in order to make sure that it covered quasi-public organizations. The literal reading of the law would have a far greater reach than Congress intended. Since the constitutionality of FACA would be arguable under a broad reading, it is appropriate to use a construction that will avoid such problems. Therefore, FACA should be read more narrowly and does not encompass such private groups as the ABA.

CONCURRENCE: (Kennedy, J.) [The Federal Advisory Committee Act applies to the American Bar Association Committee but unconstitutionally interferes with the President's authority under the Appointments Clause.]

ANALYSIS

The Court noted that the district court had declared the Federal Advisory Committee Act unconstitutional when it found that it applied to the American Bar Association. Justices Kennedy, Rehnquist, and O'Connor also agreed with this position. However, the majority seemed intent on somehow saving the law by looking past a literal reading of the statute.

Quicknotes

FEDERAL ADVISORY COMMITTEE ACT (FACA) Law intended to open up executive branch advisory groups to the public and make them more accountable.

In re Cheney

Opponents of national energy policy (P) v. Vice President of the United States (D)

406 F.3d 723 (D.C. Cir. 2005) (en banc)

NATURE OF CASE: Suit for disclosure of documents related to a group formed to help the President of the United States establish a national energy policy.

FACT SUMMARY: The President assigned several federal officials to a "development group" to help him formulate a national energy policy. Two citizen organizations (P) sought documents related to the President's development group.

RULE OF LAW

The Federal Advisory Committee Act does not require disclosure of committee documents if only federal officials compose the committee.

FACTS: President Bush established the National Energy Policy Development Group (NEPDG) to develop a national energy policy. Vice President Cheney (D) and other federal officials were named to the NEPDG. Two citizen groups, Judicial Watch (P) and the Sierra Club (P), filed separate suits against Cheney (D), among others, for declaratory and injunctive relief ordering that documents related to the NEPDG be disclosed. Both suits alleged that persons who were not federal officials regularly participated in the NEPDG, thereby giving such persons de facto membership on the NEPDG. The plaintiffs alleged further that the NEPDG was therefore an "advisory committee" whose documents were disclosable under the Federal Advisory Committee Act (FACA) because FACA's disclosure provisions exempted only groups composed solely of full-time or permanent part-time federal officials. The trial court dismissed most of the suits, leaving only a mandamus claim against Cheney (D) asking the court of appeals to order the trial court to order Cheney (D) to comply with the FACA's disclosure provisions.

ISSUE: Does the Federal Advisory Committee Act require disclosure of committee documents if only federal officials compose the committee?

HOLDING AND DECISION: (Randolph, J.) No. The Federal Advisory Committee Act (FACA) does not require disclosure of committee documents if only federal officials compose the committee. Neither the National Energy Policy Development Group (NEPDG) nor its so-called subgroups were "advisory committees," within the meaning of FACA, because only federal officials had a vote on the committee or could veto the committee's decisions. This strict construction of FACA is necessary because of the grave separation-of-powers problems in a case such as this one. Even if some persons who were not federal officials did assist the NEPDG, they did not vote on the NEPDG or have ability to veto the committee's decisions; like congressional aides, such persons might have had extensive influence on the committee's decisions, but that influence alone does not make them de facto members of the committee. In this case, neither complaint alleged that a nonfederal official voted on the NEPDG or could have vetoed the committee's decisions. Accordingly, the NEPDG was not an "advisory committee" under FACA. Furthermore, Cheney (D) did not use his delegated authority to create "subordinate working groups," and Judicial Watch (P) made no allegation that an unofficial subgroup voted on the NEPDG or could have vetoed the committee's decisions. Therefore, the subgroups were also not "agency committees" under FACA. Writ of mandamus denied.

ANALYSIS

The reporting requirements of the Federal Advisory Committee Act (FACA) are onerous. The statute itself acknowledges separation-of-powers concerns, however, and FACA permits the President the latitude of establishing advisory bodies not governed by FACA, an option that President Bush exercised in this case. Separation-of-powers concerns then play another role in the court, where the "constitutional avoidance" canon of construction requires judges to make all reasonable efforts to avoid interpreting a statute as unconstitutional. See, e.g., *Clark v. Martinez*, 543 U.S. 371, 380-81 (2004). In this case, that canon of construction guided the court of appeals to read FACA as respecting the core functions of the highest office in a coordinate branch of government.

Quicknotes

DE FACTO In fact; in reality; actual. Existing in fact but not officially approved or engendered.

FEDERAL ADVISORY COMMITTEE ACT (FACA) Law intended to open up executive branch advisory groups to the public and make them more accountable.

Northwest Forest Resource Council v. Espy

Trade organization (P) v. Government agencies (D)

846 F. Supp. 1009 (D.D.C. 1994)

NATURE OF CASE: Suit challenging the legality of an advisory committee under the Federal Advisory Committee Act.

FACT SUMMARY: The Forest Ecosystem Management Assessment Team (D) was established by the executive branch to make recommendations with regard to forest uses, but there was a dispute as to whether it was covered by the Federal Advisory Committee Act.

RULE OF LAW

State employees without federal duties may not be considered officers of the federal government for purposes of the Federal Advisory Committee Act.

FACTS: The Forest Ecosystem Management Assessment Team (FEMAT) (D) was composed of many subteams and subgroups, encompassing as many as 700 people, in order to study uses of federal forests and identify the best solutions. An interagency group, the Forest Conference Executive Committee, was established to direct and supervise the work of FEMAT (D). At least five people who worked for FEMAT (D) were faculty members at state public universities. The Northwest Forest Resource Council (D), a trade group representing the timber industry, claimed that FEMAT (D) was an advisory committee that had to meet the requirements of the Federal Advisory Committee Act (FACA).

ISSUE: May state employees without federal duties be considered officers of the federal government for purposes of the Federal Advisory Committee Act?

HOLDING AND DECISION: (Jackson, J.) No. State employees without federal duties may not be considered officers of the federal government for purposes of the Federal Advisory Committee Act (FACA). That law defines an advisory committee as any group established by the executive branch to provide advice. There is no doubt that the Forest Ecosystem Management Assessment Team (FEMAT) (D) meets these general conditions. However, FACA does exempt certain groups if they are composed wholly of full-time officers or employees of the federal government. The agencies involved with FEMAT (D) claim that the outside faculty members should fit within this exception because they are state employees who could have been assigned a federal function. However, it is obvious that their presence precludes FEMAT (D) from fitting within the FACA exception. The argument that FEMAT (D) was not providing policy advice to the President is also clearly wrong. The record shows that the administration looked only at FEMAT (D) proposals in choosing a policy to implement. Therefore, FEMAT (D) was an advisory committee and its use violated FACA.

ANALYSIS

Other courts have also rejected the contention that the Federal Advisory Committee Act (FACA) should not apply to advisory committees that consist only of technicians who supply data. In another case, a court was faced with the legality of President Clinton's task force on health care reform. That group was composed of all full-time federal employees except for the First Lady. That court decided that the First Lady should be considered a federal employee for FACA purposes.

Quicknotes

FEDERAL ADVISORY COMMITTEE ACT (FACA) Law intended to open up executive branch advisory groups to the public and make them more accountable.

Federal Communications Commission v. ITT World Communications, Inc.

Government agency (D) v. International telecommunications company (P)

466 U.S. 463 (1984)

NATURE OF CASE: Review of order challenging international conferences.

FACT SUMMARY: ITT World Communications, Inc. (P) contended that certain international conferences attended by Federal Communications Commission (D) members were covered by the federal Sunshine Act.

RULE OF LAW

The Sunshine Act applies only to discussions that effectively predetermine official actions.

FACTS: Three members of the Federal Communications Commission (the FCC) (D) attended a series of informal conferences with overseas telecommunications regulators. The FCC (D) had participated in the conferences in the hope that an information exchange might persuade European nations to encourage competition. ITT World Communications, Inc. (ITT) (P) filed a rulemaking petition with the FCC (D), contending that the meetings were within the scope of the Sunshine Act and should have been held in public. The court of appeals held that the Sunshine Act did apply to the conferences. The United States Supreme Court granted review.

ISSUE: Does the Sunshine Act apply only to discussions that effectively predetermine agency actions?

HOLDING AND DECISION: (Powell, J.) Yes. The Sunshine Act applies only to discussions that effectively predetermine official actions. Section 552b(a)(2) of the Sunshine Act only defines "meetings" as "the deliberations of at least the number of individual agency members required to take action on behalf of the agency where such deliberations determine or result in the joint conduct or disposition of official agency business." Although the Federal Communications Commission (FCC) (D) commissioners who attended the conferences did not constitute a quorum, they did have the power to approve common carrier applications, and therefore the Sunshine Act would normally apply to such conferences. However, the conferences did not result in any formal action by the FCC (D) regarding applications, nor did they result in any firm agency positions on any matter before the commissioners. Therefore, the conferences were not meetings "of an agency" since they were not convened by the FCC (D) nor subject to its unilateral control. For these reasons, the Sunshine Act does not apply. Reversed.

ANALYSIS

The Sunshine Act strikes a balance between the public's "need to know" and agency process. On the one hand, "meetings" must be open. On the other hand, the term "meetings" is narrowly defined.

Quicknotes

SUNSHINE ACT, 5 U.S.C. § 552B(B) Requires that meetings of agencies be open to the public.

CHAPTER 9

Attorney's Fees

Quick Reference Rules of Law

Buckhannon Board and Care Home, Inc. v. West Virginia Department of Health and Human Resources

Assisted-living provider (P) v. State agency (D)

532 U.S. 598 (2001)

NATURE OF CASE: Suit to invalidate a state regulation for assisted-living providers.

FACT SUMMARY: An assisted-living provider sued a state agency to invalidate a state regulation for assisted-living providers. While the suit was pending, the state legislature eliminated the requirement. The trial court granted the state's motion to dismiss the suit for mootness and denied the assisted-living provider's request for an award of attorney's fees.

RULE OF LAW

The "catalyst theory" does not justify an award of attorney's fees under the Fair Housing Amendments Act of 1988 (FHAA) or under the Americans with Disabilities Act of 1990 (ADA) where a party achieves its desired result, but the court enters no judgment on the merits or court-ordered consent decree.

FACTS: The West Virginia Office of the State Fire Marshal found that some residents who were cared for by Buckhannon Board and Care, Inc. (P) were not capable of "self-preservation" as required by state law. Buckhannon (P) sued the State of West Virginia (D) and several others, alleging that the "self-preservation" requirement violated the Fair Housing Amendments Act of 1988 (FHAA), 42 U.S.C. § 3601 et seq., and the Americans with Disabilities Act of 1990 (ADA), 42 U.S.C. § 12101 et seq. While the suit was pending, the West Virginia legislature eliminated the "self-preservation" requirement. The State (D) then moved to dismiss Buckhannon's (P) suit on grounds of mootness. The trial court granted the motion, and Buckhannon (P) requested an award of attorney's fees, arguing that it was entitled to the award under the "catalyst theory" because the suit indirectly achieved Buckhannon's (P) desired result by encouraging the West Virginia legislature to eliminate the challenged requirement. The Fourth Circuit Court of Appeals, which had squarely rejected the "catalyst theory" in an earlier case, affirmed the trial court's denial of attorney's fees. Buckhannon (P) petitioned the United States Supreme Court for further review.

ISSUE: Does the "catalyst theory" justify an award of attorney's fees under the Fair Housing Amendments Act of 1988 (FHAA) or under the Americans with Disabilities Act of 1990 (ADA) where a party achieves its desired result, but the court enters no judgment on the merits or court-ordered consent decree?

HOLDING AND DECISION: (Rehnquist, C.J.) No. The "catalyst theory" does not justify an award of attorney's fees under the Fair Housing Amendments Act of 1988 (FHAA) or under the Americans with Disabilities Act of 1990 (ADA) where a party achieves its desired result, but the court enters no judgment on the merits or court-ordered consent decree. The "American Rule" generally requires each side to bear its own litigation expenses, including attorney's fees, unless a statute explicitly permits an award of attorney's fees. Here, the FHAA and ADA both permit attorney's fees to a "prevailing party," and the question is therefore whether a party "prevails," within the meaning of these statutes, if a court does not grant the party some form of relief. Our case law has consistently held that a party is a "prevailing party," for fee-shifting purposes, only if the result bears a judicial imprimatur by entering a judgment or a court-ordered consent decree. Buckhannon's (P) several policy arguments thus have no weight, and Buckhannon (P) is not entitled to an award of attorney's fees in this case. Affirmed.

DISSENT: (Ginsburg, J.) Contrary to clear majority of federal appellate courts, the Court today permits defendants to escape attorney-fee liability even when a plaintiff "prevails" under a less restrictive definition of the term.

ANALYSIS

Buckhannon highlights a tension inherent in courts for dispute resolution. This decision encourages plaintiffs to make extra efforts to try to resolve their differences with defendants outside the judicial system, where legal fees are more likely to remain relatively low. At the same time, defendants often will not take plaintiffs' complaints seriously unless and until a judicial figure oversees the dispute's resolution. Although the prior law presented in the casebook excerpt seems to require judgment against the plaintiffs in this case, as a practical matter Justice Ginsburg is also surely correct that *Buckhannon* will "impede access to court for the less well heeled"—that is, for the parties most likely to need attorneys who will risk taking a meritorious case on only the mere likelihood that they will be able to collect fees after the case concludes.

Continued on next page.

Quicknotes

CONSENT DECREE A decree issued by a court of equity ratifying an agreement between the parties to a lawsuit; an agreement by a defendant to cease illegal activity.

JUDGMENT ON THE MERITS A determination of the rights of the parties to litigation based on the presentation evidence, barring the party from initiating the same suit again.

Barrios v. California Interscholastic Federation

Paraplegic coach (P) v. State athletic association (D)

277 F.3d 1128 (9th Cir. 2002)

NATURE OF CASE: Suit for alleged discrimination under federal and state law.

FACT SUMMARY: A state athletic association prevented a paraplegic baseball coach from coaching after he had been permitted to coach for seven years. The coach sued, and the parties eventually reached a private settlement agreement.

RULE OF LAW

A party is a "prevailing party" entitled to attorney's fees under the Americans with Disabilities Act (ADA) where a case concludes with a stipulated dismissal and a settlement agreement expressly entitling the party to an award of attorney's fees.

FACTS: From 1992 to 1999, Victor Barrios (P), who was paraplegic and used a wheelchair, coached baseball, without incident, at a California high school. In 1999, umpires inexplicably started prohibiting Barrios (P) from coaching games simply because he used a wheelchair. Through counsel, Barrios (P) made extensive efforts to resolve the matter informally, without filing suit against the California Interscholastic Federation (CIF) (D). The CIF (D), through its counsel, repeatedly assured Barrios's (P) counsel that Barrios's (P) use of a wheelchair was not a problem and that the umpires apparently did not understand the situation. Nevertheless, umpires continued to prevent Barrios (P) from coaching, even after he filed suit against the CIF (D). Out of court, the CIF's (D) counsel continued to assure Barrios's (P) counsel that all was well, although the CIF's (D) counsel also repeatedly refused to sign written stipulations memorializing his oral assurances about Barrios's (D) ability to continue coaching baseball. Eventually the parties did enter a long-written settlement agreement that required the CIF (D) to pay Barrios (P) $10,000 in compensatory damages; the agreement also expressly reserved, for the trial court's determination, the issue of whether any party was a "prevailing party" for purposes of awarding attorney's fees. Barrios (P) moved for an award of attorney's fees and costs. Following the terms of the settlement agreement, the trial court entered a judgment and order. One month later, the CIF (D) moved to vacate the judgment, arguing that the parties had not agreed on whether a judgment or a stipulation of dismissal would be filed to terminate the case. Barrios (P) conceded that point but argued that a judgment was necessary for the agreed compensatory damages. The trial court vacated the original judgment and [despite also finding Barrios (P) to be the "prevailing party,"] denied Barrios's (P) request for attorney's fees. The parties then filed a stipulation for dismissal with prejudice, with the filing silent on the question of attorney's fees. Barrios (P) appealed.

ISSUE: Is a party a "prevailing party" entitled to attorney's fees under the Americans with Disabilities Act (ADA) where a case concludes with a stipulated dismissal and a private settlement agreement?

HOLDING AND DECISION: (Tashima, J.) Yes. A party is a "prevailing party" entitled to attorney's fees under the Americans with Disabilities Act (ADA) where a case concludes with a stipulated dismissal and a private settlement agreement. Ninth Circuit law holds that a legally enforceable settlement agreement is sufficient to confer "prevailing party" status. Like a judgment or consent decree, an enforceable settlement agreement materially alters the legal relationship between the parties such that a party can be said to "prevail" in the litigation. The United States Supreme Court's recent decision in *Buckhannon Board and Care Home, Inc. v. West Virginia Dept. of Health and Human Resources*, 532 U.S. 598 (2001), does not affect this case. In *Buckhannon*, the United States Supreme Court rejected the "catalyst theory" for awarding attorney's fees—as has the Ninth Circuit—but Barrios grounds his argument for "prevailing party" status on the settlement agreement, not on his having encouraged policy change. Moreover, *Buckhannon*'s apparent restriction of "prevailing party" status to favorable judgments or consent decrees was not only dictum but also dictum that does not reach this Circuit's law on enforceable settlement agreements. Reversed and remanded.

ANALYSIS

Barrios's reading of *Buckhannon* should be approached with caution. *Buckhannon* can easily–perhaps even most justifiably–be read as directly holding that "prevailing party" status is available only when a court enters a favorable judgment or orders and adopts a consent decree. See, e.g., *Union of Needletrades, Industrial & Textile Employees v. INS*, 336 F.3d 200, 204-05 (2d Cir. 2003) (so reading *Buckhannon*).

Quicknotes

CONSENT DECREE A decree issued by a court of equity ratifying an agreement between the parties to a lawsuit; an agreement by a defendant to cease illegal activity.

JUDGMENT A determination of the rights among the parties by a court having jurisdiction over the matter.

Roberson v. Giuliani

Applicants for public assistance (P) v. City mayor (D)

346 F.3d 75 (2d Cir. 2003)

NATURE OF CASE: Suit challenging a city's disposition of applications for various forms of public assistance.

FACT SUMMARY: Applicants for public aid sued New York City (the City) (D) to challenge its means of disposing of public-aid applications. The trial court entered summary judgment for the City (D) on one count, and the parties resolved the remaining six counts through a private settlement agreement over which the trial court retained enforcement jurisdiction.

RULE OF LAW

A trial court's retention of enforcement jurisdiction over a private settlement agreement is a sufficient judicial sanction to confer prevailing-party status on the plaintiffs.

FACTS: Roberson (P) and others sued New York City (the City) (D) to challenge the manner in which the City (D) disposed of applications for various forms of public assistance. The trial court entered summary judgment for the City (D) on one count of the complaint, and the parties resolved the complaint's other six claims through a private settlement agreement. According to the agreement, Roberson (P) agreed to dismiss the remaining six counts in consideration of the City's (D) agreement to extensive modifications of its procedures. The agreement also reserved Roberson's (P) entitlement to attorney's fees for a later determination by the trial court. Roberson (P) eventually submitted a proposed dismissal order to the trial court, with that order expressly reserving to the court enforcement jurisdiction over the parties' private settlement agreement. Three months later, Roberson (P) moved for an award of attorney's fees, and the City (D) resisted, arguing that Roberson (P) was not a prevailing party. The trial court interpreted the recent decision in *Buckhannon Board and Care Home, Inc. v. West Virginia Dept. of Health and Human Resources*, 532 U.S. 598 (2001), as limiting prevailing-party status to instances in which a court enters a judgment or adopts and orders a consent decree. Accordingly, the trial court denied Roberson's (P) request for attorney's fees. Roberson (P) appealed.

ISSUE: Is a trial court's retention of enforcement jurisdiction over a private settlement agreement a sufficient judicial sanction to confer prevailing-party status on the plaintiffs?

HOLDING AND DECISION: (Feinberg, J.) Yes. A trial court's retention of enforcement jurisdiction over a private settlement agreement is a sufficient judicial sanction to confer prevailing-party status on the plaintiffs. Although *Buckhannon* somewhat restricted the availability of prevailing-party status, that opinion's reference to judgments and consent decrees was only illustrative, not exhaustive. A majority of appellate courts have, therefore, read *Buckhannon* to permit other indications of judicial approval that are sufficient to confer prevailing-party status on plaintiffs. One such judicial imprimatur is a retention of enforcement jurisdiction like the one present in the dismissal order in this case. Such a retention of jurisdiction is similar to an approved consent decree: breaching the agreement would constitute a violation of a court order; at most, requiring compliance in this case would necessitate an intermediate order of specific performance, which would properly be followed by an enforceable finding of contempt upon noncompliance. Accordingly, Roberson (P) is a prevailing party for purposes of attorney's fees. Vacated and remanded.

ANALYSIS

As the *Roberson* court notes, the determination of prevailing-party status remains the same from one federal statutory scheme to another. Although this case decided the question with reference to the fee-shifting provisions at 42 U.S.C. § 1 988, the analysis is the same as that engaged in by the U.S. Supreme Court under the Fair Housing Amendments Act of 1988, 42 U.S.C. § 3601 et seq., and the American with Disabilities Act, 42 U.S.C. § 12101 et seq., in *Buckhannon Board and Care Home, Inc. v. West Virginia Dept. of Health and Human Resources*, 532 U.S. 598 (2001).

Quicknotes

CONSENT DECREE A decree issued by a court of equity ratifying an agreement between the parties to a lawsuit; an agreement by a defendant to cease illegal activity.

SUMMARY JUDGMENT Judgment rendered by a court in response to a motion made by one of the parties, claiming that the lack of a question of material fact in respect to an issue warrants disposition of the issue without consideration by the jury.

Doe v. Boston Public Schools

Disabled student (P) v. Public school system (D)

358 F.3d 20 (1st Cir. 2004)

NATURE OF CASE: Suit to require a student with disabilities' placement in a private therapeutic school.

FACT SUMMARY: A student with severe mental disabilities negotiated with a public school system under the Individuals with Disabilities Education Act (IDEA) for placement in a private therapeutic school. The parties eventually resolved their differences purely through a private settlement agreement, and the trial court dismissed the student's subsequent complaint in which she requested an award of her attorney's fees.

RULE OF LAW

Plaintiffs suing under the Individuals with Disabilities Education Act (IDEA) who achieve their desired result through a private settlement agreement do not qualify as "prevailing parties" for purposes of attorney's fees if a court does not sanction the case's resolution.

FACTS: Jane Doe (P) was a student with severe mental disabilities in the Boston public school system (Boston) (D). Her father informally asked Boston (D), without judicial assistance, to place her in a private therapeutic school, but the parties could not agree on such a placement. They then could not resolve the matter through mediation or during a pre-hearing conference held before a scheduled administrative hearing on the case. Three months after the pre-hearing conference, and just before the scheduled hearing, Boston (D) proposed to place Doe (P) in a different private school from the one she originally requested, and Doe (P) agreed to the placement. After further administrative proceedings, Doe (P) filed a complaint in federal court for an award of her attorney's fees in the matter. The trial court dismissed her complaint because, the judge reasoned, she was not a "prevailing party" as defined by *Buckhannon Board and Care Home, Inc. v. West Virginia Dept. of Health and Human Resources*, 532 U.S. 598 (2001). Doe (P) appealed.

ISSUE: Do plaintiffs suing under the Individuals with Disabilities Education Act (IDEA) who achieve their desired result through a private settlement agreement qualify as "prevailing parties" for purposes of attorney's fees if a court does not sanction the case's resolution?

HOLDING AND DECISION: (Stahl, Sr. J.) No. Plaintiffs suing under the Individuals with Disabilities Education Act (IDEA) who achieve their desired result through a private settlement agreement do not qualify as "prevailing parties," for purposes of attorney's fees, if a court does not sanction the case's resolution. No court or administrative agency sanctioned the result achieved by Doe (P). Her result, accordingly, is only a private settlement agreement that lacks the judicial imprimatur required by *Buckhannon*. The Ninth Circuit's reading of *Buckhannon* in *Barrios v. California Interscholastic Federation*, 277 F.3d 1128 (9th Cir. 2002), seems to contradict the U.S. Supreme Court's express disapproval of private settlements in *Buckhannon* and, thus, does not support a ruling for Doe (P) in this case. Doe (P) is, therefore, not a "prevailing party" under the IDEA, and she is not entitled to an award of attorney's fees. Affirmed.

ANALYSIS

Note the crucial distinction between *Doe* and *Roberson v. Giuliani*, 346 F.3d 75 (2d Cir. 2003). In *Roberson*, the dismissal order expressly reserved enforcement jurisdiction to the trial court over the parties' settlement agreement. The Second Circuit therefore treated the dismissal order in *Roberson* as a consent decree that met the "judgment or consent decree" standard for determining prevailing-party status arguably announced in *Buckhannon*. In *Doe*, however, the purely private settlement agreement enjoyed no judicial sanction, and the First Circuit accordingly held that Doe (P) was not a prevailing party and, therefore, not entitled to an award of attorney's fees.

Quicknotes

CONSENT DECREE A decree issued by a court of equity ratifying an agreement between the parties to a lawsuit; an agreement by a defendant to cease illegal activity.

Pierce v. Underwood

Secretary of Housing and Urban Development (D) v. [Party not identified]

487 U.S. 552 (1988)

NATURE OF CASE: Appeal of an award of attorney's fees.

FACT SUMMARY: A district court awarded attorney's fees to a party because it found that the Housing and Urban Development agency had taken a position that was not substantially justified.

RULE OF LAW

Attorney's fees may be awarded against a party whose position was not justified to a degree that would satisfy a reasonable person.

FACTS: The Equal Access to Justice Act (EAJA) allows for the awarding of attorney's fees to the prevailing party in litigation when the other party's position was not "substantially justified." In a suit against the Secretary of Housing and Urban Development (the Secretary) (D), the case was settled on grounds very unfavorable to the agency and the trial court ruled that the Secretary's (D) position was not substantially justified because of the objective indicia of the case, including the terms of the settlement, and awarded attorney's fees. The Ninth Circuit Court of Appeals affirmed, finding that a position is "substantially justified" if it "had a reasonable basis both in law and fact." The Secretary (D) appealed to the United States Supreme Court.

ISSUE: May attorney's fees be awarded against a party whose position was not justified to a degree that would satisfy a reasonable person?

HOLDING AND DECISION: (Scalia, J.) Yes. Attorney's fees may be awarded against a party whose position was not justified to a degree that would satisfy a reasonable person. Courts should not try to substitute for the formula that Congress has laid out in the statute. Accordingly, the "substantially justified" test is the only one that matters. There are a few different meanings of the word "substantial," so the test is susceptible to different interpretations. However, in this field of law there are other tests that use similar phrases and we should use them in interpreting the language of the Equal Access to Justice Act (EAJA). It is clear from these other phrases that substantial justification was not meant to mean "justified to a high degree." Rather, it was meant to be interpreted as "justified in substance." This is essentially the same as the Ninth Circuit's formulation of "reasonable basis both in law and fact." The Court is less sure that the district court should have looked only at the objective indicia of the case to determine whether the Secretary's (D) position was substantially justified. The terms of a settlement may be the result of other factors than a poor legal position. It is better to look directly at the merits of the position taken. After considering the merits, the Court cannot find that the district court abused its discretion in finding that there was no substantial justification for the Secretary's (D) position. Affirmed.

ANALYSIS

The Court noted that looking only at settlement terms to determine justification might discourage settlements in the future. The standard of review in looking at the award of attorney's fees is abuse of discretion. Accordingly, it is not easy for an appellate court to overrule the trial court's initial determination.

Quicknotes

ABUSE OF DISCRETION A determination by an appellate court that a lower court's decision was based on an error of law.

EQUAL ACCESS TO JUSTICE ACT (EAJA) Provides for the awarding of attorney's fees to a prevailing party, other than the government, when the opposing side took a position that was not substantially justified.

Martinez v. Secretary of Health & Human Services

Injured worker (P) v. Government agency (D)

815 F.2d 1381 (10th Cir. 1987)

NATURE OF CASE: Appeal from an award of attorney's fees.

FACT SUMMARY: The Government's (D) position in a disability benefits case was against the position adopted in the jurisdiction after the suit was filed.

RULE OF LAW

Private litigants are not entitled to attorney's fees from the government under the Equal Access to Justice Act (EAJA) if the governing law at the time was unclear or in flux.

FACTS: Martinez (P) was injured in a work accident in 1978 and began receiving disability benefits under the Social Security Act. An investigation led to the cessation of the benefits in 1981 and the termination was upheld by an administrative law judge. In 1983, Martinez (P) sought judicial review in district court and argued that termination of the benefits required evidence that his medical condition had improved and that failure to apply that standard commanded reversal. The Secretary of Health and Human Services (the Secretary) (D) asserted that this was not the proper test. In 1984, in a separate case, the Tenth Circuit Court of Appeals ruled that benefits could not be discontinued without a showing that the claimant's medical condition had improved. Based on this ruling, the district court ruled that Martinez (P) should have his benefits reinstated. Martinez (P) then applied for attorney's fees under the Equal Access to Justice Act (EAJA). The Secretary (D) argued that the medical improvement standard was not adopted until after the litigation and thus there was substantial justification for their position. The district court agreed and denied attorney's fees. Martinez (P) appealed.

ISSUE: Are private litigants entitled to attorney's fees from the government under the Equal Access to Justice Act (EAJA) if the governing law at the time was unclear or in flux?

HOLDING AND DECISION: (Per curiam) No. Private litigants are not entitled to attorney's fees from the government under the Equal Access to Justice Act (EAJA) if the governing law at the time was unclear or in flux. The more clearly established the governing norms are, the less justified a position in litigation will be. Where there are contrary interpretations by district courts and no clear precedent on a particular issue, it would be unfair to say that one position is not substantially justified because the other position is later adopted as law. In the present case, other circuit courts had adopted the medical improvement standard, but the governing law in this circuit was less certain. There were some indications that this standard would be used, but some district courts had ruled differently on the issue prior to our definitive 1984 ruling. Accordingly, the Secretary of Health and Human Services (D) was substantially justified in taking an opposing position in the *Martinez* litigation, which was prior to the 1984 decision. Therefore, the district court's ruling denying an award of attorney's fees is affirmed.

DISSENT: (McKay, J.) The government's position was not substantially justified.

ANALYSIS

Martinez finds the governing law must be fairly well settled before a court will find that an opposing position is not justified. Where there is any controversy or ambiguity, parties will not be punished for taking a position later ruled wrong. The courts permit flexibility particularly where there are contrary district court interpretations and the government is relying on an extrapolation of the court's eventual decision.

Quicknotes

EQUAL ACCESS TO JUSTICE ACT (EAJA) Provides for the awarding of attorney's fees to a prevailing party, other than the government, when the opposing side took a position that was not substantially justified.

JUDICIAL REVIEW The authority of the courts to review decisions, actions, or omissions committed by another agency or branch of government.

Friends of the Boundary Waters Wilderness v. Thomas

Public interest group (P) v. Government agency (D)

53 F.3d 881 (8th Cir. 1995)

NATURE OF CASE: Appeal from denial of attorney's fees.

FACT SUMMARY: The Chief of the United States Forest Service (D) argued that its position in a losing case was justified because a district court had agreed before being reversed on appeal.

RULE OF LAW

A party must show that its position was clearly reasonable and well founded in law and fact in order to prove substantial justification for an incorrect legal position in litigation.

FACTS: In 1978, Congress passed the Boundary Waters Canoe Wilderness Area Act providing that the termination of existing motorboat transport operations at a certain waterway was required unless it was determined that there was no "feasible" nonmotorized means available. In 1986, the United States Forest Service (Forest Service) authorized continued motorboat operations of various portages because it found that it was not feasible to use nonmotorized portage wheels. The Friends of the Boundary Waters Wilderness (Friends) (P) brought an administrative appeal of this ruling and the Chief of the Forest Service (D) affirmed. The Friends (P) filed suit in district court, which found that the Chief's (D) interpretation of the Act was reasonable and also affirmed. The Friends (P) appealed and the court of appeals reversed, finding that the Chief's (D) interpretation was contrary to the definition of "feasible." The Friends (P) applied for an award of attorney's fees under the Equal Access to Justice Act (EAJA) as the prevailing party, but the district court denied the award, finding that the Chief's (D) position was substantially justified given the ambiguity of the statute. The Friends (P) once again appealed.

ISSUE: Must a party show that its position was clearly reasonable and well founded in law and fact in order to prove substantial justification for an incorrect legal position in litigation?

HOLDING AND DECISION: (Gibson, Sr. J.) Yes. A party must show that its position was clearly reasonable and well founded in law and fact in order to prove substantial justification for an incorrect legal position in litigation. In order for the government's position to be substantially justified, it must be justified to a degree that would "satisfy a reasonable person" and have "a reasonable basis both in law and fact." The most powerful indicator of the reasonableness of an ultimately rejected position is a decision on the merits and the rationale supporting that decision. The decision of the district court and dissenting judges may be considered. However, when the superior appellate court finds that a position was clearly contrary to the law, this must be given greater weight. In this case, this court concluded that the position of the Chief of the Forest Service (the Chief) (D) was contrary to clear congressional intent and the plain meaning of "feasible." Given this unequivocal rejection of the Chief's (D) position in the earlier litigation, it cannot now be said that the position was reasonable or well founded. Thus, the district court abused its discretion in concluding that the Chief (D) was substantially justified, and the attorney's fees should have been awarded to the Friends (P). Reversed.

ANALYSIS

The court also noted that the Chief of the Forest Service (D) had not always interpreted the statute in the same way prior to the litigation with the Friends of the Boundary Waters Wilderness (P). One judge dissented from the majority position when the original litigation reached the court of appeals. This decision here is rather biting in that it implies strongly that the dissenting judge took a clearly unreasonable position in the dissent.

Quicknotes

ABUSE OF DISCRETION A determination by an appellate court that a lower court's decision was based on an error of law.

EQUAL ACCESS TO JUSTICE ACT (EAJA) Provides for the awarding of attorney's fees to a prevailing party, other than the government, when the opposing side took a position that was not substantially justified.

Pierce v. Underwood

Secretary of Housing and Urban Development (D) v. [Party not identified]

487 U.S. 552 (1988)

NATURE OF CASE: Review of award of attorney's fees.

FACT SUMMARY: A district court awarded attorney's fees in excess of the statutory cap because of allegedly special circumstances.

RULE OF LAW

For attorneys to be awarded fees under the Equal Access to Justice Act (EAJA) that exceed the statutory cap, they must be qualified for the proceedings in some specialized sense.

FACTS: When a lawsuit against the Secretary of Housing and Urban Development (D) was settled, attorneys for the plaintiff were awarded attorney's fees under the Equal Access to Justice Act (EAJA). The amount of the fees awarded was higher than the limit set by the statute. The district court based the amount of the award on an exception in the statute for cases involving allegedly special factors, such as the limited availability of qualified attorneys for the proceedings involved. The Government (D) appealed, claiming that no special factors were present in this case to warrant the higher award.

ISSUE: For attorneys to be awarded fees under the Equal Access to Justice Act (EAJA) that exceed the statutory cap, must they be qualified for the proceedings in some specialized sense?

HOLDING AND DECISION: (Scalia, J.) Yes. For attorneys to be awarded fees under the Equal Access to Justice Act (EAJA) that exceed the statutory cap, they must be qualified for the proceedings in some specialized sense. The exception should be applied only when attorneys have some distinctive knowledge or specialized skill related to the litigation in question, such as an identifiable practice specialty or knowledge of a foreign language. The factors considered by the court below were too generally applicable to be regarded as special reasons for exceeding the statutory cap. It was an abuse of discretion for the court to rely on those factors. Reversed.

ANALYSIS

The district court had based its award on the novelty and difficulty of the issues, the undesirability of the case, the work and ability of counsel, the results obtained, and the customary fees and awards in other cases. The Court here found that none of those factors justified the higher award. The special factors to be considered for a higher award must not be of broad and general application.

Quicknotes

EQUAL ACCESS TO JUSTICE ACT (EAJA) Provides for the awarding of attorney's fees to a prevailing party, other than the government, when the opposing side took a position that was not substantially justified.

Pirus v. Bowen

Class representative (P) v. Secretary of the Department of Health and Human Services (D)

869 F.2d 536 (9th Cir. 1989)

NATURE OF CASE: Appeal of an award of attorney's fees.

FACT SUMMARY: The Government (D) complained that an award of attorney's fees should not have been enhanced past the statutory maximum rate.

RULE OF LAW

Attorneys with distinctive knowledge in a practice specialty are entitled to fees higher than the maximum rate under the Equal Access to Justice Act (EAJA) where those qualifications are necessary to the litigation and there are no other lawyers to take the case at the statutory rate.

FACTS: Pirus (P) brought a class action against the Secretary of the Department of Health and Human Services (the Secretary) (D) on behalf of a class that was denied Social Security benefits. The district court granted summary judgment to Pirus (P) and the class. Pirus (P) then petitioned for an award of attorney's fees under the Equal Access to Justice Act (EAJA). The court awarded the fees and determined that special factors justified an award of fees in excess of the EAJA maximum cap. The factors considered by the court were the attorney's expertise, the lack of other lawyers willing to take the case, and the unique ability of the attorneys in this particular area of the law. The Secretary (D) appealed.

ISSUE: Are attorneys with distinctive knowledge in a practice specialty entitled to fees higher than the maximum rate under Equal Access to Justice Act (EAJA) where those qualifications are necessary to the litigation and there are no other lawyers to take the case at the lower rate?

HOLDING AND DECISION: (Norris, J.) Yes. Attorneys with distinctive knowledge in a practice specialty are entitled to fees higher than the maximum rate under Equal Access to Justice Act (EAJA) where those qualifications are necessary to the litigation and there are no other lawyers to take the case at the statutory rate. The Supreme Court has decided that Congress intended for courts to deviate from the statutory cap only if the attorney had some distinctive knowledge or specialized skill needed for the litigation. Although the Supreme Court pointed out patent law as an example of a practice specialty and specialized skill, there is no reason to believe that this standard would not apply to other areas of the law. In the present case, Pirus's (P) attorneys developed a specialty in Social Security law and had expertise pertaining to the complex statutory scheme of the law. The district court found that this special expertise was needed in the case, which was highly complex and required substantial knowledge about a narrow area of the law. Accordingly, the district court acted properly in awarding an enhanced fee. Affirmed.

ANALYSIS

The reasoning of this decision seems to open up many types of cases to fee enhancements. In many, if not most, cases the prevailing party's attorneys will have some expertise in the legal area of the case.

Quicknotes

EQUAL ACCESS TO JUSTICE ACT (EAJA) Provides for the awarding of attorney's fees to a prevailing party, other than the government, when the opposing side took a position that was not substantially justified.

Chynoweth v. Sullivan

Benefits recipient (P) v. Government agency (D)

920 F.2d 648 (10th Cir. 1990)

NATURE OF CASE: Appeal from denial of enhancement of attorney's fees award.

FACT SUMMARY: Chynoweth (P) claimed her attorneys were entitled to a fee enhancement under the Equal Access to Justice Act (EAJA) because of their special expertise in Social Security disability law.

RULE OF LAW

The Equal Access to Justice Act (EAJA) statutory cap on attorney's fees may be exceeded only in unusual situations where the legal services rendered require specialized training and expertise unattainable by an ordinary competent attorney.

FACTS: After winning a Social Security disability case, Chynoweth (P) petitioned the district court for attorney's fees of $130 per hour under the Equal Access to Justice Act (EAJA). Chynoweth (P) claimed that her attorney was a specialist in Social Security Disability benefits law. The district court held that Chynoweth (P) was entitled to attorney's fees since the Secretary's denial of disability benefits was not substantially justified. However, the district court concluded that Chynoweth's (P) attorney was not entitled to a fee enhancement based on the absence of a special factor. Chynoweth (P) appealed this aspect of the award.

ISSUE: May the Equal Access to Justice Act (EAJA) statutory cap on attorney's fees be exceeded only in unusual situations where the legal services rendered require specialized training and expertise unattainable by an ordinary competent attorney?

HOLDING AND DECISION: (Baldock, J.) Yes. The Equal Access to Justice Act (EAJA) statutory cap on attorney's fees may be exceeded only in unusual situations where the legal services rendered require specialized training and expertise unattainable by an ordinary competent attorney. The EAJA mandates a maximum rate unless a special factor justifies a higher fee. Expertise in a particular legal field alone does not justify the higher rate. Merely because some scholarly effort or professional experience is required to attain proficiency in a particular practice area does not automatically require a fee enhancement. Social Security law is not beyond the grasp of a typical competent practicing attorney. In the present case, the district court also made no findings that Chynoweth's (P) action was a particularly difficult case or that she would have been unable to obtain other competent representation at the statutory rate. Affirmed.

ANALYSIS

Although this case would seem to turn mostly on the court's opinion that expertise with Social Security law is not a specialized skill, there may be more important factors. The court was reviewing the district court's denial of the fee enhancement under an abuse of discretion standard. Also, the district court obviously made no effort to put on the record facts about Chynoweth's (P) case that would make it seem difficult and unique.

Quicknotes

ABUSE OF DISCRETION A determination by an appellate court that a lower court's decision was based on an error of law.

EQUAL ACCESS TO JUSTICE ACT (EAJA) Provides for the awarding of attorney's fees to a prevailing party, other than the government, when the opposing side took a position that was not substantially justified.

Raines v. Shalala

Benefits recipient (P) v. Secretary of Health and Human Services (D)

44 F.3d 1355 (7th Cir. 1995)

NATURE OF CASE: Appeal from award of attorney's fees.

FACT SUMMARY: Raines's (P) attorney was awarded fees in excess of the Equal Access to Justice Act (EAJA) statutory cap in a Social Security benefits case.

RULE OF LAW

Attorney's fees in excess of the Equal Access to Justice Act (EAJA) statutory maximum rate are only appropriate in unusual cases where the case requires someone with specialized training and expertise unattainable by a standard competent attorney.

FACTS: Raines (P) filed suit against Health and Human Services (D) for his entitlement to Social Security disability benefits and prevailed. Raines's (P) petition requested $175 per hour for attorney's fees, claiming that this was the prevailing market rate due to the limited availability of qualified Social Security lawyers. The district court awarded attorney's fees pursuant to EAJA, deciding that special factors were present in order to award fees in excess of the statutory cap. The court found that the attorney had expertise with a complex statutory scheme, familiarity with a particular agency, and understood the needs of a particular class of clients. Health and Human Services (D) appealed, claiming that if such practice specialties were routinely found to be special factors, fee awards subject to the statutory cap would be rare.

ISSUE: Are attorney's fees in excess of the Equal Access to Justice Act (EAJA) statutory maximum rate only appropriate in unusual cases where the case requires someone with specialized training and expertise unattainable by a standard competent attorney?

HOLDING AND DECISION: (Ripple, J.) Yes. Attorney's fees in excess of the Equal Access to Justice Act (EAJA) statutory maximum rate are only appropriate in unusual cases where the case requires someone with specialized training and expertise unattainable by a standard competent attorney. The United States Supreme Court has clearly held that a fee enhancement under EAJA cannot be based simply on the limited availability of qualified attorneys. The nature of the case must also make it necessary to have an attorney with a specialized skill in an identifiable practice specialty. This special skill requirement means something not easily acquired by a reasonably competent attorney or a special non-legal skill such as knowledge of a foreign language. Additionally, it will be an exceptional or unusual situation when the special factors will apply. The test applied by the district court in the instant case was a bit too lenient. Although Raines's (P) attorney was undoubtedly very proficient in the area of Social Security benefits law, this isn't the type of skill and expertise that is unattainable by a competent attorney through diligent study. Furthermore, the principal issues arising in Raines's (P) case are issues that arise not infrequently in disability litigation. Accordingly, the award in excess of the statutory cap was improper and must be reversed.

ANALYSIS

The weight of authority in attorney fee cases pursuant to the Equal Access to Justice Act (EAJA) declines to award fees in excess of the statutory cap. Indeed, "[i]f expertise acquired through practice justified higher reimbursement rates then all lawyers practicing administrative law in technical fields would be entitled to fee enhancements." *F.J. Vollmer Company, Inc. v. Magaw*, 102 F.3d 591 at 598 (D.C. Cir. 1996). To receive a fee award exceeding the statutory cap, an attorney must have an identifiable practice specialty such as patent law, or knowledge of foreign law or language. See, *Pierce v. Underwood*, 487 U.S. 552 (1988).

Quicknotes

EQUAL ACCESS TO JUSTICE ACT (EAJA) Provides for the awarding of attorney's fees to a prevailing party, other than the government, when the opposing side took a position that was not substantially justified.

Glossary

Common Latin Words and Phrases Encountered in the Law

A FORTIORI: Because one fact exists or has been proven, therefore a second fact that is related to the first fact must also exist.

A PRIORI: From the cause to the effect. A term of logic used to denote that when one generally accepted truth is shown to be a cause, another particular effect must necessarily follow.

AB INITIO: From the beginning; a condition that has existed throughout, as in a marriage that was void ab initio.

ACTUS REUS: The wrongful act; in criminal law, such action as is sufficient to trigger criminal liability.

AD VALOREM: According to value; an ad valorem tax is imposed upon an item located within the taxing jurisdiction calculated by the value of such item.

AMICUS CURIAE: Friend of the court. Its most common usage takes the form of an amicus curiae brief, filed by a person who is not a party to an action but is nonetheless allowed to offer an argument supporting his or her legal interests.

ARGUENDO: In arguing. A statement, possibly hypothetical, made for the purpose of argument.

BILL QUIA TIMET: A bill to quiet title (establish ownership) to real property.

BONA FIDE: True, honest, or genuine. May refer to a person's legal position based on good faith or lacking notice of fraud (such as a bona fide purchaser for value) or to the authenticity of a particular document (such as a bona fide last will and testament).

CAUSA MORTIS: With approaching death in mind. A gift causa mortis is a gift given by a party who feels certain that death is imminent.

CAVEAT EMPTOR: Let the buyer beware. This maxim is reflected in the rule of law that a buyer purchases at his or her own risk because it is the buyer's responsibility to examine, judge, test, and otherwise inspect what he or she is buying.

CERTIORARI: A writ of review. Petitions for review of a case by the United States Supreme Court are most often done by means of a writ of certiorari.

CONTRA: On the other hand. Opposite. Contrary to.

CORAM NOBIS: Before us; a writ of error directed to the court that originally rendered the judgment.

CORAM VOBIS: Before you; a writ of error directed by an appellate court to a lower court to correct a factual error.

CORPUS DELICTI: The body of the crime; the requisite elements of a crime amounting to objective proof that a crime has been committed.

CUM TESTAMENTO ANNEXO, ADMINISTRATOR (ADMINISTRATOR C.T.A.): With will annexed; an administrator c.t.a. settles an estate pursuant to a will in which he or she is not appointed.

DE BONIS NON, ADMINISTRATOR (ADMINISTRATOR D.B.N.): Of goods not administered; an administrator d.b.n. settles a partially settled estate.

DE FACTO: In fact; in reality; actually. Existing in fact but not officially approved or engendered.

DE JURE: By right; lawful. Describes a condition that is legitimate "as a matter of law," in contrast to the term "de facto," which connotes something existing in fact but not legally sanctioned or authorized. For example, de facto segregation refers to segregation brought about by housing patterns, etc., whereas de jure segregation refers to segregation created by law.

DE MINIMUS: Of minimal importance; insignificant; a trifle; not worth bothering about.

DE NOVO: Anew; a second time; afresh. A trial de novo is a new trial held at the appellate level as if the case originated there and the trial at a lower level had not taken place.

DICTA: Generally used as an abbreviated form of obiter dicta, a term describing those portions of a judicial opinion incidental or not necessary to resolution of the specific question before the court. Such nonessential statements and remarks are not considered to be binding precedent.

DUCES TECUM: Refers to a particular type of writ or subpoena requesting a party or organization to produce certain documents in its possession.

EN BANC: Full bench. Where a court sits with all justices present rather than the usual quorum.

EX PARTE: For one side or one party only. An ex parte proceeding is one undertaken for the benefit of only one party, without notice to, or an appearance by, an adverse party.

EX POST FACTO: After the fact. An ex post facto law is a law that retroactively changes the consequences of a prior act.

EX REL.: Abbreviated form of the term "ex relatione," meaning upon relation or information. When the state brings an action in which it has no interest against an individual at the instigation of one who has a private interest in the matter.

FORUM NON CONVENIENS: Inconvenient forum. Although a court may have jurisdiction over the case, the action should be tried in a more conveniently located court, one to which parties and witnesses may more easily travel, for example.

GUARDIAN AD LITEM: A guardian appointed by the court to represent a minor or incompetent person in a legal action.

HABEAS CORPUS: You have the body. The modern writ of habeas corpus is a writ directing that a person (body) being detained (such as a prisoner) be brought before the court so that the legality of his or her detention can be judicially ascertained.

IN CAMERA: In private, in chambers. When a hearing is held before a judge in his or her chambers or when all spectators are excluded from the courtroom.

IN FORMA PAUPERIS: In the manner of a pauper. A party who proceeds in forma pauperis because of his or her poverty is one who is allowed to bring suit without liability for costs.

INFRA: Below, under. A word referring the reader to a later part of a book. (The opposite of supra.)

IN LOCO PARENTIS: In the place of a parent.

IN PARI DELICTO: Equally wrong; a court of equity will not grant requested relief to an applicant who is in pari delicto, or as much at fault in the transactions giving rise to the controversy as is the opponent of the applicant.

IN PARI MATERIA: On like subject matter or upon the same matter. Statutes relating to the same person or things are said to be in pari materia. It is a general rule of statutory construction that such statutes should be construed together, i.e., looked at as if they together constituted one law.

IN PERSONAM: Against the person. Jurisdiction over the person of an individual.

IN RE: In the matter of. Used to designate a proceeding involving an estate or other property.

IN REM: Signifies an action against the res, or thing. An action in rem is basically one that is taken directly against property, as distinguished from an action in personam, i.e., against the person.

INTER ALIA: Among other things. Used to show that the whole of a statement, pleading, list, statute, etc., has not been set forth in its entirety.

INTER PARTES: Between the parties. May refer to contracts, conveyances, or other transactions having legal significance.

INTER VIVOS: Between the living. An inter vivos gift is a gift made by a living grantor, as distinguished from bequests contained in a will, which pass upon the death of the testator.

IPSO FACTO: By the mere fact itself.

JUS: Law or the entire body of law.

LEX LOCI: The law of the place; the notion that the rights of parties to a legal proceeding are governed by the law of the place where those rights arose.

MALUM IN SE: Evil or wrong in and of itself; inherently wrong. Describes an act that is wrong by its very nature, as opposed to one which would not be wrong but for the fact that there is a specific legal prohibition against it (malum prohibitum).

MALUM PROHIBITUM: Wrong because prohibited, but not inherently evil. Describes something that is wrong because it is expressly forbidden by law but that is not in and of itself evil, e.g., speeding.

MANDAMUS: We command. A writ directing an official to take a certain action.

MENS REA: A guilty mind; a criminal intent. A term used to signify the mental state that accompanies a crime or other prohibited act. Some crimes require only a general mens rea (general intent to do the prohibited act), but others, like assault with intent to murder, require the existence of a specific mens rea.

MODUS OPERANDI: Method of operating; generally refers to the manner or style of a criminal in committing crimes, admissible in appropriate cases as evidence of the identity of a defendant.

NEXUS: A connection to.

NISI PRIUS: A court of first impression. A nisi prius court is one where issues of fact are tried before a judge or jury.

N.O.V. (NON OBSTANTE VEREDICTO): Notwithstanding the verdict. A judgment n.o.v. is a judgment given in favor of one party despite the fact that a verdict was returned in favor of the other party, the justification being that the verdict either had no reasonable support in fact or was contrary to law.

NUNC PRO TUNC: Now for then. This phrase refers to actions that may be taken and will then have full retroactive effect.

PENDENTE LITE: Pending the suit; pending litigation underway.

PER CAPITA: By head; beneficiaries of an estate, if they take in equal shares, take per capita.

PER CURIAM: By the court; signifies an opinion ostensibly written "by the whole court" and with no identified author.

PER SE: By itself, in itself; inherently.

PER STIRPES: By representation. Used primarily in the law of wills to describe the method of distribution where a person, generally because of death, is unable to take that which is left to him or her by the will of another, and therefore his or her heirs divide such property between them rather than take under the will individually.

PRIMA FACIE: On its face, at first sight. A prima facie case is one that is sufficient on its face, meaning that the evidence supporting it is adequate to establish the case until contradicted or overcome by other evidence.

PRO TANTO: For so much; as far as it goes. Often used in eminent domain cases when a property owner receives partial payment for his or her land without prejudice to his or her right to bring suit for the full amount he or she claims the land to be worth.

QUANTUM MERUIT: As much as the party deserves. Refers to recovery based on the doctrine of unjust enrichment in those cases in which a party has rendered valuable services or furnished materials that were accepted and enjoyed by another under circumstances that would reasonably notify the recipient that the rendering party expected to be paid. In essence, the law implies a contract to pay the reasonable value of the services or materials furnished.

QUASI: Almost like; as if; nearly. Essentially used to signify that one subject or thing is almost analogous to another but that material differences between them do exist. For example, a quasi-criminal proceeding is one that is not strictly criminal but shares enough of the same characteristics to require some of the same safeguards (e.g., procedural due process must be followed in a parole hearing).

QUID PRO QUO: Something for something. In contract law, the consideration, something of value, passed between the parties to render the contract binding.

RES GESTAE: Things done. In evidence law, this principle justifies the admission of a statement that would otherwise be hearsay when it is made so closely to the event in question as to be said to be a part of it, or with such spontaneity as not to have the possibility of falsehood.

RES IPSA LOQUITUR: The thing speaks for itself. This doctrine gives rise to a rebuttable presumption of negligence when the instrumentality causing the injury was within the exclusive control of the defendant, and the injury was one that does not normally occur unless a person has been negligent.

RES JUDICATA: A matter adjudged. Doctrine that provides that once a court of competent jurisdiction has rendered a final judgment or decree on the merits, that judgment or decree is conclusive upon the parties to the case and prevents them from engaging in any other litigation on the points and issues determined therein.

RESPONDEAT SUPERIOR: Let the master reply. This doctrine holds the master liable for the wrongful acts of his or her servant (or the principal for his or her agent) in those cases in which the servant (or agent) was acting within the scope of his or her authority at the time of the injury.

STARE DECISIS: To stand by or adhere to that which has been decided. The common-law doctrine of stare decisis attempts to give security and certainty to the law by following the policy that once a principle of law as applicable to a certain set of facts has been set forth in a decision, it forms a precedent that will subsequently be followed, even though a different decision might be made were it the first time the question had arisen. Of course, stare decisis is not an inviolable principle and is departed from in instances where there is good cause (e.g., considerations of public policy led the Supreme Court to disregard prior decisions sanctioning segregation).

SUPRA: Above. A word referring a reader to an earlier part of a book. (The opposite of infra.)

ULTRA VIRES: Beyond the power. This phrase is most commonly used to refer to actions taken by a corporation that are beyond the power or legal authority of the corporation.

Addendum of French Derivatives

CHATTEL: Tangible personal property.

CY PRES: Doctrine permitting courts to apply trust funds to purposes not expressed in the trust but necessary to carry out the settlor's intent.

IN PAIS: Not pursuant to legal proceedings.

PER AUTRE VIE: For another's life; during another's life. In property law, an estate may be granted that will terminate upon the death of someone other than the grantee.

PROFIT A PRENDRE: A license to remove minerals or other produce from land.

VOIR DIRE: Process of questioning jurors as to their predispositions about the case or parties to a proceeding in order to identify those jurors displaying bias or prejudice.

www.ingramcontent.com/pod-product-compliance
Lightning Source LLC
LaVergne TN
LVHW060036210926
848481LV00013B/3878